100 THINGS NATIONALS FANS
SHOULD KNOW & DO
BEFORE THEY DIE

100 THINGS NATIONALS FANS SHOULD KNOW & DO BEFORE THEY DIE

Jake Russell

TRIUMPH
BOOKS

Library of Congress Cataloging-in-Publication Data

Names: Russell, Jake, author.
Title: 100 things Nationals fans should know & do before they die / Jake Russell.
Other titles: One hundred things Nationals fans should know and do before they die
Description: Chicago, Illinois : Triumph Books, 2016.
Identifiers: LCCN 2015041351 | ISBN 9781629371917 (paperback)
Subjects: LCSH: Washington Nationals (Baseball team)—History. | Washington Nationals (Baseball team)—Miscellanea. | BISAC: SPORTS & RECREATION / Baseball / General. | TRAVEL / United States / South / South Atlantic (DC, DE, FL, GA, MD, NC, SC, VA, WV).
Classification: LCC GV863.W18 R87 2016 | DDC 796.357/6409753—dc23 LC record available at http://lccn.loc.gov/2015041351

This book is available in quantity at special discounts for your group or organization. For further information, contact:
  Triumph Books LLC
  814 North Franklin Street
  Chicago, Illinois 60610
  (312) 337-0747
  www.triumphbooks.com

Printed in U.S.A.
ISBN: 978-1-62937-191-7
Design by Patricia Frey
Photos courtesy of AP Images

To my mother, Terri; grandmother, Betty; sisters, Brandi and Shannon; niece, Madison; and nephews, Jaxon and Westin.

Contents

Foreword *by Dusty Baker* xi

Introduction xiii

1 The Announcement—September 29, 2004 1

2 A New Beginning 3

3 Bryce Harper's MVP Season 6

4 Strasmas 9

5 Jayson Werth's Game 4 Walk-Off Homer 12

6 Strasburg's Shutdown 15

7 Nationals Park Opens with Dramatic Flair 17

8 Walter Johnson's Feats 20

9 Jordan Zimmermann's No-Hitter 22

10 Cheer on the Racing Presidents 25

11 Rivalry with the Orioles 28

12 America's Team—The 1924 Senators 31

13 The Riot 34

14 Max Scherzer Throws Two No-Hitters in 2015 37

15 The 2012 NL East Champions 40

16 Presidential First Pitches 42

17 The Longest Game in Playoff History 48

18 The Curious Case of Smiley Gonzalez 51

19 Ted Williams' Reign as Manager 53

20 Frank Howard's 10 Home Runs in Six Games 56

21 The Last Expo 58

22 The 2014 NL East Champions 61

23 Walter Johnson's Three Shutouts in Four Days 64

24 Mr. Walk-Off 65

25 That's a Clown Question, Bro. 68

26 Matt Williams 71

27 The Derivation of Natitude. 74

28 The Kid Managers. 77

29 Mike Rizzo 80

30 The Kiss 82

31 Take a Nationals Road Trip 84

32 The Washington...Padres? 87

33 Jim Riggleman Quits. 90

34 The 2015 Letdown 93

35 Davey Johnson 97

36 Gio Gonzalez. 99

37 How to Get Autographs 102

38 Livo. 106

39 National Guardsman/Senators Shortstop 107

40 Alfonso Soriano Founds 40-40-40 Club 109

41 The Cardiac Nats' Wild 10-Game Winning Streak. 112

42 When Owen Wilson Played for the Nationals 116

43 Mickey Vernon 117

44 The Homestead Grays 119

45 Get Ready for the 2018 All-Star Game 123

46 Senators No-Hitters 125

47 The Chief 128

48 The Mysterious Demise of D.C.'s First Batting Champion. . . 130

49 World Series or Bust. 133

50 Brad Wilkerson and the Nats' Cycles 136

51 Bryce's Benching 138

52 The Senators' Spy 140

53 Scott Boras' Ties to the Nationals 142

54 An Owner Sells Off His Relatives 145

55 "Hammering" Grand Slams in Consecutive Innings 147

56 Visit Cooperstown 150

57 The Big Donkey 152

58 The Origins of the Senators Name 154

59 Great Trades 156

60 The Amputee Pitcher 160

61 The Combustible Jose Guillen 163

62 D.C. Baseball Stadium History 166

63 Why Getting Swept by the Padres Was a Good Thing 169

64 The Six Aces 173

65 Visit RFK Stadium 176

66 A Fan's Quest to Torment a Former Senators Owner 178

67 The Kidnapped Catcher 181

68 The Bryce Harper Timeline 183

69 The Only Player to Play in Both of the Senators' Last Games . . 188

70 Watch the Nats' Minor League Teams 190

71 The Deaf Center Fielder 193

72 Nats Superfans 196

73 Meet the Lerners 198

74 The Future 201

75 The Natinals 205

76 Is Killebrew MLB's Logo? 207

77 Tony Plush 210

78 Sit in the Lexus Presidents Seats 212

79 Frank Robinson's Showdown with Mike Scioscia 214

80 The Midseason Parade for "The Wondrous Nats" 216

81 Uniforms and Logos 217

82 Nationals All-Stars. 220

83 Sam Rice's Secrets 226

84 Interesting Draft Picks and Minor Leaguers 228

85 2005's 10-Game Winning Streak 233

86 The Fan Who Died from a Wild Throw. 236

87 Michael Morse's Phantom Grand Slam. 237

88 Did the Senators Nearly Sign Josh Gibson and Buck Leonard? . 241

89 Inviting Phillies Fans to Nationals Park. 243

90 Learn the Names on the Ring of Honor 244

91 Hang Out with Screech. 251

92 Call Me Maybe 252

93 D.C. Baseball's Clowns 254

94 The Origins of the Curly W 256

95 Go to Nationals Park on Opening Day and Fourth of July. . . 258

96 Jayson Werth Goes to Jail 259

97 Watch a Concert at Nationals Park. 262

98 Villains 264

99 Hiring Dusty Baker. 267

100 The Presidential Statistician 269

Acknowledgments 271

Sources 273

Foreword

The decision to lead the Washington Nationals was not hard for me. I wanted to be back in baseball, and the opportunity to lead a team that had won its division twice in the last four years in the most powerful city in the world was too good to pass up.

When I was introduced as the team's manager, I said that for once I wanted to do more with more. I've managed some of the biggest superstars to step on a Major League Baseball diamond— Moises Alou, Barry Bonds, Ellis Burks, Jeff Kent, Matt Williams, Sammy Sosa, Greg Maddux, Ken Griffey Jr., and Joey Votto, just to name a few. But of my 20 years of leading teams, I've never inherited a team with as much talent and depth as this Nationals club has. I know a lot of managers wish they could be so lucky to lead a team stacked with players like reigning National League MVP Bryce Harper, Cy Young candidates Stephen Strasburg and Max Scherzer, Mr. National Ryan Zimmerman, Anthony Rendon, and Jayson Werth. I'm thrilled to lead this group of men.

A lot of these players, especially Bryce, are on pace to become some of the all-time greats. They remind me of myself because I played with an unparalleled passion and love for the game. During my playing career, I've been surrounded with some of the best to play the game. I was on deck when Hammerin' Hank Aaron hit his record-breaking 715th career home run in 1974. I also played with Phil Niekro, Don Sutton, Fernando Valenzuela, Mark McGwire, Dave Stewart, and others who went on to become managers like Joe Torre, Davey Johnson, Johnny Oates, Mike Scioscia, and Davey Lopes. I went to three World Series with the Los Angeles Dodgers, winning one.

If my 20 years as manager and 19 years as a major league ballplayer have taught me anything, it's to adapt to my surroundings and the people around me. As a leader of men, I get to know my players' strengths and I understand their weaknesses. Having accomplished that, I can help them become the best version of themselves on and off the diamond. My friends like to call me "the Chameleon" because I can fit in just anyplace, anytime, anywhere.

Many people have questioned my age and if I can get things done at this stage in the game. That's baloney. I feel like I'm the youngest 66-year-old around. As the saying goes, age ain't nothing but a number. I don't think of myself as 66 years old. I don't know *how* old I am sometimes. It really doesn't matter. Not to sound cocky, but as I joked during my initial press conference, I don't see a whole bunch of dudes out there who look better than me.

I've won a division title with all three teams I've managed and took the San Francisco Giants to the 2002 World Series. In my 20 years as a manager, my teams had winning seasons in 12 of them. I've taken teams to seven playoff appearances, something only eight other managers have done more frequently since 1900. The only thing missing from my mantle is a World Series trophy and World Series ring as a manager.

My time in Washington, D.C., will be a true learning experience and a challenge I very much look forward to taking on. It's a great city and one that deserves a winner, and the diversity and history in and around the Beltway makes me feel right at home. My stint with the Nationals probably will be my last as a Major League Baseball manager, so I will make the most out of it. Our goal is to win a World Series, and I know we have the talent to accomplish that.

Stay tuned, Nats fans. You're going to enjoy the ride!

—Dusty Baker
January, 2016

Introduction

September 29, 2004 was a momentous day for me for many reasons. It was my 17th birthday and a month into my senior year of high school and it will forever be known as the day baseball officially returned to Washington, D.C., after a 33-year absence.

Writing this book spurred me to research the history of baseball in the nation's capital. Yeah, I knew of Frank Howard, Walter Johnson, Clark Griffith, Mickey Vernon, and so on. But delving deeper meant learning the real impact these men had on the city during their time here. The whole process of writing this book was an amazing learning experience about an era of baseball that ended 16 years before I was even born. It also provided for a fun refresher course on the Nationals' memorable first 11 seasons of existence.

Watching Bryce Harper win National League Player of the Month in May 2015 after blasting 13 home runs and 28 RBIs made Howard's 10 home runs in six days in May of 1968 that much more impressive. Max Scherzer's hot streak in June of 2015 that included a one-hitter at the Milwaukee Brewers and a no-hitter against the Pittsburgh Pirates goes down as one of the best back-to-back pitching performances of all time. That conjured up thoughts of Walter Johnson's three shutouts in four days in 1908.

Growing up, it was always understood that when it came to D.C. sports, it was the Redskins first, and everyone else would fight for second—no matter how the burgundy and gold fared. The Wizards were perennial losers long removed from their glory days as the Bullets in the 1970s. The Capitals reached the 1998 Stanley Cup Finals but were swept. That was the closest they have gotten to bringing hardware to D.C. in my lifetime.

When it came to baseball, there were the Baltimore Orioles and Bowie Baysox. I may not have realized it as a youngster, but it was strange in retrospect. How can Washington, D.C., the world's most powerful city, not have a baseball team?

That all changed in 2004.

The anticipation for baseball's return to D.C. was so high that the team received 10,000 season ticket deposits before Major League Baseball even formally approved the move of the Montreal Expos. As someone who grew up accustomed to D.C. sports teams losing, it was awkwardly comforting to know the Washington Senators' motto for the 20th century was "first in war, first in peace, last in the American League."

The Nats surprised everybody by spending 63 days of the 2005 season in first place, peaking at 19 games above .500, and settling to 52–36 at the All-Star break. The team closed out the season with a 29–45 record to finish the season 81–81. It would have been nice to start their new run in D.C. above .500, but no one expected 80 wins with that hodgepodge group, especially after the Expos went 67–95 the year before. The team wouldn't reach 80 wins again until 2011 after enduring 91, 89, 102, 103, and 93-loss seasons in between.

Despite a disappointing 2015 season, the Nationals still have stars like Harper, Stephen Strasburg, Ryan Zimmerman, and Max Scherzer. They won two National League East titles in three years and are perennial World Series contenders. That's an embarrassment of riches for a city robbed of a generation of baseball.

Enjoy it. Embrace it. Be grateful. It wasn't always like this.

1 | The Announcement— September 29, 2004

One day shy of the 33rd anniversary of the final Washington Senators game, the baseball-starved fans of the nation's capital received the news for which they had been waiting more than a generation. An agonizing span of 12,045 days of emptiness was now over. Standing in front of a podium at the City Museum's Great Hall and donning a red Senators cap, D.C. mayor Anthony A. Williams proudly proclaimed: "After 30 years of waiting…and waiting…and waiting and lots of hard work and more than a few prayers, there will be baseball in Washington in 2005!"

Charlie Brotman, the Senators' public address announcer from 1956–1971, was a part of the ceremony to welcome baseball back to the District. "Shout it from the rooftops—let's play ball!" yelled Brotman, who led the jubilant crowd in a chorus of "Take Me Out to the Ballgame."

Major League Baseball commissioner Bud Selig made it official earlier in the day during a call to an eager group consisting of Williams, council members, and city sports officials at city hall. "Congratulations," Selig told them. "It's been a long time coming."

Selig's statement read: "Washington, D.C., as our nation's capital, is one of the world's most important cities, and Major League Baseball is gratified at the skill and perseverance shown by Mayor Williams throughout this process."

The mood at City Museum and throughout the District of Columbia was light and filled with a certain joy that hadn't been experienced in decades. The banner above the dais read: "A HOME RUN FOR DC." John Fogerty's "Centerfield" blasted over the loudspeakers as the media, former Senators players, and

1

excited fans in attendance took in the environment. Youth baseball players who had known of no professional baseball team in the city at any point in their lifetime stood behind officials during the press conference.

Washington, D.C., would finally have a Major League Baseball team to call its own, inheriting the National League East's Montreal Expos. Washington, D.C., beat out Las Vegas; Portland, Oregon; Norfolk, Virginia; Monterrey, Mexico; and a site in Loudoun County, Virginia, that proposed a new stadium and building a city around it.

Even Vice President Dick Cheney chimed in, saying during a campaign stop in Minnesota that he was looking forward to seeing D.C. become a "ball town again." "This will be a great boon to the community," Cheney added. "It will force a lot of us to reorient our loyalties. We've all picked up, acquired, become fans of other teams."

The Expos had been owned by Major League Baseball since 2002 and were not a top priority to the league. They even split home games between Canada and San Juan, Puerto Rico, in 2003 and 2004. None of that mattered now. They were D.C.'s team. "The sun is setting in Montreal, but it's rising in Washington," Expos president Tony Tavares said during a news conference at Olympic Stadium.

D.C. baseball fans fully understood what fans in Montreal were experiencing, having lost the Senators twice in an 11-year span. Local fans also understood that their new team would be a reclamation project.

The Expos had dropped to 65–94 the night of the announcement after a 9–1 loss to the Florida Marlins in their last game at Montreal's Olympic Stadium. They finished the season 67–95. The Expos hadn't won more than 83 games since the 1996 season. Long gone from that franchise were the likes of stars such as Vladimir Guerrero, Cliff Floyd, Pedro Martinez, Larry Walker, Moises Alou, and Marquis Grissom. A strike-shortened 1994 season ended what was primed to be a dominant postseason run for the Expos, who sat atop baseball at 74–40. The current crop moving to Washington boasted the likes of Livan Hernandez, Brad Wilkerson, Chad Cordero, Jose Vidro, Nick Johnson, Jamey Carroll, and Brian Schneider—all managed by Hall of Famer Frank Robinson.

The team, whose new name and identity were yet to be determined, was set to play at RFK Stadium for three seasons and then move to a new home nestled along the Anacostia River in Southeast D.C. in 2008. A new era had begun. There was baseball in Washington, D.C.

A New Beginning

It was the moment millions of Washingtonians had all been waiting for. After 12,250 days—almost 34 years—of anticipation since the Washington Senators last stepped foot on RFK Stadium grounds, the Washington Nationals filled the void experienced by those longing for the national pastime in their city.

On April 14, 2005, a crowd of 45,596 was on hand to witness the Nationals take on the Arizona Diamondbacks in their first home game. President George W. Bush, protected by Secret Service members disguised as Nationals coaches, set the tone for a raucous night. After a few minutes of small talk, the commander in chief told Nationals catcher Brian Schneider just before taking the field, "Here we go. Just catch it." *It* was the ball lent to President Bush by former Senators pitcher Joe Grzenda and was the final ball used in Washington Senators history. It was the one Grzenda held on while standing on the mound as fans at RFK rushed the field with one out to go on September 30, 1971.

Sporting a red Nationals jacket, the president headed onto the grass, took his place on the mound, and tossed the ceremonial first pitch to Schneider at 6:52 PM. Former Senators such as Frank Howard, Mickey Vernon, Roy Sievers, Eddie Brinkman, and Chuck Hinton stood at their old positions to hand out the gloves to the current crop of Nationals as they took their places on the field for the first pitch. At 7:06 PM on that chilly Thursday night, with cameras and flashbulbs readying around the park, Nationals ace Livan Hernandez threw the first pitch, a fastball past Diamondbacks second baseman Craig Counsell, for a strike. Schneider tossed the ball to the dugout for the beginning of its journey to the National Baseball Hall of Fame in Cooperstown, New York.

Hernandez pitched a gem—at least until the ninth inning. The workhorse tossed a one-hitter and had a 5–0 lead going into the final inning until surrendering a one-out, three-run home run to Chad Tracy.

It had been more than three decades since baseball was a daily occurrence at RFK, but fans were well aware of what third baseman Vinny Castilla was on the verge of accomplishing in his fourth at-bat. He had already doubled in the second inning, tripled in the fourth inning, and hit the first Nationals home run at RFK in the sixth inning.

Castilla batted second in the eighth inning against Arizona reliever Lance Cormier. The 15-year veteran was just a single away from the cycle. Cormier plunked Castilla on the first pitch. The capacity crowd realized that—with a 5–0 lead and four plate appearances already behind him—getting hit by a pitch ended any chance of a cycle. Boos rained down on Cormier from the RFK faithful.

But when Castilla tripled in the fourth inning to score second baseman Jose Vidro and right fielder Jose Guillen to give the Nats a 2–0 lead, RFK Stadium erupted. It rocked and shook like it had whenever the Redskins scored a touchdown or sacked opposing quarterbacks.

That kind of home-field advantage was new for Major League Baseball, and those in attendance who had never felt a stadium move before. "Holy shit," Nationals president Tony Tavares said.

The Montreal Expos, the franchise that gave way to the Washington Nationals, totaled just 748,550 fans in 2004, averaging just 9,356 per game, the lowest in the majors by almost 7,000 per game. Left fielder Brad Wilkerson, who spent his first four seasons with the Expos, said after the game that he was impressed with the D.C. crowd. "It was amazing to see," he said. "Honestly, it was more than I expected. They lived and died with every pitch. You know it's going to be a great place to play."

Outfielder Terrmel Sledge, who hit the first home run and RBI in Nats history in the season opener against the Philadelphia Phillies on April 4, echoed Wilkerson's sentiments following the game. "I just looked at the fans and thought, *We finally have a home-field advantage*," Sledge said.

Chad Cordero, the 23-year-old closer nicknamed "the Chief," ended the game, recording the final two outs—the last one being a fly out from Tony Clark to right fielder Ryan Church.

Kool & the Gang's "Celebration" played throughout the stadium, ushering in not just another win in the record books but a new feeling in the city. "The win put the icing on the day, especially with the team playing its first game in Washington, where it had no baseball for 34 years," Nationals manager Frank Robinson said after the game. "To go out here and win with this atmosphere—the president out here, other dignitaries in the stands, and real baseball fans out there cheering—it was a special situation where you wanted to win the game. It's nice when you go out there and do it. It keeps the enthusiasm as high, and the expectations even higher."

3 Bryce Harper's MVP Season

Before the 2015 season began, *ESPN The Magazine* anonymously polled 117 major leaguers. Of that group 41 percent voted Bryce Harper as the most overrated player in baseball. It was the second straight season that distinction was bestowed upon the young phenom who has carried the burden of lofty expectations since high school. Though said in jest, Harper's spring training declaration of "Where's my ring?" in response to the Washington Nationals adding Max Scherzer to the starting rotation didn't help matters.

However, the 22-year-old silenced his doubters early on. In the fourth inning of Opening Day, Harper walked to the plate with Frank Sinatra's "The Best is Yet to Come" blaring loud and clear through the Nationals Park loudspeakers. It was foreshadowing at its finest. On the second pitch, Harper hit his first home run of the season.

The Nats labored through April, but May was a different story. Washington went 18–9 in the month of May, and Harper was a catalyst. He earned National League Player of the Month after batting .360 with 13 homers (a Nats single-month record) and 28 RBIs while scoring 24 runs and drawing 22 walks. He also reached base at least twice in 12 straight games. He became the third player in the last 100 years to hit 15 home runs in his first 40 games at age 22 or younger. The last to do it before him was Harmon Killebrew with the 1959 Washington Senators.

In June, Harper faced the Yankees in New York for the first time in his career. Early in his pro career, he was vocal about his lifelong affinity of the Bronx Bombers. Yankees die-hards were well aware and made it clear they'd welcome him in pinstripes. Referencing Harper's Nationals contract ending after the 2018

The brash but sensational Bryce Harper celebrates after scoring in 2015, a year in which he hit .330 with 42 home runs, 99 RBIs, and a .460 on-base percentage.

season, fans in the Yankee Stadium bleachers chanted "Fu-ture Yankee!" and "20-19!" During that series in New York, Harper managed to face a pitcher younger than he for the first time in his professional career. In Harper's 2,303rd plate appearance and his 554th game between the minors and majors, he faced Yankees prospect Jacob Lindgren, who is 147 days younger, and flew out to left field on the second pitch of the at-bat.

Despite his youth Harper was voted to his third All-Star Game in four seasons. By the All-Star break, he had already hit 26 home runs with a .339 average, 61 RBIs, and 63 walks.

Heading into the final game of the season, Harper was locked in a dead heat for the NL batting title with Miami Marlins second baseman Dee Gordon. Both men boasted .331 averages going into their respective finales. Harper went 1-for-4 against the New York Mets while Gordon went 3-for-4 against the Philadelphia Phillies, dropping Harper's average to .330 and raising Gordon's to .333.

Over the course of the 2015 season, millions witnessed Bryce Harper's transformation from very good to great. His development

Bryce Harper's Fantastic Four

In a 2015 season filled with many firsts for Bryce Harper, he continued to amaze even without swinging a bat. During a 15–1 rout of the Atlanta Braves on September 3, Bryce took 20 pitches without swinging his bat.

Harper walked on all four of his plate appearances and scored four times, becoming the fourth player in MLB history to go 0-for-0 and score at least four runs and record four walks, joining Larry Doby (1951), Joe Morgan (1973), and Rickey Henderson (1989).

He also registered an RBI in the second inning when he was walked with the bases loaded, becoming the first player with no hits, four walks, four runs, and one RBI since RBIs became a statistic in 1920.

Harper was replaced by Matt den Dekker in the sixth inning while the Nats were up 12–1. Who knows what further damage he could have done if he played the rest of the game?

into a more well-rounded player translated to a .330 batting average, 42 home runs, 99 RBIs, and a staggering .460 on-base percentage. He became just the ninth player in baseball history to hit 42 home runs with a .330 batting average and .460 on-base percentage. Only Babe Ruth, Ted Williams, Lou Gehrig, Jimmie Foxx, Mickey Mantle, Todd Helton, Jason Giambi, and Barry Bonds had previously accomplished those numbers.

Health played a lead role in Harper's 2015 production. Harper never landed on the disabled list after missing 62 games in 2014. His maturation at the plate became apparent in the 2014 National League Division Series against the San Francisco Giants. As his teammates' bats disappeared, his came to life. He led the team with three home runs, four RBIs, and four runs. His five hits were second only to Anthony Rendon's seven. Harper also walked twice. With Harper the Nationals offense went 26 for 159 (.164). Without Harper the rest of the offense went 21 for 142 (.148).

Harper's patience at the plate was on display throughout the 2015 season. He broke the Nationals/Expos franchise single-season record with 124 walks. He walked in 88 of the 153 games he played in and walked at least twice in 26 games. Harper was also intentionally walked a career-high 15 times in 2015. He had been intentionally walked just eight times in his three previous seasons combined.

4 Strasmas

It was Washington, D.C.'s most anticipated baseball game since the national pastime returned to the nation's capital. Nationals Park experienced an unparalleled buzz—or as it's commonly referred to—"Strasmas," leading up to June 9, 2010, the debut of rookie phenom Stephen Strasburg. The first overall pick in the 2009 MLB Draft out of San Diego State would blow away not only his opponents—the Pittsburgh Pirates—but also the loft expectations that preceded the contest.

Nicknamed "Slothburg" by his college strength coach Dave Ohton because of his lack of proper conditioning and 6'4", 255-pound frame in high school, Strasburg proved the pace of the major league game wouldn't be an issue. In 11 minor league starts with the Double A Harrisburg Senators and Triple A Syracuse Chiefs, Strasburg was 7–2 with a 1.30 ERA, 65 strikeouts, 13 walks, and a .80 WHIP. It was time for him to show what he was made of at the highest level.

There was no lack of coverage for this monumental debut. MLB Network broadcast the game nationally, and reporters from every local and national media outlet were in attendance. More than 200 credentials were handed out for a Tuesday night game in early June against the Pirates. It was clear to even the most passive of baseball fans that things had certainly changed in Washington, D.C. "The anticipation before first pitch was the loudest I've ever heard at Nationals Park," Nationals radio play-by-play man Charlie Slowes said during the hour-long special *National Pastime: Baseball's Return to Washington.*

Strasburg received a standing ovation while walking from the bullpen to the dugout after warming up. "It was like a World Series game," MASN's play-by-play man Bob Carpenter said on *National Pastime: Baseball's Return to Washington.* "It was October in June."

"Strasmas" was such a big event that his West Hills (California) High School coach Scott Hopgood and teammates gathered in a Santee, California, sports bar to catch the action. One of those teammates, Aaron Richardson, called in sick from work and attended the get-together. A TV station interviewed Richardson and his old teammates at the viewing party. Richardson's boss saw it and subsequently fired him. That's the risk Richardson was willing to take to see his former teammate shine on the big stage.

At 7:06 PM Strasburg's new life began with a 97-mph offering inside to center fielder Andrew McCutchen before forcing him to line out. He then forced Neil Walker to ground out and ended the inning striking out former National, Lastings Milledge.

It would be the first of a team-record 14 strikeouts for the 21-year-old.

He struck out three in the second inning—with the only hit coming on a two-out single from future National Adam LaRoche. His fastball reached 100 mph on the radar gun that inning. Strasburg's roll continued as he struck out two in the third. His biggest hiccup of the night came in the fourth inning when he allowed three hits, including a two-out, two-run home run to Delwyn Young to give Pittsburgh a 2–1 lead.

After that, Strasburg shifted into another gear, not allowing another runner on base through the seventh inning, striking out his last seven batters and electrifying a sold-out, standing-room only crowd of more than 40,000. Following his last pitch, a seventh-inning strikeout to LaRoche, the stadium chanted "Ste-phen Stras-burg!" (clap-clap, clap-clap-clap).

In the middle of the inning, with the team's new strikeout record announced, Strasburg saluted the crowd with a curtain call. "If you'd have told me any kid would ever come up to the big leagues and strike out 14 hitters in his major league debut, I would have said you are absolutely crazy," Carpenter said.

Washington regained the lead in the bottom of the sixth and won the game 5–2, giving Strasburg a 1–0 record to start his career. His final line was seven innings pitched, 94 pitches, 14 strikeouts, four hits, and two runs. Just 58 days removed from his first minor league appearance and 364 days removed from signing a record $15.1 million contract, he met and surpassed the tremendous buildup. "The Strasburg game had to be the biggest game played in this town in maybe almost 75 years or so," said Bethesda, Maryland, native and ESPN baseball reporter Tim Kurkjian in a 2012 interview for Frederic Frommer's book *You Gotta Have Heart*. "And for that kid to do what he did was unbelievable. No one in history had ever walked none and struck out 14 in their major league debut ever. And with all the hype, and I can't remember any one player being hyped quite like this kid, to exceed the expectations, to go beyond the hype, was remarkable."

This was a banner night for baseball in the city, a new chapter marking what many consider its true arrival, resonating across generations and reeling in a new wave of fans. "It's a red-letter day for the franchise," Nationals principal owner Mark Lerner said that night. "Fans one day will look back and say, 'I was here the day the franchise took the next step.'"

5 Jayson Werth's Game 4 Walk-Off Homer

When Jayson Werth made the decision to sign a seven-year, $126 million contract with the Washington Nationals in December 2010, it created a lot of industry buzz to say the least. Two years removed from winning a World Series title with the Philadelphia Phillies, the 31-year-old Werth chose to sign with a team that had lost 196 games in that span.

After putting pen to paper on what was at the time the 13th largest contract in baseball history, national media pundits scratched their heads and asked: "He signed *where*? And for *how* much?" The Philadelphia media had a field day. The *Philadelphia Daily News* ran a back page cover saying "Nats Are Nuts" while their front cover took a shot at Washington Redskins fans with its headline: "Hey Washington: If you liked McNabb…You'll love Werth!"

Meanwhile, Nats fans were second-guessing what they had read and said to themselves: *Wait, he signed with us?* His acquisition changed how future free agents viewed the up-and-coming Nationals. After enriching their depleted minor league system with good young talent, the Nationals' signing of Werth marked the beginning of, as the front office called it, "Phase Two," where the team would make calculated free-agent signings in their bid to contend for National League East titles.

Werth was brought to D.C. for his winning track record and clubhouse leadership. No moment in Werth's Nationals tenure will surpass his epic 13-pitch at-bat in the bottom of the ninth in Game 4 of the 2012 National League Division Series against the St. Louis Cardinals.

The Nats, down 2–1 in the five-game series, battled for their playoff lives in a home contest that had been knotted at one run apiece since the third inning. The only runs came from Nats first baseman Adam LaRoche's 417-foot home run in the second inning and Carlos Beltran responding a half-inning later with a sacrifice fly that sent Pete Kozma home to tie the game.

In the bottom of the ninth—with the season on the line and tensions rising throughout Nationals Park—Werth engaged in a battle with Cardinals pitcher Lance Lynn that will forever be remembered by Nats fans. Here's how it went:

Pitch 1: 95-mph fastball. Low down the middle. Strike 1. (0–1)
Pitch 2: 94-mph fastball. Low and away. Strike 2. (0–2)
Pitch 3: 81-mph curveball. Wild pitch outside. Ball 1. (1–2)
Pitch 4: 96-mph fastball. High and outside. Ball 2. (2–2)
Pitch 5: 97-mph fastball. High and inside. Fouled to the first base side. (2–2)

Pitch 6: 97-mph fastball. High down the middle. Fouled to the first base side. (2–2)

Pitch 7: 97-mph fastball. Outside toward the middle. Fouled to the first base side. (2–2)

Pitch 8: 96-mph fastball. High and outside. Fouled into the Nationals dugout. (2–2)

Pitch 9: 82-mph curveball. Low and away. Foul. (2–2)

Pitch 10: 96-mph fastball. Fouled straight back. (2–2)

Pitch 11: 79-mph curveball. Low and away. Ball 3. (3–2)

Pitch 12: 97-mph fastball. Fouled to the first base side. (3–2)

Pitch 13: 96-mph fastball. Home run 406 feet to left field.

With no outs and a full count, Werth delivered the most memorable shot in the Nationals postseason history to the delight

Play-By-Play Call

Nationals fans listening on the radio to 106.7 The Fan, the team's flagship station, were in for a treat with play-by-play announcers Dave Jageler and Charlie Slowes on the call. Slowes essentially predicted the home run before it even happened. What happened next still gives Nats fans goosebumps every time they hear it.

Jageler: "This is an epic battle."
Slowes: "Remember the at-bat after the rain delay, Dave?"
Jageler: "I do."
Slowes: "Remember what happened culminating that at-bat?"
Jageler: "I do."
Slowes: "Wouldn't that be nice?"
Jageler: "I hope you're the summoner."
Slowes: "I hope I can steal a little summoning from you, Dave."
Slowes: "Three balls. Two strikes. The pitch. Swing and a long drive! Deep left field! Going! Going! It's gooooone! Good-bye! Game over! It's a walk-off, game-winning, season-saving home run for Jayson Werth! And the Nationals have won the game 2–1! Unbelievabllllllle!"

of the raucous crowd of 44,392. "That was loud as I've ever heard a place," Cardinals pitcher Adam Wainwright said. Washington had tied the series 2–2 with a 2–1 walk-off win. "That's the way that game should have ended—Jayson Werth hitting a home run," Nats manager Davey Johnson said.

6 Strasburg's Shutdown

Washington was leading the Philadelphia Phillies 5–1 in the bottom of the fifth inning on Saturday, August 21, 2010. But after his 56th pitch, rookie phenom Stephen Strasburg knew something was wrong. He shook his right arm to jostle the problem away. When he stood back on the mound, he motioned to the Nats dugout for assistance. Manager Jim Riggleman, pitching coach Steve McCatty, catcher Ivan Rodriguez, and head athletic trainer Lee Kuntz spoke with Strasburg at the mound, and after brief deliberation, Strasburg left the game with an apparent arm injury just 13 days after returning from a disabled list with inflammation in his right shoulder.

A couple days after leaving the game, Strasburg was placed on the 15-day DL with a strained flexor tendon in his right forearm after the first round of MRI results. Four days later a second MRI revealed that Strasburg was nursing a torn ligament in his right elbow. He would have to undergo the dreaded Tommy John surgery and take a year off from baseball to recover.

Fellow pitcher Jordan Zimmermann, who missed half the 2009 season and most of the 2010 season, replaced Strasburg on the roster. Zimmermann's innings in 2011 were capped at 160. He eventually pitched 161⅓ innings and was shut down in September.

Strasburg returned September 6, 2011, against the Los Angeles Dodgers, striking out four and allowing only two hits in five shutout innings. The Nats improved as a club, climbing from 69–93 in 2010 to 80–81 in 2011. Strasburg pitched 24 innings in four more games in 2011. But how many would he pitch in 2012? Would the Nats put Strasburg on an innings limit or continue to pitch him if they made the postseason? That question fueled a firestorm of debate that would rage the entire length of Strasburg's career.

In 2012 the Nationals were expected to have their first winning record since moving to D.C. Strasburg's innings and pitch count were tracked by every media member and by countless fans throughout his 2012 All-Star campaign. Unlike Zimmermann's situation, Strasburg is a former first overall pick, and the Nats were in a pennant race all season.

Ultimately, general manager Mike Rizzo stuck with his plan to limit Strasburg's innings. "It's not on [manager] Davey Johnson or Mr. [team owner Ted] Lerner. It's on me," Rizzo told *The Washington Post*. "I know it may stain my reputation or my career. There's no way it can ever be proved if I was right. The easy thing for me is just to do nothing. But I'm hardheaded. The decision was made five months ago because it was the best decision for Stephen and the Nationals. And nothing is going to change it."

After pitching 159⅓ innings in 28 games, Strasburg expected to pitch one more time. He was 15–6 with a 3.16 ERA—not bad for someone who had missed almost a whole year the season before. However, on September 8, with a 6½ game lead in the National League East, the Nats decided to shut down Strasburg just weeks away from Washington's first postseason baseball appearance since 1933.

This was the beginning of the most controversial moment in Nationals history.

Johnson believed Strasburg had become distracted by the media coverage of the innings limit at that point and felt it was best to end his season. "I don't know if I'm ever going to accept it, to be honest," Strasburg said after the decision was made. "It's something that I'm not happy about at all. That's not why I play the game. I play the game to be a good teammate and win. You don't grow up dreaming of playing in the big leagues to get shut down when the games start to matter. It's going to be a tough one to swallow."

Years after the shutdown, critics still proclaimed Strasburg's innings limit was a bad idea. In June 2014 former Nationals player Michael Morse voiced his disagreement with the move to *USA TODAY.* "A lot of people don't realize you might only get one shot," Morse said. "That could have been the only shot. I just wish we could have given it everything we had, but we didn't."

Author and columnist John Feinstein said in 2015 that Strasburg's struggles that year were karma for Rizzo's cockiness in believing he could shut the young pitcher down in 2012 and still win the World Series.

The pitcher, himself, has since moved on from the decision. "As you get older, it becomes easier for you to relax out there," Strasburg said in September 2014. "I've become more comfortable with myself, where I'm at physically."

Nationals Park Opens with Dramatic Flair

After 243 games resulting in a 122–121 record at RFK Stadium from 2005 to 2007, the Washington Nationals and their fans were ready for a change. Out was the 46-year-old lovable relic. In was the brand-spanking new $693 million baseball stadium eloquently named Nationals Park. Not since American League Park II (1904–1911) had a stadium in Washington, D.C., been used specifically for professional baseball. In March 1911 a plumber's blowtorch burned the wooden structure to the ground while the Washington Senators were still in spring training.

Now it was time for baseball in D.C. to have a true home, a true location to call its own.

Nationals Park, built next to the Washington Navy Yard along the Anacostia River, officially opened on March 30, 2008, with the Nationals and the Atlanta Braves facing off in a rare one-game series on national television.

Nationals TV announcer Don Sutton emceed the pregame ceremonies following a video montage of the history of baseball in Washington, D.C., and a time-lapse of Nationals Park's construction on the stadium's 4,532-square-foot video board. The Braves' lineup was introduced followed by the unfurling of two large American flags in the outfield, the Nationals' team introduction, and the singing of the national anthem by D.C. native Denyce Graves.

Just as he had in RFK's 2005 opener, President George W. Bush threw out the ceremonial first pitch. Just as he had in 2005, he threw it high and inside. This time Nats manager Manny Acta was the recipient. After the president's pitch, Washington, D.C., mayor Adrian Fenty yelled out: "Play ball!"

The Nats struck quickly, taking a 2–0 lead in the first inning. Nick Johnson scored Cristian Guzman on a double to right, and Austin Kearns knocked Johnson home with a single to right. Nationals starting pitcher Odalis Perez threw 70 pitches in five innings, striking out two and allowing just four hits, one run, and one walk.

Chipper Jones put the Braves on the board with a solo home run to left-center field in the fourth inning. With two outs in the top of the ninth and Martin Prado on third, Nationals pitcher Jon

Rauch delivered a pitch past catcher Paul Lo Duca, allowing Prado to tie the game.

The game entered the bottom of the ninth tied 2–2. Cristian Guzman struck out, and Lastings Milledge grounded out. Third baseman Ryan Zimmerman, the face of the Nationals, stepped to the plate. Sitting on a 1–0 pitch against Braves pitcher Peter Moylan, Zimmerman christened Nationals Park by taking a 93-mph fastball to the Red Porch seats in left-center field just over the wall that read "Welcome Home."

Having endured the 50-degree weather, the opening night capacity crowd of 41,888 erupted, knowing the team would start the season and the tenure of their new home with a win over their National League East rivals. "You can't really write up a script better than that," Zimmerman said after the game. "It turned out perfect."

Zimmerman stared the ball down, talked to it until it landed, and raised his right arm as he touched first base. After rounding third he casually tossed his helmet toward the infield and was mobbed by his teammates at home plate. With a smile on his face, he dashed toward first base to escape the chaos. "We've waited for so long for a place that can be our own," Zimmerman said of the stadium. "There are just too many people on this team that are tired of being mediocre."

The Nats catcher compared Zimmerman to two of the greatest basketball players of all time. "Zim seems to be the guy when the spotlight is on him, something good happens," Lo Duca said. "You can't teach that...Some guys have it—Kobe Bryant, Michael Jordan. The elite athletes have a way of coming through when you need it the most. Zim is definitely one of those guys."

Zimmerman's fourth career walk-off home run was commemorated during the 2015 season with a fist-raising bobblehead.

8 Walter Johnson's Feats

Walter Johnson's Hall of Fame career in Washington is nothing short of amazing. The humble, quiet Kansas native didn't even play baseball until high school, where he started out as a catcher. His active sidearm fastball got the attention of those around him, and he transitioned to pitcher. In an era before radar guns, all batters could go off of was the sound of the ball while fans heard the thud of the baseball reaching the catcher's mitt. Although in Johnson's day, some mitts were less reliable than others. His first game as a pitcher was a 21–0 loss primarily because the catchers couldn't hold onto the ball during third strikes.

In 1907, at the age of 19, he reportedly pitched 75 consecutive scoreless innings and threw two straight no-hitters in the Idaho State League. He and base-stealing specialist Clyde Milan were scouted in Idaho by Washington and joined the team shortly after. New York Highlanders manager Clark Griffith got wind of Johnson from a friend in Idaho. By the time Griffith requested his friend send Johnson to New York for a tryout, the Nats had already snatched him up.

Still technically not under contract, Johnson made his Major League Baseball debut with the Senators on August 2, 1907, against the vaunted Detroit Tigers. He left a lasting impression on Hall of Famer Ty Cobb that day. "The first time I faced him, I watched him take that easy windup, and then something went past me that made me flinch," Cobb said. "I hardly saw the pitch, but I heard it. The thing just hissed with danger. Every one of us knew we'd met the most powerful arm ever turned loose in a ballpark." Cobb later admitted he would crowd the plate because he knew Johnson was a nice guy and didn't want to hit him.

Johnson boasted a 1.88 ERA in 110⅓ innings his rookie season. In 1908, his second season with the Senators, Johnson accomplished arguably his most impressive feat by tossing three shutouts in a span of four days against the Highlanders.

On July 1, 1920, against the Boston Red Sox, Johnson threw his only MLB no-hitter, striking out 10 batters and walking none. The only Boston baserunner reached on an error by rookie second baseman Bucky Harris, spoiling Johnson's bid for a perfect game. Four years later on August 25, Johnson held the St. Louis Browns hitless through seven innings before rain stopped the game.

Johnson's Staggering Stats

Walter Johnson finished his playing career having accomplished the following:

- 110 shutouts—most in MLB history
- Seven shutout titles
- 417 wins—second in MLB history
- Led AL in wins six times
- 55⅔ consecutive scoreless innings pitched—third in MLB history
- 5,914⅓ innings pitched—most in AL history, third in MLB history
- 531 complete games—fourth in MLB history
- 205 hit batters—fourth most in MLB history
- 2.17 ERA—seventh in MLB history
- Five ERA titles
- 3,508 strikeouts—ninth in MLB history
- 12 strikeout titles
- Hit .433 in 1925, the best single-season batting average for a pitcher
- 802 MLB games as a player, 966 as a manager
- Led AL in innings pitched five times—tied for league record with Bob Feller
- Pitched 14 Opening Day games
- Highest paid pitcher in baseball from 1912 to 1928
- Pitched three seasons without allowing a home run

Johnson's arm was so well-respected that during a game he had thrown a second strike to Cleveland Indians infielder Ray Chapman, who tossed his bat and began to walk back to his team's dugout. Umpire Billy Evans told Chapman that he still had one strike left. "You can have it. It wouldn't do me any good," Chapman reportedly replied over his shoulder.

Johnson appeared in two World Series, closing out Game 7 in 1924 against the New York Giants to give Washington its only title. Dubbed "The Big Train" by legendary sportswriter Grantland Rice, Johnson played 21 seasons in Washington and managed them for four seasons (1929–1932), three of which saw at least 90 wins. He finished his managerial career with the Cleveland Indians from 1933 to 1935. In seven seasons he managed 966 games, winning 529 of them.

Johnson passed away in 1946, and a memorial was unveiled by President Harry Truman outside of Griffith Stadium. Truman called Johnson "the greatest baseball player who ever lived." The memorial now stands at Walter Johnson High School in Bethesda, Maryland.

9 Jordan Zimmermann's No-Hitter

Not since Senators southpaw Bobby Burke threw an eight-strikeout gem on August 8, 1931, had D.C. baseball fans experienced a no-hitter. Fast forward 30,367 days to September 28, 2014, the day of the Nationals' regular season finale. Washington's status as the best team in the National League had been cemented, along with their spot in the postseason. Fans arriving at Nationals Park on a bright and sunny Sunday weren't expecting much more than a win against the Miami Marlins, whom the Nats had beaten 12 times before that season. The Redskins were off that day, having lost to the New York Giants 45–14 on national TV three nights before. The Nats' regular season finale gave D.C. sports fans not only a reprieve from their football team, but also a chance to salute their baseball team for a strong regular season and a glimpse into an upcoming postseason filled with hope.

But no one expected to be a part of history.

Jordan Zimmermann entered the final game with a 13–5 record and a 2.78 ERA. His last appearance also came against the Marlins. Miami won that game eight days earlier 3–2.

It was a different story at Nationals Park, where Zimmermann put on the best performance of his career. He retired the first 14 batters he faced before walking Justin Bour on a two-out, 3–2 pitch in the fifth inning, erasing a perfect game. Zimmermann forced the next batter to line out.

The Auburndale, Wisconsin, native mowed through the sixth inning, striking out one and causing two ground-outs. Garrett Jones reached base safely in the seventh inning on a third-strike wild pitch from Zimmermann. It was Zimmermann's third strike-out of the inning. He responded by picking off Jones at first base to end the seventh.

Zimmermann made quick work of the eighth inning, which ended with his 10th and final strikeout of the day. Resting on a 1–0 lead thanks to an Ian Desmond home run in the second inning, Zimmermann was three outs away from history in the top of the ninth.

Adeiny Hechavarria fell victim to a second base ground-out. Jarrod Saltalamacchia flied out to center field. Entering the game was Christian Yelich, Miami's leadoff hitter. Yelich worked his way to a 2–1 count and drove Zimmermann's 104th pitch to left-center field. Resigned to the fact that he just allowed a double, Zimmermann spun around and begrudgingly watched the ball to see where it would land. Center fielder Michael A. Taylor and left fielder Steven Souza Jr. both sped up to reach the ball. Only Souza, who entered the game in the ninth inning, was close enough to make a play. Before the ball was hit, he was ready to do whatever it took to secure Zimmermann's place in baseball lore. "The more you grasp the reality of the moment, the more you can be ready for anything that comes at you," Souza said after the game.

Souza raced toward the Marlins bullpen, leaped in the air as if he was posing for a Superman comic book cover, stuck out his glove as the ball made its way in, and pulled his right hand in to secure the catch—and the no-hitter—in dramatic fashion. "The 2–1 pitch lined to left-center field," Nationals radio play-by-play announcer Charlie Slowes belted out over the airwaves. "Souza moving over, can he get there? HE MAKES A DIVING CATCH! HE MAKES A DIVING CATCH! He holds on! It's a no-hitter! It's a no-hitter for Jordan Zimmermann!"

Top Pitchers in Nationals History

Jordan Zimmerman is the winningest pitcher in Nats history. Here are the leading pitchers in four different categories through Washington's first 11 seasons based on their Nationals tenure.

Wins
1. 70—Jordan Zimmerman
2. 54—Stephen Strasburg
3. 53—Gio Gonzalez
4. 44—Livan Hernandez
5. 42—John Lannan

Innings Pitched
1. 1,094—Jordan Zimmermann
2. 828—Livan Hernandez
3. 783—John Lannan
4. 776—Stephen Strasburg
5. 729—Gio Gonzalez

Saves
1. 113—Chad Cordero
2. 95—Drew Storen
3. 75—Rafael Soriano
4. 34—Tyler Clippard
5. 26—Matt Capps

Games
1. 414—Tyler Clippard
2. 355—Drew Storen
3. 305—Chad Cordero
4. 245—Sean Burnett/Saul Rivera
5. 239—Jon Rauch

Souza rolled over on his back and immediately lifted his glove to show he had made the catch. Zimmermann became the first player in Nats history to record a no-hitter.

Looking to left field as the events unfolded, Zimmermann raised his arms. The Nationals' dugout cleared, and his teammates mobbed him at the mound. The scoreboard at Nationals Park displayed "NO-HITTER!" with Zimmermann's digital signature under it, and video of fireworks playing in the background.

After the game Zimmermann said: "whatever [Steven] wants, he can have. I'll buy him anything." Souza jokingly requested a BMW but did receive a Best Buy gift card from Zimmermann.

10 Cheer on the Racing Presidents

One of the most anticipated moments of every Nationals game is the Presidents Race, a tradition that began during the 2006 season. The race started off with the representatives of Mount Rushmore—George Washington, Thomas Jefferson, Abraham Lincoln, and Teddy Roosevelt. Each wears the order of their presidency as their jersey number.

During the fourth inning of every home game, the presidents sneak out from behind the center-field wall and sprint around the warning track with their giant heads (perhaps a shot at politicians in itself) swaying back and forth as they make their way down either the first or third-base side to reach the finish line.

One president became a fan favorite for an obvious reason.

Teddy Roosevelt was a big loser. For seven years he hadn't won a race in more than 500 attempts. This became such an outrage that the "Let Teddy Win" campaign was formed and quickly gained steam. Fans constantly held out hope with each race that it would be his time to earn a Curly W. In September of 2012, ESPN produced a satirical video about Roosevelt's shortcomings with the race. One of Roosevelt's biggest supporters was United States senator and 2008 Republican presidential nominee John McCain. "I'm paying a lot of attention to the fact that one of the truly great presidents in history has never won a race," McCain said in the video. "I'm outraged. That's why I'm calling for congressional hearings to right this horrible wrong."

On October 3, 2012, Teddy fell behind in the early stages of the race, but a fake Philly Phanatic, aka Fakenatic, took out George, Tom, and Abe, allowing Teddy to take the lead. With his competitors left in his dust, the Fakenatic followed Teddy to the finish line, which led to a thunderous ovation from the crowd at Nationals Park. Fans celebrated, and politicians rejoiced. McCain tweeted: "#Teddy won! #Teddy won! #Teddy won! We've defeated the massive left wing conspiracy!"

Nationals third baseman Ryan Zimmerman was less enthused. "I am so glad Teddy won so we can stop talking about Teddy," Zimmerman said sarcastically in his standard dry tone. "People get more excited for a mascot race than a game. Yes, I'm excited Teddy won. I'm ecstatic."

Washington's deliberate ploy to hold Roosevelt down for so long could be retaliation for the real life president's view of the sport. The proud outdoorsman, who enjoyed hunting and football, called baseball a "mollycoddle" game. In today's vernacular that translates to pampered or overprotected.

Following the 2012 season, the team unveiled William Howard Taft or "Bill," as the name on the back of his jersey indicates, as the fifth racing president. Taft became the first president to throw out the first pitch on Opening Day, tossing a baseball from his seats on the first-base side to legendary pitcher Walter Johnson on April 14, 1910, before the Washington Senators hosted the Philadelphia

Part of a Nationals tradition, the Racing Presidents sprint during the fourth inning of an August 26, 2015, game against the San Diego Padres.

Athletics. Taft went on to win 12 races in 2013, tying Teddy for last. Teddy went on to win 26 races in 2014, the most of any of the presidents that season.

Every year since 1909, Democrats and Republicans have faced off for charity in the congressional baseball game. In June of 2015, President Barack Obama stopped by Nationals Park to enjoy the game. As he was leaving the stadium, he spotted the racing presidents and stopped the motorcade to greet them. He posed for a picture with George, Tom, Abe, Teddy, and Bill and tweeted the picture with the message: "I challenged them to a race." It was retweeted more than 10,000 times.

Weeks later, the Nationals introduced Calvin Coolidge as the sixth racing president. Coolidge was president when the Senators won the 1924 World Series. He even tossed out the first pitch of Game 1 as well as the home opener of the 1925 World Series. It didn't take long for Silent Cal to make an impact in his debut as a running caricature of himself. On July 3, 2015, he sprinted in front of George to catch up to Teddy. As Teddy was about to cross the finish line, Calvin knocked him out of the way to capture his first win.

11 Rivalry with the Orioles

A dream scenario for local baseball fans would be a Washington Nationals-Baltimore Orioles World Series in what would unequivocally be the most important "Battle of the Beltway" in local sports history. That matchup would play host to a dynamic number of fans: those who grew up Orioles fans and converted to Nationals fandom when the Montreal Expos moved to D.C. in 2004; Orioles fans who never converted; Senators fans who converted to become Orioles fans during baseball's absence in D.C.; Senators fans who never converted; and the large contingent of fans who still root for both teams and sport both teams' gear when they meet up every season. Even Nationals star Bryce Harper declared that a Baltimore-Washington World Series would be "epic." No matter where your allegiance lies, it's impossible to argue with that.

The Orioles are the Nationals' biggest non-division rival. Well, they're about as big of a rival as one team could be, considering they face off only four to six times a year over the course of a 162-game season. Geography plays the primary role in this rivalry. Nationals Park is less than 40 miles away from Oriole Park at Camden Yards, making both parks accessible to supporters of either side. Banter between Baltimore and Washington sports fans is a local pastime.

Orioles owner Peter Angelos plays the biggest role of any person. Senators owner Clark Griffith agreed to waive his territorial rights for a fee to allow the St. Louis Browns to move to Baltimore to become the Orioles in 1954. However, Angelos put up much more of a fight to keep the sport out of the nation's capital. After years of ardent opposition to baseball returning to D.C., he said in a 2004 radio interview that "there are no real baseball fans in D.C." That contradicted his resounding fear of losing fans to the bigger D.C. market. Major League Baseball owners voted 29–1 to approve the Expos' move to D.C. in December 2004. Angelos was the only dissenting vote. He was displeased with the decision and eventually negotiated a TV deal heavily favoring his pocketbooks.

Orioles manager Buck Showalter stoked the rivalry's flames during a series between the two teams at Nationals Park in 2014. "Our owner was kind enough to let them have a team here," Showalter said. "A lot of people that are here are people that used to come over to Baltimore."

Nationals fans wouldn't use "kind" to describe the way Angelos went about Montreal's move to D.C. Even Orioles fans aren't fond of their litigious owner.

A popular fan video produced in 2012 titled "Baltimore vs. Washington: An Orioles fan and a Nationals fan walk into a bar..." still holds up even if some of the players referenced are no longer on their respective teams. The video depicts two friends sitting at a bar joking back and forth about each other's clubs. One fan is sporting a red Nationals polo with a red Curly W cap while the other wears a black T-shirt and an Orioles hat. One of the more memorable lines in the video comes when the Nats fan points to his hat and says: "You know what I see when I see this? Another Curly W in the books." His friend quips: "You know what I see? Walgreens." For anyone who wants to get a few laughs in before the two teams meet again, be sure to check it out.

The lasting image of the Nats-O's series in 2015 came when Nats closer Jonathan Papelbon delivered a pitch up and in that plunked Orioles third baseman Manny Machado in the second game of their last series. It was the first pitch delivered to Machado since his seventh-inning, two-run go-ahead home run. That won't be forgotten by the Orioles. The teams will play a home-and-home series from Monday, August 22 through Thursday, August 25 in 2016. The first two games will be at Oriole Park at Camden Yards, and the final two will take place at Nationals Park.

D.C. baseball teams haven't had much luck against the Orioles over their history. The original Senators were 65–89 against the Charm City birds from 1954 to 1960. The expansion Senators fared even worse, going 61–135 from 1961 to 1971. The Nationals are 23–33 all time vs. the Orioles. Amidst the bad overall record, the Senators managed to have some memorable moments against their brethren just a hop, skip, and a jump northeast.

The original Senators played their final game, a 2–1 home loss against the Orioles on October 2, 1960. On September 12, 1962, Senators pitcher Tom Cheney set an MLB record with 21 strikeouts over the course of 16 innings in Baltimore's Memorial Stadium on the way to a 2–1 Washington win. He threw more than 200 pitches, which is double today's typical limit. The next night Senators outfielder Jimmy Piersall went into the stands to confront an Orioles fan who was taunting him about his battles with mental illness. Both men were taken to the police station. The 32-year-old center fielder was charged with disorderly conduct but was never convicted.

The current Nationals have also had their own moments against the Orioles. On June 12, 2007, in a 7–4 victory in Camden

Yards, Chad Cordero became the second youngest pitcher in MLB history to reach 100 career saves. Nats fans certainly remember the convincing 17–5 win in Baltimore on May 20, 2011. The game featured six Washington home runs and two triples. The 17 runs are still the most in Nationals history. Exactly one year later at Nationals Park, pitcher Stephen Strasburg hit his first career home run, an offering he took to deep left-center field off of Orioles starter Wei-Yin Chen. Regardless of whether you support the red, white, and blue or the orange and black, these games should certainly be circled on your calendar.

12 America's Team— The 1924 Senators

Over the course of D.C.'s only World Series championship season, the 1924 Washington Senators transformed into America's team. The cast of Nationals (the name was used interchangeably with Senators back then) characters was led by 36-year-old pitching sensation Walter Johnson, 34-year-old Sam Rice, 30-year-old first baseman Joe Judge, 27-year-old first-year manager/second baseman Bucky Harris, and 23-year-old outfielder Goose Goslin. After starting the 1924 season 24–26, the Senators went on a tear, winning 10 straight games. Babe Ruth wrote in his autobiography that, "Washington got hot quicker than almost any club I ever saw."

The Senators weren't based off a power offense, hitting just 21 home runs as a team that season. Ruth alone had 46. The team preferred to get on base and manufacture runs. Six players, who played at least 45 games that season, hit .300 or better on the year. Washington swept Ruth's Yankees in New York en route to their ninth straight win and sole possession of first place in the American

League. The team returned home to 8,000 giddy fans at Union Station.

In early September President Calvin Coolidge invited the team to the White House to congratulate them on the season. The president, still mourning the death of his 16-year-old son from blood poisoning two months earlier, told them he'd be pleased to root them on in person at the World Series.

The team then embarked on a crucial 20-game road trip to close out the regular season, facing seven of the eight American League clubs: Philadelphia, Detroit, Cleveland, St. Louis, Chicago, and Boston. Knowing this, Harris told his team: "Let's not make any enemies if we can help it. Most of the western clubs would rather see us win the pennant than the Yankees. Let's beat 'em, but treat 'em nice."

Washington went 14–6 on the road trip and clinched the AL pennant on September 29 in Boston's Fenway Park. "The celebration at Fenway Park must have made the Senators feel like they had been playing at home," author Frederic Frommer recalled in a 2014 *Politico* article. "Hundreds of fans rushed onto the field to mob the Senators, and thousands more cheered the team as it left the field. They tossed straw hats into the air and waved handkerchiefs, and some lifted Senators owner [Clark] Griffith from his seat in the stands and ferried him down to the dugout. Griffith, Harris, and Johnson received standing ovations."

An editorial from *The New York Times* highlighted the team's national admiration. "There is no doubt as to the popularity of a Washington victory," it stated. "All over the major league circuits, the fans have been cheering for the Senators. In Boston the crowd stood up and cheered every time they scored." *The Boston Globe* celebrated Washington's first pennant on the next day's front page with a cartoon of Harris standing on top of the Capitol building and holding a pennant that said "champions" with tiny fans jumping for joy. "We knew that the country wanted us to win, and that's what helped to keep us fighting," Judge said on the train ride back from Boston.

Coolidge telegrammed Harris with the following message: "Heartiest congratulations to you and your team for your great work in bringing Washington its first pennant. We of Washington are proud of you and behind you. On to the world's championship."

More than 2,000 fans camped out at Union Station to greet the newly-crowned American League champs the morning of October 1. That afternoon 100,000 people packed Pennsylvania Avenue for a celebratory parade.

Johnson, Washington's star attraction, was known as a nice, humble man. He was in his 17th season in D.C., having only played on six winning teams before his first World Series appearance. In a syndicated column titled "Everybody is pulling for Walter" that was published in late September, Will Rogers wrote, "There is more genuine interest in him than there is in a presidential election."

Detroit's Ty Cobb hopped on the Nats bandwagon, expressing his allegiance to Washington as they took on the nine-time National League champion New York Giants in the 1924 World Series. "They are imbued with the competitive spirit and they'll fight hard," he said.

Having seen the Yankees battle the Giants in the three previous World Series, baseball fans wanted some new blood to contend for a championship. "Harris and his players are liked everywhere because they are young and dashing and enthusiastic," *The New York Times* proclaimed. "New York is hated because it has won too many pennants and possesses too much money and is too powerful."

Johnson started Games 1 and 5, losing both contests and disappointing fans everywhere. But when Game 7 came around, he delivered when it mattered the most. Down 3–1 the Senators tied the game in the bottom of the eighth inning. Johnson came on in the ninth as a reliever. Little did he know he'd have to pitch three more shutout innings until a lucky bounce decided his team's fate.

In the bottom of the 12ᵗʰ and with Muddy Ruel at second base, Earl McNeely hit a grounder toward Giants third baseman Freddie Lindstrom. Unexpectedly, the ball bounced over Lindstrom, and Ruel hustled toward home uncontested. Some say it just took a wicked bounce; others say a pebble redirected the ball in Washington's favor. Sportswriter Fred Lieb claimed, "Perhaps the millions of fans pulling for Washington to win its first World Series championship influenced the usually fickle goddess of luck to give a little lift to the gallant Nationals." The Senators won the game—and the series—4–3. David had finally slayed Goliath. "The good Lord just couldn't bear to see a fine fellow like Walter Johnson lose again," said Jack Bentley, New York's losing pitcher and Johnson's teammate in D.C. from 1913 to 1916.

Giants manager John McGraw, who led New York to nine World Series appearances during his 31-year reign as skipper from 1902 to 1932, was humble in defeat, stating that Washington winning the series was the "greatest thing that could have happened to baseball. It was a popular victory."

The Riot

The expansion Washington Senators set up shop in 1961 to replace the original Senators, who left for Minnesota to become the Twins. The second version of the franchise experienced just one winning season, going a surprising 86–76 in 1969, Ted Williams' first season as manager. By the summer of the 1971 season, owner Bob Short was claiming that he had lost $3 million since buying the Senators in the fall of 1968. With an agreement in place to move the team to Texas, a sense of loss enveloped Washington, D.C., for the second time in 11 years. On September 30, 1971, the Senators would take on the New York Yankees for the last game in franchise history.

Fans arrived at RFK Stadium with a sense of joy, numbness, uncertainty, anger, and everything in between. They were joyful because they were witnessing history and recollecting on what had been. They were numb because they had seen this movie before. They were uncertain as to whether or not they'd see another D.C. baseball team in their lifetime. And they were angry at Short for taking what was theirs.

The resentment of Short was palpable. Fans at the stadium chanted, "We want Bob Short!" One fan wore a black armband to symbolize mourning. Others carried around dummies of Short. In the outfield's upper deck, fans unfurled two banners that read "SHORT STINKS," prompting a standing ovation from the 14,460 spectators on hand.

Wisely, Short stayed home in Edina, Minnesota, listening to the game's radio broadcast via a special phone hookup. Short took the time to call the station to complain about announcer Ron Menchine's criticism of him throughout the broadcast. Washington dug themselves out of a 5–1 deficit, which was highlighted by a four-run sixth inning that included a leadoff blast from Frank Howard. The pitch was a gift from Yankees pitcher Mike Kekich. "Let's just say I tried to throw him a straight pitch," Kekich said after the game. "I felt sorry for the fans."

Howard waved his helmet in the air, tossed his cap into the stands, and blew kisses to the crowd. Williams took Howard out of the game following the home run, telling the slugger: "You'd better get out. It's going to be a wild house."

Fans were growing restless as the game went on. Players spotted them tossing ripped pieces of Ted Williams' book, *My Turn at Bat*. The book was given away to fans along with a bunch of other promotional items such as balls, shirts, and hats. A few fans tried to rush the field but were promptly subdued. Sensing something was stirring with the rest of the crowd, umpire Jim Odom told Senators first baseman Tom McCraw that he was getting ready to leave. McCraw told Odom: "If you go, I'm going to be in your back pocket."

The Senators scored two more runs in the bottom of the eighth inning to carry a 7–5 lead into the ninth. Senators pitcher Joe Grzenda took the mound to close out the final chapter in D.C. baseball history—at least for the foreseeable future. Williams allowed the relievers in the bullpen to go to the locker room when there were two outs so that they were safe from the crowd. "They knew something was going to happen," Grzenda said. He forced Felipe Alou and Bobby Murcer to ground out.

Then, with one out standing between the Senators and their final win in franchise history, the dam broke loose. Hordes of fans hopped the fence to storm the field, picking up chunks of grass, dirt, bases, and light bulbs from the scoreboard. "They came over the fence, and there was actually dust flying," Grzenda said. "There were hundreds that came over the fence. It looked like a herd of cattle coming in those old movies when they stampede."

RFK Stadium usher captain James Findley, who began working at Griffith Stadium 28 years earlier, explained the crowd's behavior as "just one of them things. [You] can't blame 'em on a last night," Findley said. "They're sad. I'm sad. This is my life."

Howard, starting pitcher Dick Bosman, and first baseman Don Mincher gathered around in the clubhouse drinking National Bohemian until 2 AM, signing autographs for a few straggling fans outside the stadium as they made their way to the parking lot.

In typical Senators fashion, despite their "win," the game was marked as a loss and forever recorded as a forfeit by the traditional forfeiture score of 9–0 that baseball mandated.

Grzenda made sure to keep the ball from the game's final out. Little did he know that 12,250 days later, it would be used by the president of the United States for the ceremonial first pitch in baseball's official return to D.C.

14 Max Scherzer Throws Two No-Hitters in 2015

The seven-year, $210 million deal Max Scherzer signed with the Nationals in January 2015 made jaws drop throughout Major League Baseball, including his own. However, the eight-year veteran didn't let those numbers faze him during his first season in Washington. In 33 games in 2015, Scherzer struck out a Nationals-record 276 batters, tossed six shutouts, pitched into the eighth inning 12 times, struck out 10 or more batters in a game 11 times, carried a no-hitter through five innings six times, took a no-hitter through six innings four times, and, on three occasions, was one out away from becoming the 24th pitcher in history to throw a perfect game.

As if those feats weren't impressive enough, he topped off his fantastic debut season in D.C. with two no-hitters, becoming the fifth player in baseball history to do so in the same regular season. The last to accomplish that was Nolan Ryan with the California Angels in 1973. Scherzer is the sixth major league pitcher to throw two no-hitters in the same calendar season. Roy Halladay threw a regular season no-hitter and a postseason no-hitter for the Philadelphia Phillies in 2010.

The meticulous Scherzer brought a calculated blend of comedy and intensity to the Nationals clubhouse. On his off days, he can clown around and prank with the best of them. On days he's scheduled to pitch, he transforms into an ultra-focused animal with no room for jokes.

Nationals general manager Mike Rizzo was already familiar with Scherzer's makeup years before bringing him to Washington. He drafted the eventual ace in 2006 while with the Arizona Diamondbacks.

Scherzer's first no-hitter came against the Pittsburgh Pirates at Nationals Park on June 20. However, it was not without its own dose of controversy. One strike away from a perfect game and with the home crowd providing a standing ovation and awaiting the final out, Scherzer delivered a slider inside. Pirates pinch-hitter Jose Tabata appeared to lean in and was hit on the elbow pad as a result. Tabata denied intentionally leaning in to break up Scherzer's perfect game, saying it was a movement based on pure instinct with the ball quickly tailing toward him. Nationals fans beg to differ. They showed their displeasure by booing Tabata profusely the next day.

Though disappointed, Scherzer brushed it off and forced Josh Harrison to fly out three pitches later to complete the first no-hitter of his career. His final line included 82 strikes in 106 pitches and 10 strikeouts. Scherzer was drenched in chocolate syrup by his teammates in a tradition he started that season. His sterling performance came on the eve of Father's Day with his parents in attendance and six days after a dominant outing against the Milwaukee Brewers, in which he struck out a Nationals-record 16 batters and was one Carlos Gomez seventh-inning bloop single away from a perfect game.

He became the first pitcher since 1944—and the fifth pitcher of all time—to allow one hit or fewer in two consecutive complete games, conjuring up memories of Johnny Vander Meer's back-to-back no-hitters with the Cincinnati Reds in 1938. Scherzer's workmanlike performance in the month of June placed him at the top of the list for the Cy Young Award. He earned National League Pitcher of the Month in May and June and won National League Pitcher of the Week for the week of June 22.

His phenomenal first half also resulted in his first All-Star nod, but his play tailed off after the Midsummer Classic, and he struggling mightily in August. He managed to resurrect himself in September. With nothing but pride left to play for, Scherzer dazzled again by topping the team record he set in June by striking out 17 New York Mets on the way to his second no-hitter of the season, which occurred on a cold night on Saturday, October 3 at Citi Field.

Scherzer was in familiar territory, taking another perfect game into the sixth inning. That was until Mets catcher Kevin Plawecki hit a ground ball to third baseman Yunel Escobar, who hesitated and underthrew first baseman Clint Robinson for an error, ending Scherzer's perfect game bid. That didn't daunt the 31-year-old, who was so locked in that he struck out an astonishing nine straight prior to facing his final batter. He ended the night with 80 strikes on 109 pitches.

He became the first player in MLB history to throw two no-hitters without allowing a walk. He is also the first pitcher in baseball history to strike out 17 batters and walk none in a no-hitter. His dominance over the Mets was the second-best pitching performance, according to Bill James' Game Score metric. Scherzer logged a Game Score of 104, just one point shy of Kerry Wood's 20-strikeout performance with the Chicago Cubs in 1998.

In a strange twist, Scherzer finished with one hit of his own in each of his contests against Milwaukee, Pittsburgh, and New York. He had 15 hits and batted .217 on the year. On the mound Scherzer's season ended with a 14–12 record, 2.79 ERA (11th-best in baseball), 276 strikeouts (second only to Clayton Kershaw's 301), .208 opponent batting average (fifth-best in baseball), and a career-low WHIP of 0.918.

Since the franchise's first game on April 4, 2005, the Nationals went 3,464 days without throwing a no-hitter. Thanks to Jordan Zimmermann and Max Scherzer, three were thrown in a span of

370 days. Scherzer now owns 66 percent of Nationals no-hitters and 40 percent of no-hitters thrown in D.C. baseball history.

15 The 2012 NL East Champions

Following an 80–81 record in 2011, the Nationals were expected to improve with the likely call-up of outfield phenom Bryce Harper and the return of pitcher Stephen Strasburg from Tommy John surgery after pitching five games at the end of the previous season. The quantum leap, however, to National League East championship contender wasn't anticipated until 2013.

In the 2012 offseason, the Nats traded for pitcher Gio Gonzalez, who went on to win 20 games; signed reserve infielder Chad Tracy, closer Brad Lidge, and starting pitcher Edwin Jackson; and re-signed starting pitcher Chien-Ming Wang and outfielder Rick Ankiel.

The Nats had a 14–4 record by April 25, a sign they were well ahead of schedule.

Harper was called up and made his debut on April 28 in Los Angeles against the Dodgers. With his national reputation preceding him, he took the plate amid a chorus of boos. He finished 1-for-3 with a sacrifice fly in the ninth inning to give the Nats the 2–1 lead.

Harper's first true rookie test was on ESPN against the Philadelphia Phillies on May 6. Pitcher Cole Hamels hit him on his first throw to make an example of him. Harper advanced to third on a single by Jayson Werth. He exacted more revenge by stealing home on an attempted pickoff of Werth to give the Nats a 1–0 lead. Intentionally hitting Harper infuriated the Nats brass, including Nationals general manager Mike Rizzo, who called Hamels "fake tough." Harper, though, turned the other cheek, simply complimenting Hamels as a pitcher.

That night, the Nats suffered a huge loss when Werth broke his wrist attempting to catch a fly ball. He didn't play again until August 2. The former Phillies star received added incentive to return as Philadelphia fans mocked him while he walked off the field clutching his wrist. "I am motivated to get back quickly and see to it personally those people never walk down Broad Street in celebration again," Werth wrote in an email to *The Washington Post*'s Adam Kilgore after the game.

Injuries played a role in the team's identity throughout the year. Five reserve position players appeared in at least 68 games. Ankiel (68 games), Tracy (73), Tyler Moore (75), Jesus Flores (83), Steve Lombardozzi (126), and Roger Bernadina (129) all contributed in one way or another. They were the engine that kept the train rolling, though controversy ensued when Rizzo stuck with his plan to restrict Strasburg to 160 innings. On September 8, Nationals manager Davey Johnson informed Strasburg that his season was over with 24 games remaining.

Nonetheless, the team celebrated its first division title and the city's first playoff berth since 1933 in unusual fashion. With two games remaining, they lost at home to the Phillies 2–0, but news trickled out in the ninth inning that the Pittsburgh Pirates beat the Atlanta Braves 2–1, clinching Washington's first division title since moving to D.C.

For the longest time, the Washington Senators were known for being "first in war, first in peace, and last in the American League," a spin-off of Henry Lee's eulogy of George Washington, in which he said the nation's first president was: "First in war, first in peace, and first in the hearts of his countrymen."

Now, for the first time, the Nats were considered "first in war, first in peace, and first in the National League," ending the season with an MLB-best record of 98–64. The team also led baseball with three Silver Slugger Award winners: first baseman Adam LaRoche (.271, 33 home runs, 100 RBIs), shortstop Ian Desmond (.292, 25 home runs, and 73 RBIs), and Strasburg (.277). LaRoche also won a Gold Glove.

In the final game of the year, perhaps the most eagerly anticipated moment came to fruition when Teddy Roosevelt won his first Presidents Race after more than 500 losses.

Up next were the reigning World Series champions, the St. Louis Cardinals, in the National League Division Series. The Nats took Game 1 in St. Louis 3–2, dropped Game 2 by a 12–4 score, and were blanked 8–0 in Game 3 at Nationals Park. Werth played the hero in Game 4 with a 13-pitch at-bat that resulted in a walk-off homer. Game 5 proved heartbreaking as a 6–0 lead dissolved into a 9–7 loss following a four-run ninth inning by the Cardinals.

The season ended in ruthless fashion but didn't take away from the beginning of the Nats' reign of supremacy in the NL East.

16 Presidential First Pitches

Presidents have long had a fascination with baseball—even in the sport's earliest years.

In 1865 the Washington Nationals faced the Brooklyn Atlantics and the Philadelphia Athletics in a tournament at the Ellipse in front of the White House. President Andrew Johnson let government clerks out early to watch the games. Johnson even attended one himself.

The tradition of the presidential first pitch, however, did not start for another 45 years.

On April 14, 1910, William Howard Taft attended the Washington Senators season opener against the Philadelphia Athletics. Senators manager Jimmy McAleer suggested to 22-year-old phenom pitcher Walter Johnson that he catch a ball from Taft before the game. Taft tossed a ball from his seats on the first-base line to Johnson and became the first president to throw the ceremonial first pitch. Johnson then threw a complete game one-hitter in a 3–0 victory.

Taft's presence also unintentionally broke up Johnson's no-hitter. (Senators outfielder Doc Gessler admitted he was daydreaming about hitting a grand slam in front of the president when he tripped over a fan while trying to catch a fly ball that dropped for a double.) Johnson later mailed the ball to the White House with a note requesting Taft's signature. The president returned the ball with the following inscription: "For Walter Johnson, with the hope that he may continue to be as formidable as in yesterday's game. William H. Taft."

Taft threw out the first pitch of Opening Day 1911 but missed the 1912 opener, which was four days after his friend and military aide, Major Archibald Butt, died aboard the *Titanic*. At the behest of Senators owner Clark Griffith, who wanted to turn this ceremony into a tradition, Taft rescheduled and threw the first pitch on June 18, 1912.

As part of the tradition, Washington would begin its season one day ahead of the rest of the American League to commemorate the "presidential opener." The president would stand in his box and toss the ball over a crowd of photographers into a group of players from both teams. It became such an event that Congress even recessed for the day.

Woodrow Wilson—who had a "dugout" at the White House where he read and talked about baseball—carried the torch, throwing Opening Day first pitches in 1913, 1915, and 1916. He missed the 1914 opener due to a dispute with Mexican President

Victoriano Huerta, the 1917 and 1918 openers due to World War I, and the 1919 opener because of his attendance at the Paris Peace Conference.

After he left office, he suffered a stroke that partially paralyzed him, but he still wanted to attend Senators games. Griffith acquiesced, allowing him to park a car in foul territory between left field and the spectators. Griffith even had a player sit on the bumper to act as a ball boy and fend off any foul balls headed Wilson's way. Wilson owns the best record of all presidents on D.C. baseball Opening Day games. The team went 3–0 when he visited.

Warren Harding, a former minor league team owner, tossed the Opening Day pitches from 1921 to 1923. The 1921 opener was the first Senators loss after a presidential first pitch.

Harding's successor, Calvin Coolidge, threw out the first pitch of Game 1 of the 1924 World Series, becoming the first president to do so during the series. He also tossed the first pitch of the 1925 World Series home opener and the Senators openers in 1924, 1925, 1927, and 1928. He missed the 1926 opener because of his father's death. Ironically, Coolidge saw the most success despite not being a baseball fan. His wife, Grace, though, was a die-hard. She even kept score at the games.

Herbert Hoover threw the first pitch at Senators openers from 1929 to 1932 while holding the undesirable distinction of throwing first pitches during the Great Depression and prohibition.

Hoover's successor, Franklin D. Roosevelt, tossed the most Opening Day first pitches, spanning 1933–1938, 1940, and 1941. He missed the 1939 opener to attend a family gathering. His pitch in 1940 missed wildly, smashing into the camera of a photographer for *The Washington Post*. FDR was on hand for Game 3 of 1933 World Series and tossed the first pitch at the 1937 All-Star Game at Griffith Stadium.

From 1942 to 1944, no president tossed an Opening Day first pitch. FDR died eight days before Washington's 1945 home

President John F. Kennedy throws out the first pitch before the expansion Senators' first game on April 10, 1961.

opener. On September 8, 1945, six days after Japan surrendered to end World War II, Harry Truman threw the first pitch before the Senators took on the St. Louis Browns. Truman threw Opening Day first pitches from 1946 to 1952 and attended 16 Senators games, the most of any president. He became the first president to attend a night game (1948) and a game on the Fourth of July (1952).

In 1950 Truman threw one ball left-handed and one right-handed. He was booed in the 1951 opener, which took place nine days after he stripped General Douglas MacArthur of his command in the Far East. Music was played at Griffith Stadium to drown out the catcalls. MacArthur had delivered his famous line, "Old soldiers never die, they just fade away" the day before the game.

Dwight Eisenhower threw first pitches at home openers from 1953 to 1956, 1958, and 1960. He actually blew off the 1953 opener to go golfing at Augusta, Georgia. The opener was scheduled for April 13 but was rained out. Ike was luckily able to throw the ceremonial pitch on the rescheduled opener of April 16 after enduring a lot of criticism for skipping it initially. Vice president Richard Nixon threw the first pitch at the 1959 opener in Eisenhower's place.

On April 10, 1961, John F. Kennedy threw out the first pitch during the expansion Senators' first game, a 4–3 loss to the Chicago White Sox. In 1962 Kennedy tossed the first ever Opening Day pitch at D.C. Stadium, which was later renamed RFK Stadium in honor of his brother, Robert. John threw the 1963 Opening Day first pitch seven months before his assassination.

Lyndon Johnson threw Opening Day first pitches in 1964, 1965, and 1967. Vice president Hubert Humphrey hurled the Opening Day first pitch in 1968 but was booed by Senators fans when he walked to the Minnesota Twins dugout to greet his home-town team, which had moved from D.C. in 1960. (The Twins would later play their home games in the Hubert H. Humphrey Metrodome from 1982 to 2009.)

Nixon was an avid baseball fan who composed his own All-Star teams for the Associated Press. On April 7, 1969, with Senators manager Ted Williams looking on, he threw his only Opening Day first pitch in D.C. as president. When the expansion Senators left to become the Texas Rangers after the 1971 season, Nixon switched his allegiances to his home team, the California Angels. He tried to get future presidential first pitches moved to the commander in chief's hometown, but it never materialized.

George W. Bush threw out the first pitch at two very memorable openers. On April 14, 2005, he was handed the ball used for the last pitch in Senators history. Bush's pitch rang in the new era of the Washington Nationals as they made their long-awaited home debut in front of a boisterous RFK crowd. Bush also threw the first pitch on Opening Night in 2008 as Nationals Park was unveiled. Bush, a passionate baseball fan, owned the Rangers before running for president.

Barack Obama commemorated the 100th anniversary of the presidential first pitch in controversial fashion at the Nationals' home opener on April 5, 2010. As he took the mound, the Chicago native pulled out a White Sox hat from his glove, placed it on his head, hesitated to give everyone enough time to notice it, waved to the booing crowd, leaned back, and laughed. He returned two months later to watch Stephen Strasburg take on the White Sox at Nationals Park. Obama did not throw the first pitch in what was Strasburg's third career start.

Obama is the only president to throw just one Senators/Nationals Opening Day pitch.

Overall, the Senators and Nationals are 25–24 (.510) when presidents throw the Opening Day first pitch. They are 14–10 (.583) when Republicans throw the first pitch and 11–14 (.440) when Democrats do so.

17 The Longest Game in Playoff History

Game 2 of the 2014 National League Division Series between the Washington Nationals and the San Francisco Giants lasted 18 innings, which translated to six hours and 23 minutes in real time, both Major League Baseball postseason records. It was two playoff games for the price of one.

Jordan Zimmermann was on the mound at Nationals Park for the first time since his no-hitter in the regular season finale just six days before. Reminiscent of his last start, Zimmermann was in a zone and pitching a gem, throwing only 100 pitches, striking out six and only walking one.

And then everything changed.

Zimmermann's lone walk came on his 100th and final pitch. A 92-mph offering to Joe Panik that was several inches outside snapped Zimmermann's streak of 20 consecutive retired batters. The rest of the series would ride or die with what happened next. Nationals manager Matt Williams, a first-year skipper, emerged from the dugout and removed Zimmermann from the game and turned to closer Drew Storen, who had won back that role during the regular season after Rafael Soriano's inconsistencies became unbearable.

Storen, as Nats fans vividly remember, struggled in his first postseason go-round. In Game 5 of the 2012 NLDS against the St. Louis Cardinals, Storen came on to close the game in the top of the ninth. After sporting a 6–0 lead after three innings, the Nationals allowed runs in the fourth, fifth, seventh, and eighth innings. Holding on to a 7–5 lead, all Storen needed was three outs in order for Washington to advance to the city's first league championship series.

After allowing a double to Carlos Beltran, Storen then walked Yadier Molina and David Freese to load the bases. Adron Chambers was sent in to run for Molina. A Daniel Descalso single scored Beltran and Chambers to tie the game at seven. Five pitches later Pete Kozma singled to score Freese and Descalso to give St. Louis the 9–7 lead and ultimately a victory by that tally.

Fast forward two years. Storen, with one on and two out, surrendered a single to Buster Posey. With Panik at second, that meant two on and two out with Pablo Sandoval at the plate. The first pitch to Sandoval was fouled. The second turned into a double that plated Panik to tie the game 1–1. As Panik scored, Posey was rounding third and heading home. A relay throw from Nationals shortstop Ian Desmond was bounced to Nationals catcher Wilson Ramos, who then tagged Posey at the waist as he slid home for the final out of the inning in one of the closest calls anyone will ever see.

With Desmond, Bryce Harper, and Wilson Ramos unable to get on base in the bottom of the ninth, the game carried on. Tyler Clippard, Matt Thornton, Aaron Barrett, Jerry Blevins, Craig Stammen, and Soriano pitched through the 16th inning, allowing no runs and just two hits. After being the fifth pitcher on a dominant starting staff, Tanner Roark had finished the regular season with an impressive 2.85 ERA in 31 games but had to prepare himself for the life of long relief in the postseason.

Roark pitched a clean 17th inning, forcing a fly out of Posey, line out of Sandoval, and strikeout of Hunter Pence. On for the 18th, Roark gave up a devastating 413-foot home run to Brandon Belt on a full count to give the Giants a 2–1 lead. He then struck out Brandon Crawford and Gary Brown and forced a fly out of Juan Perez to close the inning, but the damage was done.

In the bottom of the 18th, Danny Espinosa struck out, and Denard Span grounded out. With two outs Anthony Rendon was walked. Jayson Werth, the hero of Game 4 in the 2012 NLDS, was at the plate, looking to replicate history and send the Nationals Park crowd home happy. It wasn't meant to be this time around. On a 2–2 count, he lined out to right field to put a stamp on the team's most heartbreaking loss since 2012's Game 5 meltdown. All Williams could do was experience the loss from the locker room. He and second baseman Asdrubal Cabrera were thrown out of the game in the 10th inning for arguing balls and strikes.

The marathon of a game morphed into a test of wills for the players, coaches and fans who remained. What began at 5:37 PM ended as the clock struck midnight, a metaphor for a new day and a commanding 2–0 series lead that represented a dramatic momentum shift for the eventual World Series champions.

After Game 2, Williams' decision to replace Zimmermann with Storen was widely criticized. Why take out your reliable starter just one out away from a complete game shutout and replace him with a quality regular season closer with a shaky playoff past? "Anytime you make a decision on something, and it doesn't work, you kick yourself," Williams said before Washington's optional workout the next day at San Francisco's AT&T Park. "I kicked myself all night. That's human nature. But we also have a reason for that move."

Williams was disappointed in the result but stuck by his decision, saying the reason was the man due up, Posey, had made solid contact off of Zimmermann all night and he felt Storen could close him out. Washington mustered a 4–1 win in Game 3 before succumbing to the battle-tested Giants in a 3–2, series-clinching loss in Game 4.

18 The Curious Case of Smiley Gonzalez

Jose Rijo, a former major league pitcher and Nationals special assistant to general manager Jim Bowden, managed and ran the Rijo Academy in San Cristobal, Dominican Republic. Nicknamed Loma del Sueno, or Hill of Dreams, the complex was a proving ground for young Dominican ballplayers. It featured seven baseball fields, five dorms, a weight room, cafeteria, a hotel designed by Rijo, and offered English and Spanish classes for the prospects. "[Nationals President] Stan [Kasten] told me to get aggressive," Rijo said in 2007. "Don't do anything illegal. Do everything by the book. But get aggressive—and get us players."

Eager to establish a presence on an island known as a hotbed of baseball talent, the Nationals signed a 16-year-old shortstop named Esmailyn "Smiley" Gonzalez to a team-record $1.4 million bonus on July 2, 2006. During the introductory press conference, Bowden compared "Smiley" to St. Louis Cardinals legend Ozzie Smith. "He's pretty impressive for a 16-year-old," Nationals manager and Dominican native Manny Acta said in 2006. "A guy like him, I would say in five years, with the proper development, he can be a good player on the Major League level."

Gonzalez joined the minor league Gulf Coast League Nationals in 2007 when the Nationals were ranked dead last in organizational talent rankings by *Baseball America*. In 2008 Gonzalez played his second season with the Gulf Coast League club. Turning 19 that September, he won the Gulf Coast League MVP and batting title, hitting .343 in 181 at-bats. In the middle of Gonzalez's eye-popping season, a *Sports Illustrated* report broke the news that the Nationals were under investigation for bonus skimming.

Gonzalez's bonus was double the second-best offer—$700,000 from the Texas Rangers.

Then in February 2009, the trajectories of both Gonzalez and the Nationals were altered further. Another *Sports Illustrated* article revealed Gonzalez was actually 23-year-old Carlos Daniel Alvarez Lugo, making him 20 years old at the time he signed with the team. With public knowledge that he was no longer a teenage prospect, his value in the organization plummeted, making the $1.4 million bonus an egregious overpayment.

The name Esmailyn Gonzalez, Alvarez said, came from an extended family member. He had used Gonzalez's birth certificate and assumed his identity. This news rocked Washington's international operations as well as their reputation throughout the league. "I'm angry. I am very angry," Kasten said. "We've been defrauded, and make no mistake—this wasn't a college kid with a fake ID that came in and did this. This was a deliberate, premeditated fraud with a lot more to this story, and we are going to get to the bottom of it."

The scandal became a distraction for the Nats, who were in the swing of spring training after a dismal 59–102 season in 2008. Rijo was fired on February 26, and Bowden resigned three days later. Current general manager Mike Rizzo stepped in as acting general manager that March until being promoted to the full-time position months later. In 2010 Alvarez testified that both Rijo and Bowden knew of the fraud.

Amazingly, Alvarez lasted in the team's minor league system through the 2013 season, finishing his Nats career where it started, in the Gulf Coast League. He never advanced past Single A Hagerstown, Maryland, where he hit .171 in 20 games with the Suns in 2012.

In 2014 Alvarez played in two games with Tigres del Licey of the Dominican Winter League, going 0-for-4 with one strikeout, tying the bow on a career that began with such promise but then quickly unraveled. In all he played in 297 games in a span of seven seasons, batting .291 with 286 hits, 11 home runs, and 129 RBI.

Since the scandal the Nats have built their Dominican academy back up to respectability. Meanwhile, Alvarez says he has grown up through the experience and is appreciative of the time he spent in the team's system and the people he met along the way. "I've learned a lot as a person," he told *The Washington Post* in 2015. "A lot of mistakes you make, you change."

19 Ted Williams' Reign as Manager

Ted Williams' 1969 arrival in D.C. ended his nine-year hiatus from baseball. It was Bob Short's biggest coup during his three years as owner of the expansion Senators. The move was unexpected but highly embraced. Just two months after buying the team, Short landed his flashy prize in an attempt to revive a downtrodden fanbase.

The expansion Senators were as lowly as lowly could get. They hadn't won more than 76 games in a season since replacing the original Senators in 1961. Short also didn't want to be outdone by the Washington Redskins, who had just hired former Green Bay Packers head coach Vince Lombardi as their head coach, general manager, and part owner in early February 1969.

Williams, the Boston Red Sox legend, showed no inclination of returning to baseball since his 1960 retirement. He was content with living comfortably in Florida and reeling in lucrative paychecks from his line of Sears fishing tackle products. In his 1969 autobiography, he had written that, "all managers are losers; they are the most expendable pieces of furniture on Earth." As a player he turned down managerial job offers from the Red Sox in 1954 and 1959 and the Detroit Tigers in 1960. Despite the lucrative offer, Williams' own words made his decision to manage the Senators surprising.

Short worked as many angles as possible to convince Williams to manage his club. Williams balked at first, saying he didn't know how to manage and had only heard of a few players on the Senators roster like Frank Howard. Short ultimately convinced "the Splendid Splinter" to come back to baseball and lead a club that finished no better than sixth in the 10-team American League in their previous eight seasons by offering a five-year, $325,000 deal with an option to buy 10 percent of the team and 10 years to exercise the option. Williams would receive such perks as an unlimited expense account and a free apartment. He was allowed to quit but could not be fired and would be named vice president. He was also given the freedom to take a front-office position at his leisure. Just a few weeks after Lombardi was announced as the Redskins' head coach, Williams was introduced as the Senators manager in front of more than 100 media members. He was asked if manager Ted Williams would be able to tolerate a player like Ted Williams. "If he can hit like Ted Williams, you're damn right," Williams replied.

The man who amassed 2,654 hits, 521 home runs, and 1,839 RBIs graced the cover of *Sports Illustrated's* March 17, 1969, issue donning his blue Senators jacket and red Curly W cap. The last player to hit .400 in a season and one of the greatest hitters of all time immediately emphasized improvement at the plate with his new team. The team's batting average jumped from .224 in 1968 to .251 in 1969. In Williams' first year as manager, every regular hitter improved his average. Howard's average went from .274 to .296, and his on-base percentage spiked from .338 to .402. He also hit a career-high 48 home runs in 1969. He went on to lead the league in home runs (44) and RBIs (126) in 1970.

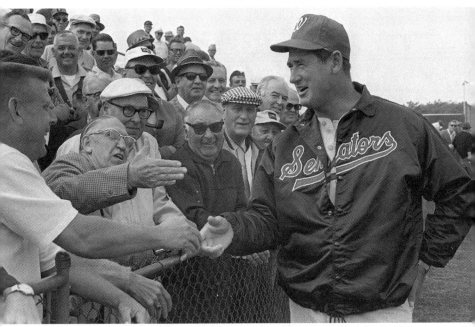

Washington Senators manager Ted Williams, whose hiring energized the D.C. fanbase, greets fans in spring training of 1969.

Williams' presence dramatically increased attendance at RFK, improving on the paltry 546,661 fans who saw them play in the District in 1968 to a respectable 918,106 in his rookie campaign as skipper. The excitement for the 1969 season was palpable on Opening Day. The record crowd of 45,113 fans at RFK gave Williams a standing ovation after he was announced with the Senators lineup. The 50-year-old was notorious for not tipping his cap, but on that day, he saluted the crowd. It was reportedly the first time he had tipped his cap since 1940.

For many reasons 1969 was a magical season despite finishing fourth in the newly formed American League East division. The Senators finished 86–76, the franchise's only winning record. It was D.C. baseball's first winning record since 1952 and last until 2012. Williams was voted AL Manager of the Year. Williams managed the club to records of 70–92 and 63–96 in 1970 and 1971, respectively. The shine gradually wore off, and Short relocated the Senators to Texas, where Williams would manage for just one season before riding off in the sunset. Teddy Ballgame supported the second departure of a D.C. baseball team in 12 years. "There was a hard core of fans here all right," said Williams referring to Senators fans, "but there were only six or 7,000 of them. Basically, Washington is a city of transient people. Most people don't give a damn."

Although Williams didn't bring a playoff appearance to D.C., his decision to manage the talent-deprived Senators represented one last bastion of hope for a town desperately in need of it.

20 Frank Howard's 10 Home Runs in Six Games

If you thought Bryce Harper's 13 home runs, 28 RBIs, and .360 batting average that earned him National League Player of the Month in May 2015 were impressive, imagine how jaw-dropping it was to witness legendary Washington Senators first baseman/outfielder Frank Howard blast 10 home runs in six games.

That's right. Ten home runs. Six games.

Howard, acquired from the Los Angeles Dodgers in December 1964, was known "the Capital Punisher," "Hondo," and "the Washington Monument," but he was not known for being shy at the plate.

His streak began at D.C. Stadium on May 12, 1968, against the Detroit Tigers' Mickey Lolich in the sixth inning and Fred Lasher in the seventh inning. After a day off, the Senators were in Boston to face the Red Sox for a two-game series. While at Fenway

Park, Howard mashed a two-run homer off of Ray Culp in the first inning and polished a sixth-inning shot off of Lee Stange. He closed the series the next day with another two-run, first-inning blast against Jose Santiago.

On May 14 at Cleveland Stadium, Howard hit a pair of two-run shots off of the Indians' Sam McDowell in a 4–1 Senators win. He began a four-game series in Detroit the next day by hitting a two-run home run off of Joe Sparma in the top of the ninth inning to give the Senators a 3–2 lead. They lost after allowing five runs in the bottom of the ninth.

His streak concluded on May 18 with two home runs off of Lolich. The last was a three-run bomb in the fifth inning that bounced off the left-field roof of Tiger Stadium. He is one of only four players in MLB history to hit a ball off of that stadium's roof. Harmon Killebrew, Cecil Fielder, and Mark McGwire are the others.

In that six-game span, Howard hit 17 RBIs and scored 10 runs. His batting average rocketed from .300 to .347—thanks to the 13 hits he accumulated in 24 at-bats during that week. Strangely enough, in the previous six games before his hot streak, Howard's average dropped from .351 to .300 after only getting three hits.

The Senators, who finished the season 65–96 and last in the American League, went 3–3 in Howard's amazing stretch. Howard finished his 1968 campaign as the league leader with 44 home runs. It was his first of four consecutive All-Star nods and his first of three straight 40-home run seasons.

When Ted Williams, arguably the greatest hitter in baseball history, joined the Senators as their new manager for the 1969 season, it meant big things were on the horizon for Washington's big bat. When they were introduced in spring training, Williams shook his hand and told the 6'7" star: "Geez, are you strong. If I'd been as strong as you, I would have hit 1,000 home runs…You hit the ball harder than anyone I've seen, though you don't hit it as far as two I've seen—[Mickey] Mantle and Jimmie Foxx."

Once Williams arrived, Howard became a more selective hitter, waiting for the right pitch to materialize rather than swinging on instinct alone. Howard set new career benchmarks in 1969 with 48 home runs, 111 RBIs, 102 walks, and 96 strikeouts—the latter being the fewest in a season since 1961. His average jumped from .274 to .296, and his on-base percentage topped .400 for the first time in his career. In 1970 he led the AL with 44 home runs, 126 RBIs, and 132 walks.

Hondo's presence at the plate was matched by his innate humor, which had the ability to keep Williams in check. One day, after a lackadaisical loss, Williams locked the Senators' clubhouse door and said, "Gentlemen, that was the worst exhibition of baseball I have ever witnessed. I'm afraid we're going to have to start over from the beginning."

Williams reached for a ball and told the team, "Now this, gentlemen, is a baseball." From the back of the room, Howard raised his hand to interrupt the lecture. "Uh, Skip?" Howard said. "Would you mind taking that a little slower?"

The Last Expo

Shortstop Ian Desmond epitomized the concept of homegrown talent during a time when the Washington Nationals needed such players to ripen. Selected in the third round of the 2004 Major League Baseball Draft out of Sarasota High School, Desmond remained the Washington Nationals' final connection to the

Montreal Expos. No one knew exactly what kind of career was in store for the teenager. Fortunately, he was given time to blossom.

Early in his career, Desmond struggled defensively, recording six errors in just 21 games during his 2009 debut season. At 23 he was raw, but the talent was there, and fans, evaluators, and media alike noticed it. He became Washington's regular shortstop in 2010 and recorded 57 errors in 308 games from 2010 to 2011. His breakout season, though, came during Washington's 2012 division title run. He hit .292 with 25 home runs and 73 RBIs, earning his first All-Star nod, the first of three consecutive Silver Sluggers, and a 16th-place finish in National League MVP voting. He stole at least 20 bases a season from 2011 to 2014. The shortstop with the rare combination of highlight-reel defensive ability and power at the plate was as impressive off the field as he was on it. Desmond gave his time to charities and the youth of Washington, D.C., even becoming a board member of the Nationals Youth Baseball Academy, located about one mile from RFK Stadium. Desmond made it a point to interact with fans and develop a connection.

After the 2013 offseason, Desmond made a career-altering decision, turning down a reported seven-year, $107 million contract offer from the Nationals. The infield centerpiece anticipated his numbers would ascend. That, however, was not the case in 2015. He batted a career-low .233 with 27 defensive errors, the second-most of his career.

It was a tale of two halves. Through 87 games he was in an enormous slump, batting .204 with seven home runs, 24 RBIs, and 21 errors. However, during a series in late-July against the Los Angeles Dodgers, Desi had a chat with Baltimore Orioles legend Cal Ripken Jr. in the Nationals Park parking lot. Ripken gave him encouragement and reminded him of a time when he struggled early in his career and managed to turn things around. Desmond did exactly that, batting .272 with 12 home runs, 38 RBIs, and only six errors through his final 69 games of the year. With free agency approaching, the reality of his eventual departure began to sink in as Washington's season came to a close. When the season was all said and done, Desmond ranked second in Nationals history in games (927), hits (917), home runs (110), and RBIs, (432).

Playing in his final home game at Nationals Park, he was pulled in the top of the ninth against the Philadelphia Phillies to a standing ovation. Even though it was overshadowed by the Jonathan Papelbon/Bryce Harper skirmish that happened just minutes before, Desmond was grateful for the appreciation from the crowd that had supported him the previous six years. "That was pretty special, bittersweet," Desmond said. "I've spent a lot of time here and I have a lot of special memories…I thank the organization and the fans for supporting me and for investing their emotion in me over the last 12 years."

After the team played its final game, a 2–1 loss to the Mets in New York, Desmond could barely contain his emotions in the locker room. "When I got drafted by the Expos, they didn't know where the team would be," Desmond told reporters. "But they couldn't have found a better home." Desmond had to pause and collect himself in order to fight back tears. With his voice breaking, he added: "I'm extremely proud to say that I was a Washington National."

Two days later, Desmond tweeted a screenshot of a 214-word message he typed. The beginning of the message was a retrospective of his career: "Twelve years. Practically half my life shaped by unbelievable men and women within the Washington Nationals organization," Desmond wrote. "I came in 'raw,' and leaving, I couldn't be more certain of who I am or what I stand for. Words can't describe how grateful I am for that."

22 The 2014 NL East Champions

Despite a disappointing 2013 campaign that resulted in a second-place, 86-76 finish and no postseason appearance, the Nats were considered World Series favorites by many pundits heading into the 2014 season. Matt Williams was hired to replace the likeable Davey Johnson after the latter led the team to its first National League East championship in 2012 but failing to deliver on his 2013 "World Series or bust" proclamation.

The team surprised the baseball world by acquiring Detroit Tigers pitcher Doug Fister in exchange for second baseman Steve Lombardozzi and pitchers Ian Krol and Robbie Ray. They also signed Nate McLouth to improve the bench and traded for relief pitcher Jerry Blevins from the Oakland Athletics. The season started slow, and Washington entered June 2 with a record of 27–28.

Then they reeled off eight wins in their next nine games and never went back below .500. Ryan Zimmerman experienced an injury-riddled and career-altering season. He broke his right thumb on April 12 and missed 44 games. After spending his whole career at third base, he returned on June 3 as a left fielder. He took the move in stride, realizing his body wasn't able to absorb the wear and tear of playing the hot corner like it used to. On June 23 he suffered another setback when he strained his right hamstring. He didn't return again until September 20.

Coupled with the addition of Fister, who ended his season with 16 wins and a 2.41 ERA, the emergence of Tanner Roark rounded out arguably the best five-man rotation in baseball. Roark was phenomenal in his first full season of work, striking out 138 batters in 31 games on his way to a 2.85 ERA. The staff finished the season with phenomenal numbers. Stephen Strasburg pitched

34 games, struck out 242 batters, and ended the year with a 3.14 ERA. Jordan Zimmermann finished with a 14–5 record and 2.66 ERA. Gio Gonzalez struck out 162 in 27 games and ended up with a 3.57 ERA.

Anthony Rendon, the sixth overall pick in the 2011 MLB Draft, underwent a renaissance season, batting .287 with 21 home runs and 83 RBIs and a National League-leading 111 runs scored. His season was so impressive that he finished fifth in NL MVP voting. Bryce Harper's season did not go as planned. He batted .273 and reached career lows in games (100), home runs (13), RBIs (32), hits (96), runs (41), and walks (38). On April 25 he tore a ligament in his left thumb sliding into third base. He didn't return until June 30. Perhaps his biggest lowlight came when he was benched by Williams on April 19 for a lack of hustle when he didn't run out a grounder to first with his typical zip.

In August the team went on an unbelievable 10-game winning streak. In that streak they became the first team since the 1986 Houston Astros to win five games on a walk-off in a six-game span. A midseason trade that sent Zach Walters to the Cleveland Indians for Asdrubal Cabrera helped stabilize their infield and offensive lineup. Cabrera provided solid defense and hit five home runs and 21 RBIs after his acquisition. Ian Desmond was the model of consistency at shortstop, leading the league in games played at the position with 154. For the third straight season, he hit at least 20 home runs (24) and stole at least 20 bases (24). He also registered career highs in RBIs (91, ranking seventh in the NL) and walks (46). These accolades helped him earn his third straight Silver Slugger Award.

The rest of the Nats bats were strong throughout the season. First baseman Adam LaRoche hit 26 home runs and 92 RBIs. Outfielder Jayson Werth knocked in 82 runs, batted .292, and walked 83 times to finish 18th in NL MVP voting. Center fielder Denard Span led the league with 184 hits, hit .302, and finished tied with Los Angeles Dodgers star Yasiel Puig at 19th in NL MVP voting. Closer Rafael Soriano grew more unpredictable as the season went on. That resulted in Drew Storen winning the job back on September 7. Storen went on to earn 10 saves the rest of the season.

On September 16 the team celebrated its second NL East title with a 3–0 win against the Atlanta Braves at Turner Field. Zimmermann put an exclamation point on the end of a phenomenal regular season by throwing the first no-hitter in Nationals history, blanking the Miami Marlins 1–0 on September 28. The Nats closed the season with 13 wins in their last 16 games.

In the National League Division Series against the San Francisco Giants, the Nats' bats went silent, scoring just nine runs in the series, four of which were scored by Harper. He was the team's primary source of offense, batting .294 with three home runs and four RBIs. Cabrera was the only other player to hit a home run that series. Harper's Game 4 homer was just the third to be hit into McCovey Cove in postseason history and just the second by an opposing hitter.

The most controversial move came in Game 2 when Williams took out Zimmermann with a 1–0 lead after throwing eight and two-thirds shutout innings. Storen came in with one out left and gave up the tying run. The Nats lost 2–1 in 18 innings in the longest postseason game in MLB history. Washington recovered to win Game 3 in San Francisco 4–1 but lost the series in Game 4 by a count of 3–2. It was the second time in three seasons the team failed to make it out of the NLDS. A new motivation consumed the team going into the 2015 season: prevent another 2013-like performance and make it out of the first round of the postseason.

23 Walter Johnson's Three Shutouts in Four Days

The 1908 season was a dud for the Washington Senators. They finished 67–85 and 22½ games back, but one of their lone bright spots was second-year pitcher Walter Johnson. The "Big Train" ended 1908 with a 14–14 record and provided a glimpse of what the rest of his 21-year Senators career would look like. That year he threw 23 complete games in 30 starts, struck out 160 batters, and walked just 53.

In a four-day stretch that season, the 20-year-old put his Hall of Fame stuff on display, tossing three shutouts against the New York Highlanders (later known as the Yankees). On Friday, September 4, Johnson took the mound to toss a six-hitter at New York's Hilltop Park on the way to a 3–0 Nats win. The next day, Johnson warmed up and took the mound after no other Washington pitcher made an effort to. All he did was allow just four hits in a 6–0 victory. "Maybe he'll go again Monday," manager Joe Cantillon remarked.

New York's Sabbath laws prevented games from being played on Sundays. This led to a Monday doubleheader. Having pitched the last two games, Johnson took the field before Game 1 to simply play catch with catcher Gabby Street. He noticed he was the only pitcher warming up and looked toward the Senators bench and received an emphatic nod from Cantillon. After warming up, Johnson made his way to Cantillon and said, "It's all right with me if it's all right with you."

His third consecutive shutout performance amazingly topped his first two. Johnson allowed just two hits during Washington's 2–0 victory. Johnson injured his arm in Game 1 and hid until Cantillon found someone else to pitch Game 2.

Johnson went on to appear in 802 career games with Washington. It's astonishing to fathom that 531 of them were complete games, and 110 were shutouts. His 110 shutouts are still a Major League Baseball record. The next closest pitcher is Grover Cleveland "Pete" Alexander with 90 shutouts. Tossing three shutouts in four days may be the most impressive of Johnson's feats, especially when put in context with this generation's infatuation with pitch counts and innings limits to rest overly taxed arms. Before there was such a premium on five-man pitching rotations and the specialization of bullpens, pitchers regularly threw complete games and weren't pulled after going a solid six or seven innings. Starters were also used interchangeably as relievers.

Mr. Walk-Off

Ryan Zimmerman is one of the most unassuming players in baseball. The 31-year-old baby-faced first baseman is the epitome of the phrase "speak softly and carry a big stick." His monotone delivery, dry sense of humor, and humble demeanor would never let you know of his accomplishments throughout his 11-year career. The numbers speak for themselves.

The Virginia native is also a man of many names, most notably "Mr. National" and "Mr. Walk-Off." The latter moniker is believed to have been started by sports blogger William Yurasko after Zimmerman opened up Nationals Park with a walk-off home run against the Atlanta Braves on March 30, 2008.

Over the course of his career, Zim has hit 16 walk-offs. His first walk-off of any kind—pros, college, high school, little

Top Hitters in Nationals History

Here are the leading batters in four different categories through Washington's first 11 seasons based on their Nationals tenure.

Hits
1. 1,412—Ryan Zimmerman
2. 917—Ian Desmond
3. 596—Jayson Werth
4. 581—Cristian Guzman
5. 528—Bryce Harper

RBIs
1. 783—Ryan Zimmerman
2. 432—Ian Desmond
3. 295—Jayson Werth
4. 269—Adam LaRoche
5. 248—Bryce Harper

Home Runs
1. 200— Ryan Zimmerman
2. 110—Ian Desmond
3. 97—Bryce Harper
4. 82—Adam LaRoche
5. 78—Jayson Werth

Walks
1. 510—Ryan Zimmerman
2. 297—Jayson Werth
3. 286—Nick Johnson
4. 279—Bryce Harper
5. 246—Adam LaRoche

league—came in 2006. Here is a list of his game-winners in chronological order:

- **June 18, 2006 vs. New York Yankees**
  A two-run home run in the bottom of the ninth inning against Chien-Ming Wang gives the Nationals the 3–2 win.
- **July 4, 2006 vs. Florida Marlins**
  A three-run home run in the bottom of the ninth against Joe Borowski gives the Nationals the 6–4 win.
- **July 6, 2006 vs. Florida Marlins**
  A one-run single in the bottom of the 11th against Jason Vargas gives the Nationals the 8–7 win.
- **September 2, 2006 vs. Arizona Diamondbacks**
  A bases-loaded walk in the bottom of the 11th against Brandon Lyon gives the Nationals the 7–6 win.
- **May 12, 2007 vs. Florida Marlins**
  A grand slam in the bottom of the ninth against Jorge Julio gives the Nationals the 7–3 win.

- **August 3, 2007 vs. St. Louis Cardinals**
  A one-run single in the bottom of the ninth against Ryan Franklin gives the Nationals the 3–2 win.
- **September 2, 2007 vs. San Francisco Giants**
  A one-run single in the bottom of the ninth against Brian Wilson gives the Nationals the 2–1 win.
- **March 30, 2008 vs. Atlanta Braves**
  A solo home run in the bottom of the ninth against Peter Moylan gives the Nationals the 3–2 win.
- **September 6, 2009 vs. Florida Marlins**
  A two-run home run in the bottom of the ninth against Juan Carlos Oviedo (also known as Leo Nunez) gives the Nationals the 5–4 win.
- **July 1, 2010 vs. New York Mets**
  A sacrifice fly in the bottom of the ninth against Ryota Igarashi gives the Nationals the 2–1 win.
- **July 6, 2010 vs. San Diego Padres**
  A solo home run in the bottom of the ninth against Luke Gregerson gives the Nationals the 6–5 win.
- **July 31, 2010 vs. Philadelphia Phillies**
  A three-run home run in the bottom of the ninth against Brad Lidge gives the Nationals the 7–5 win.
- **August 19, 2011 vs. Philadelphia Phillies**
  A grand slam in the bottom of the ninth against Ryan Madson gives the Nationals the 8–4 win.
- **September 3, 2011 vs. New York Mets**
  A two-run single in the bottom of the ninth against Bobby Parnell gives the Nationals the 8–7 win.
- **July 26, 2013 vs. New York Mets**
  A solo home run in the bottom of the ninth against LaTroy Hawkins gives the Nationals the 2–1 win.

- **May 19, 2015 vs. New York Yankees**
  A two-run home run in the bottom of the ninth against Andrew Miller gives the Nationals the 8–6 win.

Zimmerman's 2015 walk-off put him in elite company. He became the 19th player in MLB history to hit 10 career walk-off home runs. That feat tied him with Barry Bonds, Mike Schmidt, and Albert Pujols for third all-time in National League history. Only Stan Musial (12) and Tony Perez (11) have more. Almost half of Zimmerman's career walk-offs came during his first two full seasons (2006–2007). Of his 16 walk-offs, 10 have come against NL East opponents. He has four walk-offs against the Marlins, but none have occurred since the team changed its name to the Miami Marlins.

The name Mr. National is well-deserved. The first ever Nationals draft pick (fourth overall in 2005) is the only player to appear in at least one game in every season in team history. He leads the franchise in games played (1,293), hits (1,412), home runs (200), RBIs (783), runs (733), doubles (320), and walks (510).

25 That's a Clown Question, Bro

If our friends north of the border hadn't gotten a good grasp on Bryce Harper's personality during the first two months of his 2012 rookie season, they sure got a taste of it when the Nationals swept the Blue Jays in Toronto that June. In the second game of the three-game series, Harper belted out a 438-foot home run to center field. The third-inning blast bounced off the massive BlackBerry sign at Rogers Centre that read "Be Bold."

The phrase was fitting, considering Harper's nature and what he was about to be asked after Washington's 4–2 victory. Surrounded by reporters at his locker following the team's fifth straight win, a Canadian reporter asked the 19-year-old Harper if he would consider celebrating the win and his seventh home run of the season with a Canadian beer. (The legal drinking age in Canada is 19.)

Harper, who is Mormon and doesn't drink alcohol, scoffed a bit and looked down in disbelief, preparing for a retort. "I'm not answering that," Harper said. Three seconds later Harper then uttered the most popular phrase in the team's short history: "That's a clown question, bro."

In the instantaneous age of social media we now live in, that phrase caught on like wildfire. Harper and his quote were trending on Twitter. Fans all over the Internet were feverishly working on the catchiest meme using that sentence. The next day either Harper or someone involved the managing his image filed for a trademark of "That's a clown question, bro," according to the U.S. Patent and Trademark database. Major League Baseball began selling "That's a clown question, bro" T-shirts while Under Armour, the sports apparel manufacturer Harper endorses, sold T-shirts that read "Don't be a clown, bro." A week later, senate majority leader and fellow Nevada native Harry Reid used that phrase to respond to a question on immigration. Fox News' Chris Wallace used it in an awkward exchange with Shepard Smith, who had no idea what he was talking about.

Just prior to Washington's road trip against the Colorado Rockies in late June, Denver Beer Co. brewed a small batch of Canadian lager. They fittingly named it "Clown Question Bro." After arriving in Colorado, Harper learned of the killing of police-woman Celena Hollis, a single mother of a 12-year-old girl. He was moved when he found this out, and someone from his camp made a call to the brewery and asked them donate a portion of the proceeds to the Celena Hollis Memorial Fund in an effort to support her daughter.

On Halloween, sure enough, Harper sported a "Don't be a clown, bro" T-shirt with rainbow colored clown wig, large red glasses, a colorful polka dot bowtie, and a bright red nose. In January 2013, the phrase was used as a *Jeopardy!* category. In January of 2015, White House press secretary Josh Earnest revived the phrase in response to a question from CBS News' chief White House correspondent Major Garrett. The veteran reporter asked Earnest if it was true that President Barack Obama called British Prime Minister David Cameron "Bro" and if he had any other nicknames for him. Earnest jokingly replied: "Well, to paraphrase a local baseball player here in Washington, D.C., that's a clown question, bro."

Harper's older brother, Bryan, a pitcher in the Nationals minor league system who was with the short-season Single A Auburn Doubledays at the time, was asked by Auburn, New York's local newspaper, *The Citizen*, where his brother came up with that phrase. The older Harper explained his friend, Donn Roach, a 2010 second-round pick by the Los Angeles Angels, frequently used the word "clown." It certainly caught on with Bryce.

Bryan, on hearing Bryce's tone when saying the phrase: "That is some saltiness. A little bit of veteran swagger right there for Bryce."

In 2014 Bryce was asked by Comcast SportsNet if he gets tired of being asked about his collision into the right-field wall of Dodgers Stadium in May 2013. He said he was and admitted he's tired of hearing about his five famous words as well. "Everyone's still on the 'clown question' and all that crap, too," he said. "I mean, it's in the past. Everyone needs to get over it. I'm not 16, 14, 13 years old anymore. I'm playing in the big leagues. I'm 21 years old and I'm ready to go."

Matt Williams

Matt Williams' relationship with Nationals general manager Mike Rizzo dated back to their time with the Arizona Diamondbacks during the franchise's inaugural season in 1998. The former was acquired from the Cleveland Indians to be the team's third baseman, and the latter was hired as the team's scouting director. So it only felt natural when Williams was introduced as the Nationals' fifth manager on November 1, 2013. "We feel like we've got the right man at the right time here in Washington, D.C.," Rizzo said that day.

"I bring passion to the game that I love," Williams said during his introductory press conference. "This game has given me a lot, and I need to return that. In whatever aspect of the game we find ourselves in, whether it's offense, defense, pitching, I'm going to approach it with passion, I'm going to approach it with enthusiasm and a sense of work that I hope will make me a good manager and make us a good team."

Rarely does "Big Marine" smile on the job. His straight-faced, workmanlike demeanor veils his fervor for the game. "I'm probably an introvert by nature," Williams told *The Washington Post* in 2014. "I think a lot and don't necessarily verbalize."

The timing of the hiring was ideal for Williams, who inherited a team with a strong nucleus that won the National League East title a year before. It also didn't hurt that his family has ties to D.C. His grandfather, Bert Griffith, played in six games for the 1924 World Series champion Washington Senators. He had one hit and one strikeout in nine plate appearances before being traded to Kansas City of the American Association that July.

Williams' father was a carpenter, and his mother was Inyo County's first female deputy. She was among the group of officers who arrested Charles Manson in 1969 at his Death Valley compound. She processed the female members of Manson's family.

During Matt Williams' 17-year playing career, he was a spectacular hitter. The third overall pick in 1986 played in 1,866 games with the San Francisco Giants, Indians, and Diamondbacks, hitting 346 home runs and 1,113 RBIs. Williams also batted at least .275 seven times, including three seasons over .300. He was a five-time All-Star and won four Gold Glove and four Silver Slugger awards. In 1994 he led the majors with 43 home runs in 112 games before the league went on strike that August. With Arizona in 2001, he became the first player to hit home runs in the World Series with three different teams.

Between 2003 (his last season as a player) and 2009, Williams spent time as a Diamondbacks minority owner, color commentator, and minor league manager. He was Arizona's first-base coach in 2010 and third-base coach from 2011 to 2013. In his first year at

Managerial Records

The Nationals will enter the 2016 season with their sixth manager in franchise history (seven if you count John McLaren's three games as interim manager in 2009). After winning 2014 National League Manager of the Year and leading the team to the 2014 NL East title, Matt Williams was fired following a disappointing 83–79 season in 2015.

Not counting McLaren's 2–1 record as interim manager, Williams is the most successful manager in team history percentage-wise. Davey Johnson has the most wins with 224. No manager has yet lasted three full seasons in Washington.

2014–2015: Matt Williams 179–145 (.593) in 324 games
2011–2013: Davey Johnson 224–183 (.550) in 407 games
2009–2011: Jim Riggleman 140–172 (.449) in 312 games
2007–2009: Manny Acta 158–252 (.385) in 410 games
2005–2006: Frank Robinson 152–172 (.469) in 324 games

the helm in Washington, Williams led the Nats to a 96–66 record and their second National League East title in three years. That earned him NL Manager of the Year.

His most controversial move came during Game 2 of the 2014 National League Division Series against the Giants. Nats pitcher Jordan Zimmermann had thrown 99 pitches in eight and two-thirds innings after striking out six. His 100th pitch was a walk with one out left in the ninth inning with a 1–0 lead. That snapped Zimmermann's streak of 20 straight retired batters. Williams replaced him with closer Drew Storen, who gave up four runs in the ninth inning of Game 5 of the 2012 NLDS against the St. Louis Cardinals. Storen allowed San Francisco to tie the game 1–1, and the Nats lost 2–1 in 18 innings. Many still question why Williams would replace Zimmermann, who had been red-hot all night.

The Nationals entered 2015 as World Series contenders for the third straight season, but things did not go as planned. After battling injuries to key players and inconsistent play, the team sputtered throughout the summer, trying to keep pace with the New York Mets in the divisional race. In August of 2015, reports of player discontent with Williams surfaced, and fans began calling for his job. After the Nationals were eliminated from playoff contention, several players were quoted as questioning the manager's leadership and direction of the franchise.

A September report in *The Washington Post* detailed how much distance had grown between Williams and his own locker room. The "introvert by nature" lacked the communication necessary to sustain such a melting pot of personalities. "He doesn't talk to people in here," a veteran said in the story. The piece provided more details on Williams' downfall. On the morning of August 22, prior to a game against the Milwaukee Brewers, Jayson Werth arrived at Nationals Park, expecting to play that night. He looked on the lineup card and saw his name wasn't listed. Not alerting a player a night in advance that he's out of the starting lineup the next day is a baseball faux pas. Seething, Werth looked at the lineup card, ripped it up, confronted Williams, and told the manager: "When exactly do you think you lost this team?"

"He's like the guy in his house who hears a sound like someone breaking in," an unnamed player said in the story. "And his reaction isn't to take care of the problem or investigate. It's to put his head under the pillow and hope it goes away." That theory seemed to be proven true when Jonathan Papelbon berated and attacked Bryce Harper in the team's dugout during the eighth inning of the second-to-last game at Nationals Park. Williams was on the other end of the dugout when the skirmish occurred and claimed he didn't have a clear view of it. Harper was sent into the clubhouse while Papelbon went on to pitch in the ninth inning. Williams did not ask anyone in the dugout what happened. He also did not see the video of the fight until after his postgame press conference. When asked why he put Papelbon in the game after the fight, Williams replied: "He's our closer."

The fight made national headlines and appeared to seal Williams' fate. On October 5, 2015, Williams was fired as Nationals manager. In two seasons he compiled a record of 179–145 (.552). His first season produced an NL East champion, but his sophomore campaign was an utter disappointment given the talented roster and World Series expectations.

27 The Derivation of Natitude

Prior to the 2012 season, the tide was turning in the National League East. The Nationals finished 2011 with an 80–81 record and were trending upward—and away from being the accustomed division doormat. The Philadelphia Phillies finished first in the NL East from 2007 to 2011, improving their record every year with two World Series appearances and a title to show for it.

That reign of dominance, along with Nationals president Stan Kasten's 2009 open invitation to Phillies fans, led to Nationals Park's transformation into "Citizens Bank Park South" whenever the Philadelphia faithful made the two-hour trip to D.C. several times a season.

After seeing this go on for a number of years, Nationals chief operating officer Andy Feffer wanted to do something about it. For his first plan of action, he sold tickets to the May 4–6 home series against the Phillies a month in advance of the rest of the season's single-game tickets. The catch? Only fans with credit cards addressed to D.C., Maryland, and Virginia could buy them. "Frankly, I was tired of seeing it," Feffer told *The Washington Post* in 2012. "Forget you, Philly. This is our park, this is our town, these are our fans, and it's our time right now…We've heard it enough, we've seen it enough, and I don't like it any more than anyone else. We're trying to build a team here, and nothing irks me personally or the people here more than to see another team's fans—particularly Philly fans—in our ballpark, holding up signs."

The second plan of action was to promote an identity that embodied this young, up-and-coming team. A marketing campaign titled "Ignite Your Natitude" was launched. "It's a young team with an edge and attitude," Feffer said before the 2012 season. "But now it's different than the past: they're talented and they've got the skills to back it up. That kind of edge and attitude is Natitude."

An "Ignite Your Natitude" video featuring Michael Morse and Danny Espinosa exemplified the confidence of a team ready to take the next step. "Some people say you're either born with it or you're not," Morse said in the commercial. "There's no pressure on me. The pressure's on the pitcher." Said Espinosa: "I don't care if

The Nationals' popular marketing campaign is displayed as outfielder Jayson Werth catches a fly ball during Game 3 of the 2012 NLDS against the St. Louis Cardinals.

you're the best, I'm gonna get you. That's why I always look into the dugout. I want to make sure they're watching."

The third plan of action was to stage a Take Back the Park weekend while the Phillies were in town. That included placing temporary banners that read "Natitude Park" at the Center Field Gate and on top of the scoreboard. The mayor of Washington, D.C., Vincent Gray, even proclaimed May 4–6, 2012 as "Natitude Week."

Nationals manager Davey Johnson didn't buy into the Natitude hype as much as everyone else. He even had a sign behind home plate removed because he felt it may be distracting to the pitcher. "If we win ballgames, that's how we're going to take this stadium back," Johnson said before the May 4 game. "We've got an attitude. I don't know how to spell Natitude, but I don't mind the attitude. The better the team you play, the more you better have it."

Philadelphia outfielder Laynce Nix, who played with the Nats in 2011, knew both sides of the rivalry and offered a unique perspective on Natitude. "They might be overdoing it a little bit," he said. "I really don't know what to make of it. I would think the Nationals' being in first place, Strasburg pitching, Bryce Harper, us—I think that's enough to sell tickets, I would think. Who knows? Marketing is marketing."

More than 106,000 fans packed the park for that series. The Nats won two of the three games on the way to a 9–9 record against their rivals up I-95. In October the Nats clinched their first NL East division crown—the first won by a team other than Philadelphia since 2006.

Feffer left the team in 2013, but his imprint is still seen in and around the ballpark. The phrase was still used throughout the next few seasons with "#NATITUDE" appearing on the left-field wall, behind home plate, and on merchandise purchased by fans.

The Kid Managers

In an era where players doubled as managers, Washington Senators owner Clark Griffith wasn't afraid to take a gamble on who would lead his squad. The Senators not only made three World Series appearances (1924, 1925, and 1933), but those postseason contests were guided by managers under the age of 30.

Second baseman Stanley "Bucky" Harris joined Washington as a 22-year-old rookie in August 1919, appearing in eight games. He developed into a reliable fielder and appeared in 589 games from 1920 to 1923, batting .285 in that span. Shortstop Donie Bush was fired as player/manager following a 1923 season that ended with a 75–78 record and a fourth-place finish. Griffith took his time naming a new manager, looking outside the franchise before reaching out to Harris with a letter offering him the job.

The 27-year-old Harris went to his nearest phone and reached Griffith, but the connection was poor and sent the would-be skipper into a panic. He could hear Griffith just fine but not the other way around. "I want that job," Harris screamed. Griffith grew agitated that he couldn't hear Harris and hung up. Harris then went to a Western Union telegraph office, gave the clerk a $20 bill, and told the clerk to wire Griffith a message once an hour for the next four hours. "I'll take that job and win Washington's first American League pennant," the message read.

That's exactly what he did. In his first season at the helm, he led the Senators to the city's only World Series title, beating the New York Giants in seven games. He became the youngest manager to win the World Series but also did his part on the field, batting .333 and tying Goose Goslin for the most hits (11) and RBIs (seven) in that series. Harris' second regular season went even better than his first, going 96–55 (.636) compared to 1924's 92–62 mark (.597). The "Boy Wonder" helped Washington win its second straight American League pennant, but the Nats fell to the Pittsburgh Pirates in seven games in the 1925 World Series.

He went on to play and manage in Washington through 1928 and was traded to the Detroit Tigers after the season. Harris returned to D.C. to manage the Senators for two more stints (1935 to 1942 and 1950 to 1954), leading the club from the dugout in four different decades. Harris was inducted into the National Baseball Hall of Fame in 1975.

Griffith replaced Harris with Walter Johnson for the 1929 season. Johnson spent 1907–1927 as the franchise's star pitcher but faltered in his first season as manager, going 71–81. The team won at least 90 games the next three seasons but never made a postseason appearance.

When 1933 rolled around, Griffith was looking to replace Johnson. He considered bringing back Harris and even making himself manager. (Griffith had managed the team from 1912 to 1920.) Ultimately, he decided to make Senators shortstop Joe Cronin his newest player/manager, just four days before his 26th birthday. Cronin had already established himself as a steady presence in Washington, batting .307 with 52 triples and 454 RBIs in his first five seasons. Now he could contribute from the dugout as well. "I like these scrappy youngsters as leaders," Griffith said after making Cronin his new skipper. "I made no mistake with Bucky Harris. I think I have another Harris."

Cronin's managerial debut season went swimmingly. The Senators set a franchise record in wins (99) and winning percentage (.651). On the field he led the league in doubles (45). Like Harris, Cronin led Washington to the World Series in his first attempt. This time the Giants came out on top, claiming the series in five games. Cronin hit .318 in that series.

His sophomore campaign was a dud. The team went 66–86 and finished in seventh place. After marrying Griffith's niece and adopted daughter, Mildred Roberston, following the 1934 season, Cronin was shipped to the Boston Red Sox in exchange for $250,000 and shortstop Lyn Lary. From 1933 to 1941, Cronin appeared in seven All-Star Games. He went on to become a general manager, American League president, and a member of the Hall of Fame's board of directors and veteran's committee. In 1956 he earned his own rightful place in Cooperstown.

29 Mike Rizzo

Toiling as a minor league infielder in the California Angels system from 1982 to 1984, Nationals general manager Mike Rizzo came to realize his talent wasn't on the field. He had developed a keen eye for talent, mechanics, and roster construction and began to craft his career as a third-generation scout with his hometown Chicago White Sox. The hundreds of lonely miles he drove to evaluate prospects put a stamp on his love for talent evaluation. That life is not for everybody, but for Rizzo baseball was (and still is) his world.

During his stint in Chicago (1986–1992), Rizzo signed Hall of Famer Frank Thomas before moving on to work with the Boston Red Sox (1992–1998). He then joined the Arizona Diamondbacks in 1998 and helped build the 2001 World Series champions. He was passed over for Arizona's GM position and moved on to the Washington Nationals in July 2006 as GM Jim Bowden's top assistant to help refurbish a barren farm system. Rizzo was the first big hire of Ted and Mark Lerner, who had just completed their purchase of the franchise. Rizzo was appointed to interim GM when Bowden resigned in March 2009, following the Smiley Gonzalez scandal. The interim label was removed that August, making Rizzo the team's top personnel man.

During his 10 seasons with the Nationals, Rizzo transformed Washington's minor league system from one of the worst to one of the best in just a few seasons. The major league club struggled mightily in 2008 and 2009, allowing the team to draft first in 2009 and 2010. Luckily for Rizzo, those drafts presented can't-miss, surefire talent in the forms of Stephen Strasburg and Bryce Harper.

Hitting on draft picks and molding talented young players was viewed as Phase One in Washington's progression toward relevance. Players such as Jordan Zimmermann (second round in 2007), Danny Espinosa (third round in 2008), Tyler Moore (16th round in 2008), Drew Storen (first round in 2009), Michael A. Taylor (sixth round in 2009), and Aaron Barrett (ninth round in 2010) developed into contributors. Signing former division rival outfielder Jayson Werth to a seven-year, $126 million deal in December 2010, which shocked many, signaled Phase Two. Werth's deal was too long and too costly, but the move showed the team felt it was on the verge of contending and were willing to spend big to bring in the necessary free agents.

The man, who has crafted more than 35 trades during his time in D.C., is used to being on the winning side of a deal. The process to complete the December 2013 acquisition of Doug Fister put Rizzo's conviction on full display. Nationals ownership did not want to part with prospect Robbie Ray in order to get Fister. Rizzo was enraged and threatened to quit. The Lerners backed down, and the deal was made. "I've been called a bull in a china shop by an executive or two," Rizzo told *The Washington Post* in 2012. "I wear that like a badge of honor."

In December of 2014, the Nats acquired shortstop Trea Turner and pitcher Joe Ross from the San Diego Padres in a three-team trade where they sent outfielder Steven Souza Jr. and pitcher Travis Ott to the Tampa Bay Rays. The Nats were roundly applauded for the move, not only for how little they gave up, but for also how much they received in return.

Rizzo's knack for drafting and developing talent led to winning 2012 MLB Executive of the Year. With a talented roster in place to annually contend for a National League East title, Rizzo's confidence grew in his drafting process. He became comfortable enough to select players in the first round with injury histories but who had very high upsides (Anthony Rendon in 2011, Lucas Giolito in 2012, and Erick Fedde in 2014). While the major league team took care of business, those players could take their time rehabbing and developing properly.

Rizzo's original approach centered on building the team around homegrown talent sprinkled with a few strategically added pieces here and there. Deviating from that plan backfired in 2015. That January he traded set-up man Tyler Clippard, who developed into a fan favorite and the Nationals' all-time leader in pitching appearances, and signed Max Scherzer to a mega-deal as opposed to retaining Zimmermann, the most consistent starter in team history who would become a free agent after the season. In July with the team in need of middle relief, Rizzo instead acquired controversial closer Jonathan Papelbon to dethrone Storen, who was pitching lights-out until that point.

Rizzo called August 2015 his "worst month ever" as the team's general manager. During a time frame in which every win is paramount, the team went 12–17. The team went on to miss the playoffs for the second time in three years. How Rizzo will define the rest of his tenure in Washington hinges upon his ability to replace an overhauled roster for 2016 and beyond.

 **The Kiss**

Bryce Harper's indoctrination to criticism as a pro baseball player began in just his 56th game with the Single A Hagerstown Suns. On June 6, 2011, at Hagerstown's Municipal Stadium, the 18-year-old prodigy took Greensboro Grasshoppers pitcher Zachary Neal deep for his 14th home run of the season one day after getting hit in the leg. Harper admired his blast for a few seconds. Neal reportedly took exception to it and gave him a piece of his mind. As Harper rounded third, he looked at Neal and blew a kiss his way. After stepping on home plate, Harper took a few steps and looked back toward the mound.

For those covering the game, it was much ado about nothing. For the national pundits, it was a feeding frenzy. Former Nationals general manager Jim Bowden wrote in a piece for ESPN.com that he would have sent his farm director to Hagerstown for a face-to-face talk and to clarify where the team stands on the incident. "Harper's future big league career is going to come quickly," Bowden wrote, "and when it does, the stadium light towers will have fewer light bulbs, and magazines will have a new player to plaster on their covers, not just for the talent but for the personality that goes with it. By then, it won't include showing up pitchers or putting teammates at risk."

Hall of Famer Mike Schmidt didn't mince words when giving his opinion on the matter, as he criticized the teenager. "I would say, 'Bryce, if you're going to hit a lot of 'em,'" Schmidt said, "'you'd better learn not to show up the pitcher because it's just going to get tougher and tougher on you if you watch your home runs. Just hit your home runs and hit 'em like you're used to hitting 'em, not like you're surprised when you hit one.'...I hate to bring this into it, but I would think at some point the game itself, the competition on the field, is going to have to figure out a way to police this young man. If indeed his manager won't, the game will end up taking care of it."

In an interview with Baltimore's 105.7 The Fan, Orioles first-round pick Dylan Bundy was asked what he would do if he was the next pitcher to face Harper after the incident. "Well, if I was pitching the next game, I'd hit him all four at-bats," Bundy said. His brother, Bobby Bundy, was also being interviewed and shared the same sentiment. "That kid can't do that," Bobby said. "That was a little over the top. I guess he did get hit in previous at-bats, and maybe he felt like it was for nothing, but still in baseball etiquette, you don't blow a kiss to the pitcher like that. It's just not something you do."

Harper was brushed back off the plate on the first pitch of his next at-bat two innings after his infamous home run.

What was not widely reported was that such an apparently braggadocio gesture was actually Harper standing up for his teammates, whom Neal had shown up earlier while glaring into the Suns dugout after throwing strikeouts.

Whether he was overly brash, taking care of his teammates, or all of the above, Harper was promoted to Double A Harrisburg on July 4 after hitting .318 with 14 home runs, 46 RBIs, 19 stolen bases, 17 doubles, and 44 walks in 72 games and 305 plate appearances with Hagerstown.

31 Take a Nationals Road Trip

One of the most underutilized but ultimately fulfilling experiences as a sports fan is taking a road trip to see your favorite team play in enemy territory. Luckily for Nationals fans, there are five options within 250 miles.

The first trip to take is the most sensible and obvious. Baltimore's Oriole Park at Camden Yards is just 38 miles from Nationals Park, a trip that would take just around 45 minutes from stadium to stadium. The Nats and Orioles meet for two series a year—one in D.C. and one in Baltimore. For Nats fans, an annual trip up I-295 for this series is a must. Chances are, dozens of your childhood friends will be there donning orange and black. A good portion of the people who make up the current Nats fanbase defected their allegiance from the American League East's Orioles.

Another contingent of fans decided to keep both by making the Nationals their National League team and the O's their American League team. It's common to see dozens of fans wearing a combination of Nats and O's gear to these games.

The pregame and postgame entertainment options are endless. The stadium is a short walk from the Inner Harbor, where fans can enjoy fine dining and entertainment on the water.

Just behind left field are the most popular pregame attractions for Baltimore baseball fans. Pickles Pub and Sliders Bar & Grille are go-to spots for fans looking for cheaper drink options than inside the ballpark. Cruise Eutaw Street for food (Boog's BBQ and Dempsey's Brew Pub and Restaurant are fan favorites) or shopping. And yes, for those who want to "Marylandize" their food, there's Old Bay as far as the eye can see.

There isn't a bad view in the stadium, and the right-field sightline of the B&O Warehouse makes Camden Yards a must-visit for anyone with an MLB stadium bucket list to check off. Opened in 1992, Oriole Park at Camden Yards set a new precedent for modern stadium architecture.

Not far up the road are the hated Philadelphia Phillies, who have called Citizens Bank Park their home since 2004. The stadium is 134 miles (two hours and 19 minutes) from Nationals Park with tolls up and down I-95. For fans in central and southern Maryland, a good alternate route requires only the $4 toll across the Chesapeake Bay Bridge up Route 301 to Route 896 North through Delaware up to I-95. That route takes about two hours and 30 minutes, but there is little to no traffic either way.

Nestled next to Lincoln Financial Field, home of the Eagles, and Wells Fargo Center, home of the Flyers and Sixers, Citizens Bank Park has plenty to keep fans occupied while inside the stadium. The Ashburn Alley concourse, located behind left field and center field, includes the Phillies All-Star Walk, Memory Lane, Phillies Wall of Fame, and rooftop bleachers. Bull's BBQ is named after Greg Luzinski, who played for Philadelphia from 1970 to 1980.

On the site of the old Spectrum directly across from Citizen Bank Park's first-base entrance, Xfinity Live transforms from a gigantic sports bar with a casual dining experience by day to a club environment by night. Chickie's & Pete's Crab House and Sports Bar is also a local favorite that's offered inside the stadium.

Pittsburgh's PNC Park provides baseball fans with the best view in Major League Baseball in my opinion. Behind center field and right field are the buildings that make up the distinct Pittsburgh skyline, the bright yellow Roberto Clemente Bridge, and the Allegheny River. The stadium, which opened in 2001, is 228 miles (four hours and 15 minutes) from Nationals Park with tolls and 240 miles (about four and a half hours) without tolls. Only two levels high with a capacity of 38,362, PNC Park gives baseball fans a uniquely intimate setting.

A popular, and perhaps the easiest, parking option is to find public parking in downtown Pittsburgh and trek across the scenic bridge while listening to Sax Man play his favorite tunes as fans walk by. Pre and postgame options include dining in the many downtown establishments as well as hitting Rivers Casino next to Heinz Field or going to the eateries and bars on the North Side between the stadiums.

Citi Field, home to the division rival New York Mets since 2009, is 245 miles away in Queens and just over a four-hour drive from Nationals Park. Visit the 3,700-square foot Mets Hall of Fame & Museum on the first-base side to learn a little bit about the opponent. Fan Fest, located behind the center-field scoreboard, has a mini-baseball diamond, moon bounce, dunk tank, and video game entertainment center. Food and drink options include Big Apple Brews, McFadden's, and Keith's Grill, which is named after Mets announcer and former first baseman Keith Hernandez.

If you don't want to park at the stadium, take the train to the Mets via Willets Point metro stop. Located just 236 miles (just under four hours) from Nationals Park is new Yankee Stadium, which replaced baseball's ultimate cathedral—old Yankee Stadium. Get to the stadium early and be sure to visit Monument Park behind center field before the game. The shrine honoring Yankees greats closes 45 minutes before each game.

Food options in and around the ballpark are plentiful. Some of the top options in and around the stadium include Hard Rock Café, Lobel's, Premio, Yankee Tavern, and Billy's Sports Bar. The Nats have played in Yankee Stadium—old and new—five times since their inaugural season in 2005 and own a 3–2 record.

The Washington...Padres?

When the Washington Senators departed for the second time to become the Texas Rangers in 1971, there was still optimism throughout the city that a new team would play at RFK Stadium in the near future. With the fledgling San Diego Padres in a state of disarray, D.C. mayor Walter Washington appointed Joseph Danzansky, owner of several local Giant Food grocery stores, to make a pitch to buy them and bring a team back home.

In May of 1973, Danzansky agreed to buy the Padres for a record price of $12 million from C. Arnholt Smith, who was in serious financial trouble. Danzansky was the same guy who partnered up with others to buy the Senators from Bob Short for $7 million. (The Danzansky-led group bumped up their offer to $9 million, but Short still refused and moved the team to Texas.) The ambitious Danzansky was so eager to bring a team back to D.C.

that the National League had to reject a plan to move the Padres in the middle of the 1973 season.

President Richard Nixon ran into Danzansky at a public event and offered to help bring the Padres to D.C. On September 7, 1973, Nixon penned a letter to National League president Chub Feeney. "I just want to cast my own vote in favor of returning Major League Baseball to the nation's capital," Nixon wrote. "You can be sure all of us in the Washington metropolitan area would enthusiastically welcome a National League team."

On December 6, 1973, the other 11 National League owners voted unanimously to approve the sale and relocation of the Padres to Washington in time for the 1974 season. Danzansky even made a $100,000 deposit. The Padres' move to D.C. was such a sure thing that Topps printed baseball cards of Padres players and labeled the team "Washington" of the "Nat'l Lea." Players such as Willie McCovey, Nate Colbert, Randy Jones, and Dave Roberts were destined for Washington, according to Topps' rare collectibles. The team even had office furniture packed in moving vans heading to RFK. Padres general manager Peter Bavasi was sent to D.C. during the short-lived relocation process and planned to name 38-year-old California Angels designated hitter Frank Robinson the manager of the 1974 Washington franchise.

Danzansky wasn't in favor of recycling the Senators name, saying the idea of continuing that name was "a little outmoded." He wanted to call the team the Stars. Rookie pitcher Dave Freisleben modeled the franchise's new jerseys, which screamed 1970s fashion. The uniforms were light blue with "Washington" across the chest in red letters outlined in white with red, white, and blue piping around the collar, sleeves, and waistband. The hat was tri-paneled with a blue back, white front, and a thin red block W with a star affixed to the top right of the W.

The new Washington club was tentatively scheduled to open the 1974 season at home against the Philadelphia Phillies. The city of San Diego, however, fought to keep its team and threatened to sue for $84 million for breaking their lease at San Diego Stadium. Eventually Ray Kroc, the businessman who helped build McDonald's into the fast food empire that it is today, bought the Padres for $12 million in January 1974 and kept the franchise in San Diego.

Over the years other attempts to reel in another baseball team were unsuccessful. Current Nationals owner Ted Lerner tried to buy the Baltimore Orioles in 1975. The next year he offered San Francisco Giants owner Horace Stoneham $10 million in cash to buy the team and move them to D.C. But the Giants owner also had a stadium deal he couldn't get out of and settled for $8 million from San Francisco bidders.

When former Washington Redskins minority owner Edward Bennett Williams bought the Orioles in 1979, word was that he wanted to move the team back to D.C. when the team's lease at Memorial Stadium was up after the 1980 season. That never materialized, and Baltimore went on to win the 1983 World Series. Washington, D.C., was also in consideration for National League expansion in 1991, but the league instead opted to develop teams in Miami and Denver.

William Collins III worked hard to bring a team to the area as baseball continued to expand in the 1990s. He helped form the Virginia Baseball Club. In 1994 the group was one of four finalists for expansion along with Tampa Bay, Phoenix, and Orlando. Major League Baseball decided on Tampa and Phoenix. Virginia Baseball Club reached an agreement to buy the Houston Astros from owner Drayton McLane for more than $150 million in 1995. The plan was to have the team play at RFK for two to three seasons until a new 45,000-seat stadium was built near Dulles Airport in Northern Virginia. McLane didn't believe he'd have the necessary votes from fellow MLB owners to sell and move the Astros out of one of the country's biggest media markets. So a proposal to build a new, retractable-roof ballpark in downtown Houston was approved, and that kept the Astros in Texas.

Collins also reached an agreement to buy the Montreal Expos in 1999, but the arrangement disintegrated. He claimed that he offered to buy the team again in 2000 for $168 million but was ignored by Major League Baseball. For fans the D.C. baseball drought that lasted more than three decades appeared quiet on the surface, but behind the scenes, many moves were made to bring the national pastime back to the world's most powerful city.

33 Jim Riggleman Quits

Before joining the Washington Nationals in 2009, Jim Riggleman was respected around Major League Baseball, having managed the San Diego Padres from 1992 to 1994, the Chicago Cubs from 1995 to 1999, and the Seattle Mariners in 2008. He grew up in Rockville, Maryland. watching the Washington Senators and Baltimore Orioles. He attended Frostburg State and was selected by the Los Angeles Dodgers in the fourth round of the 1974 MLB Draft.

Riggleman replaced Manny Acta as interim Nationals manager in the middle of the 2009 season and lost the interim title, signing a new contract in November. He was now operating on a three-year deal that was essentially a two-year deal with a team option for the third year. "I never allow myself to feel secure," Riggleman said in regard to job status before the 2010 season. "I guess it's just my nature. If you feel secure, you're going to take something for granted. You're going to slip up. It's almost like security builds overconfidence. I never want to be overconfident."

The Nats finished the 2010 season 69–93 and expected Stephen Strasburg to miss most, if not all, of the 2011 season after undergoing Tommy John surgery. However, the team drafted Bryce Harper first overall that June, and the future still looked bright despite Strasburg's questionable health. The Nationals were a team on the rise. Riggleman knew it and wanted to be part of it.

On June 23, 2011, Laynce Nix hit a sacrifice fly to score Danny Espinosa in the bottom of the ninth to beat Seattle 1–0 in an afternoon contest at Nationals Park. Jason Marquis tossed eight innings and allowed only three hits to help complete a three-game sweep. It was Washington's 11th win in its last 12 games, and the Nats were one game above .500 for the first time since late April. They were about to embark on a six-game road trip starting in Chicago against the White Sox. Fans were excited with the direction the organization was heading.

Then, in one of the most bizarre situations in D.C. sports history (and that's saying something), Riggleman quit immediately following the win. The veteran skipper was never given assurances that he would be granted an extension to see this growing team flourish despite many pleas with general manager Mike Rizzo to discuss a new deal. "I'm 58," Riggleman told *The Washington Post*. "I'm too old to be disrespected…You don't keep a manager on a one-year deal in Major League Baseball. I'm not happy about it. I just feel in my heart it's the right thing to do."

Riggleman said that the contract should have been dealt with the previous October. "This was not a rash decision," Riggleman said. "I love it here. I don't know what it is about Mike or the ownership that makes them leery of putting me on the year '12. But I've been doing it too long to still be trying to prove myself."

That night, Riggleman was spotted at Caddies, a sports bar in Bethesda, Maryland, and photos of him enjoying adult beverages and posing for pictures with attractive young women quickly went viral. "I was solving the world's problems last night at Caddies,"

Riggleman told the Sports Junkies radio show the next morning. "I'll tell you what, I had to get down there and let those girls get a look at me. There's some beautiful young ladies in that place. Unbelievable…Hey, I was big in there. My face is up on the screen and everything."

Riggleman went on a proverbial radio barnstorming tour. He told Bruce Murray on SiriusXM's Mad Dog Radio that he "kind of planted this seed with Mike for months that we need to be talking, and we weren't, so I said, 'You know what? Enough's enough.'"

On ESPN 1000's Waddle and Silvy in Chicago, Riggleman reiterated his displeasure with his deal. "When I signed this contract a couple years ago, I made it very clear that we all know this is a ridiculous contract," he said. "I have no choice but to sign it. It's unfair, it's disrespectful, we know it's not right. And I was told, 'You're right, it is a bad contract, and when the time is right, we'll fix it.' And it just appeared that the time was never gonna be right, and the determination was made that we'll get through this year, and then you probably won't be with us anyway."

He was also asked about his night at Caddies. "Man, I should never have done that," he said laughing. "Hey, the manager needs love too, you know? You know, look, I'm a single man, and you've got to let them college girls get a look at you now and then, you know?"

Jokes aside, Riggleman knew the risks he took when he left the Nats. Would anyone see him as managerial material ever again? Would someone ever give him a chance? The next year he joined the Cincinnati Reds organization to manage their Double A affiliate, the Pensacola Blue Wahoos. He then managed the Louisville Bats, their Triple A affiliate, the two following seasons and served the 2015 season as the Reds' third-base coach.

34 The 2015 Letdown

The pressure was on for the 2015 Washington Nationals. Coming off of their second National League East title in three years, an already-stacked roster added Max Scherzer to a rotation that averaged a 2.94 ERA, the best in baseball. Of the 88 ESPN experts polled before the season, 37 predicted the Nationals to win the World Series as did three of six *Sports Illustrated* writers, six of 12 Fox Sports baseball prognosticators, and one of five CBS Sports staff members.

The Nats stumbled out of the gate, dropping the season opener 3–1 to the New York Mets and beginning the year 1–4. The team finished 10–13 in April but heated up in May. Starting on April 28, the Nats won 18 of their next 22. Bryce Harper and Max Scherzer won National League Player of the Month and NL Pitcher of the Month, respectively. Scherzer went 5–1 with a 1.66 ERA and struck out 56 batters while only walking six in the month of May. Harper hit .360 with 13 home runs, 28 RBIs, 24 runs, and a .495 on-base percentage. Both players represented the team at the All-Star Game. Harper ended the season with 42 home runs, 99 RBIs, finished second in the NL with a .330 average, and broke the Nationals/Expos franchise record with 124 walks.

Amazingly, Scherzer's June was even better than his May. He pitched a complete-game shutout against the Brewers in Milwaukee, striking out 16 and allowing only one hit. Six days later he tossed a no-hitter against the Pittsburgh Pirates. Scherzer had put together one of the greatest back-to-back pitching performances in baseball history. Both games were a pitch away from being perfect games. He finished his season with a second no-hitter against the Mets.

Washington battled injuries all season, and its projected Opening Day lineup did not play together until Denard Span returned from a nearly two-month-long hiatus on August 25, the 124th game of the season. That lineup lasted two games when Span went back on the disabled list after suffering a torn labrum in his left hip. One year removed from leading the league with 184 hits, Span played in just 61 games, the fewest of his career.

Stephen Strasburg went on the disabled list twice but was dominant when healthy. Jordan Zimmermann pitched consistently but didn't produce his usual All-Star-like numbers. Doug Fister had an off year and was relegated to the bullpen thanks to the unexpected rise of rookie Joe Ross, who had a 2.80 ERA after his first seven starts. Gio Gonzalez remained the same maddening pitcher—hot one day and cold the next. He finished with a 3.79 ERA, the highest since his second season.

Ryan Zimmerman and Jayson Werth played fewer than 100 games for the third and sixth time, respectively. The absence of Span and Werth paved the way for rookie Michael A. Taylor to make a name for himself. The rangy 24-year-old hit 14 home runs, 63 RBIs, and stole a team-high 16 bases. Taylor made highlight-reel plays in center field and hit clutch home runs over the course of the season. Of his 14 home runs, eight came in the sixth inning or later. Of those eight, five either tied the game or scored the go-ahead runs.

In early September Washington entered the most important series of the season against the Mets riding a five-game winning streak and trailing New York by just four games. After the second game of that series, Nationals fans, who were fed up with the direction of the team and had access to the Presidents Club, could watch manager Matt Williams' postgame press conference through a glass wall. They proceeded to boo Williams as he exited his presser. The next day the Nats were swept at home by their NL East counterparts, falling to seven games back. They never got closer than six back the rest of the season.

The Nationals only spent 50 games in first place in the NL East, most of which occurred in June and July with the Mets on their heels. The fork in the road for both clubs came at July's trade deadline. New York acquired former Nats setup man Tyler Clippard to solidify the back end of the bullpen and Yoenis Cespedes to provide pop to their lineup. Cespedes was a juggernaut, hammering 17 home runs, 44 RBIs, and scoring 39 runs in 57 regular season games as a Met.

The Nats, meanwhile, acquired controversial closer Jonathan Papelbon from the Philadelphia Phillies in exchange for minor league pitcher Nick Pivetta on July 28. The move had ripple effects. The Nationals needed a middle reliever but chose to keep Papelbon in the ninth-inning role and bumped Drew Storen, who had been on fire up to that point, from closer to the eighth-inning setup role.

Storen was 29 of 31 in save opportunities before Papelbon's acquisition. Furious about the trade and feeling like he had proven himself in the ninth-inning role in 2015, Storen handled the move in stride. The move worked initially with Storen not allowing a hit in his next five appearances after the trade, but after those five strong outings, he then allowed 10 runs in his next four games and couldn't recover his first-half form the rest of the year. Papelbon, who refused to relent his ninth-inning role for Storen, allowed just six hits in his first nine games as a Nat. However, like Storen, he began to implode on the mound.

Papelbon's fiery temper came to a head during the team's final home stand. On September 23 Papelbon plunked Baltimore Orioles star Manny Machado two innings after the slugger hit a lead-changing seventh-inning homer off of Scherzer. Harper said after the game that he expected to "get drilled" the next day in retaliation and that the act of intentionally hitting a batter is "pretty tired." Papelbon was suspended by Major League Baseball for his actions.

Nothing symbolized the end of the 2015 season more than what happened next, the day after the team was eliminated from playoff contention. Harper, the team's best player, did not run out a pop fly to Papelbon's liking. His arms draped on the dugout railing, the veteran closer had a few choice words for the 22-year-old as he walked back to the dugout. Papelbon walked to the dugout steps as Harper made his way down them. Surprised at Papelbon's reaction, Harper had a few choice words himself. Standing above Harper on the dugout platform, Papelbon then put his left hand around Harper's neck and pushed him back all the way toward the dugout wall.

Players and coaches quickly scrambled to break up the skirmish. Not involved in the altercation was Williams, who was at the other end of the dugout. Harper was slated to take the field in the ninth and be removed to an ovation. Instead, he was in the clubhouse the rest of the game while Papelbon entered in the ninth with the score tied at four. Papelbon then allowed five runs and was booed profusely by the sparse Nationals Park crowd as he made his way to the dugout with the bases loaded.

After the game Williams said he did not see the altercation and hadn't watched video of it before speaking to the media. When asked if he knew Papelbon had his hand around Harper's throat and why he would put Papelbon in the game after that, Williams simply replied: "He's our closer." Williams also admitted he didn't ask any questions about the incident while in the dugout.

The next day Williams' pregame press conference was delayed almost two hours before he announced Papelbon dropped his appeal of his earlier three-game suspension and that the team would suspend him the remaining four games, promptly ending his season. The team also announced Harper would be suspended for that day's game despite it being a scheduled day off for him. One week later Williams was fired after the team finished with an 83–79 record.

35 Davey Johnson

Initially brought on as senior advisor to general manager Mike Rizzo in 2009, Davey Johnson was an interesting choice to take over as manager after Jim Riggleman quit and John McLaren went 2–1 on an interim basis in the middle of the 2011 season. Johnson's pedigree preceded him. As a player from 1965 to 1978, Johnson batted .261 with 1,252 hits in 1,435 games with the Baltimore Orioles, Atlanta Braves, Philadelphia Phillies, and Chicago Cubs. He finished third in 1966 Rookie of the Year voting, was a four-time All-Star, twice finished in the top 20 in MVP voting, earned three straight Gold Gloves from 1969 to 1971, and won a World Series with Baltimore. In 14 seasons as a manager, Johnson had compiled a 1,148–888–2 record with the New York Mets (1984–1990), Cincinnati Reds (1993–1995), Orioles (1996, 1997) and Los Angeles Dodgers (1999, 2000).

Johnson captured the 1986 World Series title with the Mets but hadn't worked in a major league dugout for more than a decade. Now he was set to take over a team loaded with young talent on the cusp of pennant contention.

His laid-back, observant attitude served the Nationals well in 2012 as he led the team to the best record in baseball and its first National League East title on the way to winning NL Manager of the Year. This time around his recognition was better received than when he won the 1997 American League Manager of the Year award. He resigned from his position with the Orioles because of a dispute with owner Peter Angelos as he was about to be honored. Johnson wasn't afraid to challenge people or call it like he saw it.

In a June 2012 game against the Tampa Bay Rays, Johnson had former Nats pitcher Joel Peralta thrown out of the game for keeping pine tar in his glove to gain a better grip on the baseball. This move upset Rays manager Joe Maddon, who called Johnson out for using insider info. Maddon called Johnson's decision "cowardly" and said: "It was kind of a pussy move to go out there and do that under those circumstances."

Did Cal Ripken Jr. Nearly Become the Nationals Manager?

Hiring Cal Ripken Jr. to manage the Washington Nationals is a staggering idea for a couple of reasons. One, it would be a dagger in the hearts of every Baltimore Orioles fan. Two, it would be a dream scenario for Nats fans who traded their allegiances from Baltimore to Washington. Their childhood hero would lead their favorite team.

Davey Johnson, who managed Ripken in Baltimore, was set to step down after the 2013 season. The more Ripken covered Nationals games for TBS, the more he was seen spotted with Nationals general manager Mike Rizzo and the more he delicately hinted that he would be interested in managing. And the more speculation grew rampant.

But how close was this to happening?

Ripken had said during the 2013 season that he was interested in becoming either a manager or an executive. Nationals outfielder Jayson Werth, who spent 1997–2000 as an Orioles minor leaguer while Ripken was with the big league club, said he wanted Ripken to manage the club. Former Nats GM Jim Bowden had said that the team was giving serious consideration to Ripken as a manager—not a surprise given the good relationship between the Hall of Fame player and Rizzo.

I caught up with the "Iron Man" in June 2014 and asked him how close he was to becoming the fifth skipper in Nationals history. "We never got to a formal process," Ripken said. "It was just sort of a discussion and an examination, but it didn't materialize into anything more than a formality. I think many times the media or rumors circulate, and it makes it a little bit bigger."

Rizzo ended up hiring Matt Williams, whom he knew from their time together with the Arizona Diamondbacks. Rizzo said in a radio interview that Ripken was never formally interviewed, and they mutually decided it wasn't the right time for him to manage the Nats.

Johnson stood by his decision, saying rules are rules. He added: "I didn't know [Maddon] that well, but I thought he was a weird wuss anyway…I don't want to get in a shouting match with Joe. I looked him up on the Internet and found out he has a Tweeter, so he can get to more people than me. And so I don't want to get in a shouting match with him. He's got a bigger following. But it was interesting reading. But you can tell him I have a doctorate of letters, too. Mine's from Loyola in humanities. And I'm proud of that, too."

Leading a team with World Series expectations in 2013, Johnson told MLB Network analyst and former MLB manager Larry Bowa that the upcoming season was "World Series or bust. It's going to be my last year anyway." Those comments backfired when the team underachieved and finished the season 86–76 and missed out on the playoffs. Even though Johnson's "World Series or bust" proclamation went belly up, he helped usher in a new era of Nationals baseball that will last into the near future. These days Johnson spends his time at his waterfront home in Florida, living an envious retired life of golfing, fishing, dabbling in real estate, and spending time with his children and grandchildren.

Gio Gonzalez

Whether Gio Gonzalez is calling owner Mark Lerner "the pimp with the limp," wearing a "Chicken Mode" shirt and performing a rubber chicken sacrifice to turn around a struggling Nats club, saying "meow" 10 times in a live TV interview during spring training, having his beard sponsored, or sporting a T-shirt with a picture of former pitching coach Steve McCatty from a 1984 issue

Gio Gonzalez, who has won 53 games during his four years with the Nationals, throws during an August 26, 2015, game against the San Diego Padres.

of *Playgirl*, the man undoubtedly knows how to have a good time. The happy-go-lucky Gonzalez certainly majors in humor, but he also minors in inconsistency on the mound. His trademark smile can often be followed by a dominant outing one game and an underachieving performance the next.

In his first season in D.C., Gonzalez hit the ground running after being traded from the Oakland Athletics. He signed a five-year, $42 million contract extension through 2016 with team options for 2017 and 2018 three weeks after the trade. He then proceeded to have the best season of his career. A catalyst for Washington's 2012 National League East championship team, Gonzalez boasted a team-leading 2.89 ERA and 207 strikeouts, becoming the first D.C. pitcher to strike out at least 200 batters since Walter Johnson in 1916. He led baseball with 21 wins, becoming the first lefty in D.C. to win at least 20 games since Earl Whitehill accomplished the feat in 1933. Country music star Dierks Bentley enjoyed being at Gonzalez's 20th win so much that he added a third verse to his song "Am I the Only One" during a postgame concert at Nationals Park.

Gonzalez's accolades earned him a second-straight All-Star nod and the honor of pitching against the defending World Series champion St. Louis Cardinals in D.C. baseball's first playoff game since 1933. With a 1–0 lead at St. Louis in Game 1 of the 2012 National League Division Series, Gonzalez walked four batters in the second inning, allowing two to score, one of which was on a wild pitch. He hadn't allowed a hit, but after two innings, he had given up the lead. He regained his composure and pitched through the fifth inning without allowing another run. His final line showed he walked seven batters, struck out five, and allowed two runs on 107 pitches.

Gio's Verse

Here is the verse from Dierks Bentley's song, "Am I the Only One," in which he references Gio Gonzalez:

Between the smoke and the neon, she was turning me on;
I was 'bout to make my move.
When she started talking dresses, kids and picket fences,
Diamonds and honeymoons (whoa, whoa, whoa, whoa).
I said no thanks, I really gotta go babe;
I paid up and headed out.
Yeahhhh, I went to watch Gio get his 20th win.

In Game 5 with the series on the line, Gonzalez was more erratic on a cold night at Nationals Park. He started off hot, pitching three scoreless frames. The Nats were primed for a National League Championship Series berth after taking a 6–0 lead through three innings. Then Gonzalez lost a bit of his edge. By the end of the fifth inning, he'd allowed the Cardinals to cut the lead in half and score three runs. The rest, as we all know, is history. His start in Game 4 of the 2014 NLDS against the San Francisco Giants went better than his first postseason experience. He allowed two unearned runs in the second inning. But with the Nationals down 2–1 in the series and its offense faltering all series, two runs were too many. The team went on to lose the game 3–2 and was eliminated yet again.

Over his Nationals career, Gonzalez has been the type of player to wear his emotions on his sleeve and will let a bad start affect the rest of his game. His inconsistency plagued him in the ensuing years. His ERA climbed from 3.36 to 3.57 to 3.79 over the next three seasons. He went 11–8, 10–10, and 11–8 in that span. Gonzalez is one of the more powerful hitters among pitchers. His three home runs are the second most by a pitcher in Nationals history. He's the only pitcher in Nats history to hit a home run in three consecutive seasons.

37 How to Get Autographs

As a kid, I obsessed over getting autographs on my trading cards and programs from my favorite players, so I understand the excitement and the adrenaline rush this opportunity provides.

For the kids out there, the golden rule of autograph seeking: know who you're getting the autograph from. Asking for Stephen Strasburg's autograph when it's actually Max Scherzer in front of you is embarrassing and puts the player in an awkward spot. It's an easy mistake and it happens all the time.

When you know who you're getting your autograph from, use your manners and call them "mister" followed by their last name. Players love that, and it increases your chances of getting a signature. It shows them that you respect them as adults and that you were raised well. Continue your manners by saying "please" and "thank you." Simple things like that go a long way these days. And don't pout and get mad at them if you don't get the signature you want. You never know when you may meet them again. Have your marker ready. These guys are pros so they know to improvise and use someone else's marker in a jiff, but it makes the process easier and faster.

Head to Nationals Park early. Center-field gate opens two and a half hours before each game, allowing fans to access outfield seats and a chance to catch home run balls during batting practice. The rest of the stadium's gates open one and a half hours before, giving fans access to the entire ballpark and the chance to get close to the field.

The Nats offer a promotion called Signature Sundays. Every Sunday during the season, two Nationals players sign autographs from on top of the Nationals dugout beginning an hour and 10 minutes before the game. Fans must get a free voucher from sections 109 and 140. They're available when the first gates open up and are handed out on a first-come, first-served basis. There is a chance you can catch a player biking in and out of the players' parking lot located outside the stadium behind home plate. Pitchers Drew Storen and Tyler Clippard have been known to commute that way in the past.

NatsFest is another great opportunity to meet your favorite Nat. This event takes place every winter in the heart of D.C. to get fans fired up for spring training during the offseason. NatsFest is open to all fans and offers activities like live batting cages, Q&A sessions with players and management, autograph and photo sessions, and interactive games.

A trip to spring training in February and March should be on the bucket list of any Nationals fan. The Nats play at Space Coast Stadium in Viera, Florida, but they will be moving to West Palm Beach to share a new stadium with the Houston Astros. The rosters are expanded during spring training, giving fans more opportunities for meeting players and getting autographs.

If traveling to Florida isn't in the budget, head to any of the local (or semi-local) minor league stadiums to see the Nats regulars play at their home or road park during rehab assignments. The minor league crowds are small, and the access to the players is much better than at a professional ballpark.

Browse below for the closest minor league ballparks to Nationals Park. Plan accordingly.

Prince George's Stadium—Bowie, Maryland (20.1 miles from Nationals Park, 27-minute drive), home of the Bowie Baysox (Baltimore Orioles affiliate)

The Orioles' Double A affiliate regularly plays host to the Nationals' affiliate, the Harrisburg Senators. Those games draw a good percentage of Nationals fans.

Pfitzner Stadium—Woodbridge, Virginia (29.6 miles from Nationals Park, 40 minutes), home of the Potomac Nationals

Harry Grove Stadium—Frederick, Maryland (49.8 miles from Nationals Park, 55 minutes), home of the Frederick Keys (Baltimore Orioles affiliate)

Nats fans can travel to Frederick to see the Keys take on the Potomac Nationals.

Ripken Stadium—Aberdeen, Maryland (69.4 miles from Nationals Park, one hour, 13 minutes), home of the Aberdeen IronBirds (Baltimore Orioles affiliate)

The team named in honor of Cal Ripken Jr. is in the same league as the Auburn Doubledays, the Nats' Single A short-season affiliate.

Municipal Stadium—Hagerstown, Maryland (72.1 miles from Nationals Park, one hour, 20 minutes), home of the Hagerstown Suns

The Diamond—Richmond, Virginia (107 miles from Nationals Park, one hour, 51 minutes), home of the Richmond Flying Squirrels (San Francisco Giants affiliate)

Nats fans in southern Virginia can take a trip to see the Harrisburg Senators take on the Flying Squirrels, the Double A affiliate of the San Francisco Giants.

Metro Bank Park—Harrisburg, Pennsylvania (119 miles from Nationals Park, two hours, five minutes), home of the Harrisburg Senators

Perdue Stadium—Salisbury, Maryland (121 miles from Nationals Park, two hours, four minutes), home of the Delmarva Shorebirds (Baltimore Orioles affiliate)

The Hagerstown Suns make an annual trek down south to Maryland's Eastern Shore.

 **Livo**

Livan Hernandez didn't have the stereotypical build of an athlete, but at 6'2" and roughly 250 pounds, "Livo" crafted himself into a durable workhorse whom managers frequently trusted to last through at least six innings. Hernandez was one of the more recognizable names to carry over from the Montreal Expos and was their lone All-Star representative in 2004.

He is remembered as the Nationals' first ace, pitching in the franchise's first road (April 7, 2005 at Philadelphia, which was also his 250th career contest) and home (April 14, 2005 vs. Arizona) games. He amazed the RFK Stadium crowd of 45,596 by carrying a one-hitter into the ninth inning on the way to that memorable 5–3 victory against the Diamondbacks. He allowed a three-run home run in the ninth but walked off the field to a standing ovation and tipped his cap to the fans on the way to the dugout.

His professional baseball career took off after defecting from Cuba to the Dominican Republic in 1995. In January of 1996, he signed with the Florida Marlins and appeared in one game that season. He established himself with dominant National League Championship Series MVP and World Series MVP performances in 1997 with the Florida Marlins.

In Washington's first season, Hernandez appeared in the 2005 All-Star Game and started a team-record 35 games. It was his second straight season leading the National League in starts. He ended the year with a 15–10 record, 3.98 ERA, and Nationals-record 246⅓ innings pitched. In August of 2006, Washington traded Hernandez and cash to the Diamondbacks for pitchers Matt Chico and Garrett Mock. He returned to Washington in August 2009 and played in D.C. through the 2011 season.

Livo's durability showed itself during his two stints in Washington (2005, 2006, 2009–2011). In 129 starts with the Nationals, Hernandez pitched into the seventh inning or later 82 times (64 percent). During his five seasons in Washington, Hernandez went 44–45 and even hit four home runs during his time with the Nationals, the most by a pitcher in team history.

Hernandez officially announced his retirement in 2014 when he was working with the Nats as a spring training instructor, ending a notable 17-year career. He threw more than 200 innings in 10 of those seasons. With the San Francisco Giants in 1999, he was one out away from completing 200 innings. The man who could throw every kind of breaking pitch racked up 3,189 innings, 178 wins, and a 4.44 ERA.

39 National Guardsman/ Senators Shortstop

It's not often a baseball player heckles a teammate from the stands while holding a gun.

Though it's a bit more innocuous than it sounds, that's exactly what transpired on April 10, 1968, when the Senators opened their season against the Minnesota Twins at RFK Stadium.

In the days following the assassination of Martin Luther King Jr., the U.S. National Guard assembled throughout Washington, D.C., as riots ensued, causing the postponement of the Senators opener by two days. One of those National Guard members happened to be Washington shortstop Ed Brinkman, who appeared in just 186 games over the course of the 1967 and 1968 seasons while fulfilling his obligations as a guardsman. "I'd be with the club traveling and the phone would ring, and they'd say: 'There's going to be 30,000 kids rioting against the Vietnam War this weekend, and you've got to come back,'" Brinkman recalled in an interview for Frederic Frommer's D.C. baseball retrospective, *You Gotta Have Heart.*

Brinkman's duties included enforcing curfew on the streets, protecting equipment from being destroyed at busy firehouses, and keeping order at RFK. "I hadn't realized when I signed up that Washington, D.C., is probably the worst place to join the National Guard," he added. "There's always something going on."

On Opening Day in 1968, Brinkman was at RFK but not in his usual role as the reliable defensive shortstop. He was on guard duty in the left-field stands wearing his full army regalia.

With a crowd of just 32,000 taking in the start of the team's new season, Brinkman apparently had more time on his hands than expected. The 26-year-old decided to spice things up a bit and taunt his roommate Frank Howard, who was playing left field, from the stands. "The game's going on, and I'm trying to concentrate, and he's hollering at me," Howard told Frommer, laughing. "I'm thinking if we have to depend upon this guy to save us, we're in deep trouble."

The taunts may have negatively affected Howard, who struck out in all three plate appearances against Twins starter Dean Chance, who tossed a complete game four-hitter as the old Senators beat the expansion Senators 2–0.

A high school teammate of Pete Rose, "Steady Eddie" was never known for his bat, hitting just .226 in his 10-year career in D.C. Not surprisingly, his two best seasons at the dish came under the tutelage of manager and hitting guru, Ted Williams, batting .266 and .262 in 1969 and 1970, respectively. He never hit above .229 in his eight previous seasons.

Brinkman was involved in the 1970 trade that brought controversial Detroit Tigers pitcher Denny McLain to D.C. He experienced a career resurgence in the Motor City—especially defensively. In 1972 he played in 72 consecutive errorless games (a record that was broken by Cal Ripken Jr. in 1990), earned a Gold Glove, and finished ninth in AL MVP voting. He played in his only career All-Star Game in 1973. He ended his 15-year career, having hit .224 with 60 home runs and 461 RBIs. He played 10 seasons for the Senators, four with the Tigers, and spent time with the St. Louis Cardinals, Texas Rangers, and New York Yankees in his final season.

40 Alfonso Soriano Founds 40-40-40 Club

Alfonso Soriano was a seven-time All-Star, 2004 All-Star Game MVP, four-time Silver Slugger, and played in two World Series. He was the primary piece of the 2004 blockbuster trade that sent Alex Rodriguez from the Texas Rangers to the New York Yankees. In November of 2006, he signed with the Chicago Cubs for a staggering eight-year, $136 million deal.

But Nationals fans remember him for his spectacular 2006 season that led up to that monster contract. In his lone year in Washington, he made history. He became the only 40-40-40 player in Major League Baseball history when he hit 46 home runs, stole 41 bases, and hit 41 doubles. The Nationals had acquired the seasoned veteran from the Rangers in exchange for pitcher Armando Galarraga and outfielders Terrmel Sledge and Brad Wilkerson.

On Saturday, September 16, 2006, against the Milwaukee Brewers, Soriano was sitting on 45 home runs and 39 stolen bases. Eager to etch his name in the record books, he got a great jump on a 2–0 first-inning pitch delivered by Brewers hurler Dave Bush against Felipe Lopez. As Milwaukee catcher Mike Rivera stood up to pick off Soriano, he struggled to grip the baseball and couldn't attempt the throw to second.

Soriano, sporting a smile from ear to ear, quickly pulled second base out of the ground and handed it to the bat boy. He then tipped his batting helmet to the cheering crowd of 24,252 at RFK Stadium. That moment immortalized him with baseball's best. Only three other players in MLB history had accomplished that feat: Jose Canseco (1988), Barry Bonds (1996), and Rodriguez (1998). The four men are the only members of the ultra-exclusive 40-40 Club.

The Nats went on to beat the Brewers 8–5 that night to improve to 64–84. Nationals manager Frank Robinson added some humor to the situation after the game. "I'm sure he's glad to get it out of the way," Robinson said. "He can focus on 50-50 now."

Six days later against the New York Mets at Shea Stadium, he founded his own club: the 40-40-40 Club. To this day he's the only member. Soriano entered the game in a 2-for-21 slump since stealing his 40th base, but the trip to New York resulted in a resurgence at the plate. After scoring the game's first run, Soriano doubled to deep left in the fifth inning to reach his 40th two-bagger of the season. He also stole his 41st and final base of the season in the top of the third inning in a 3–2 victory to make Washington 67–86 on the season.

He earned the 2006 National League Silver Slugger Award, the 2006 Heart & Hustle Award, and was the team's only representative at the 2006 All-Star Game. Soriano and Ian Desmond are the only players in Nats history to have hit 20 home runs and stolen 20 bases in the same season.

Less than two months later, Soriano bolted out of D.C. to sign his megadeal with the Cubs. He had turned down a five-year, $50 million offer from the Nationals before the 2006 season. He gambled on himself and won big time, nearly tripling what the Nats had originally offered. He spent the next seven years of his career in the Windy City, batting .264 with 181 homers, 526 RBIs, 218 doubles, and 13 triples in that time.

Soriano's departure was a big blow to the Nationals lineup, but they got two picks in return from the Cubs. The first of those two picks was pitcher Josh Smoker from Calhoun High School, who was taken in the first round at 31st overall. Smoker never appeared in a game for the Nats and was released after peaking with the Class A Hagerstown Suns.

Their second pick was 67th overall in the second round. With that selection the Nats made a great pick, drafting a small-town right-handed pitcher from University of Wisconsin-Stevens Point named Jordan Zimmermann. MLB.com's scouting report labeled Zimmermann as having "some intriguing arm strength with an above-average fastball, but his other offerings are well behind. There is projection to all of his offerings and the team who believes the projection the most will take a chance on Zimmermann. He could become a good back-end-of-the-rotation type down the road."

Little did MLB.com know Zimmermann would be the first pitcher to throw a no-hitter in Nationals history and would command ace money once he hit the free-agent market. He has reached double digits in victories each of his last four years.

Soriano announced his retirement from baseball in November 2014 after his second stint with the Yankees. He finished his 16-year career with 412 home runs, 1,159 RBIs, 2,095 hits, 481 doubles, 1,152 runs, and 289 stolen bases in 1,975 games.

41 The Cardiac Nats' Wild 10-Game Winning Streak

Washington's 2014 National League East championship season was memorable for many reasons, but for some fans, their crazy 10-game winning streak stands out the most. The streak, which tied a team record set in 2005 and concluded with five walk-offs in the last six games, revived the moniker of "Cardiac Nats" for an unforgettable stretch in August.

Manager Matt Williams said in late April if the Nationals went on a 10-game winning streak that he'd revive his famous 1991 Babe Ruth impersonation from his playing days with the San Francisco Giants. Just more than three months later, the team responded with three straight series sweeps. Unfortunately, he never brought back the impression.

Here's a rundown of each game:

August 12, 2014

Nationals 7, New York Mets 1

A young outfield prospect named Michael A. Taylor homered to right field in the sixth inning of his major league debut on the way to a six-run division win on the road. That blast capped off a five-run inning in which Anthony Rendon hit his 16th home run of the season and Ian Desmond pelted his 20th, the third straight season Desmond had done that. Denard Span's 36-game on-base streak and 14-game hitting streak came to an end with an 0-for-5 performance.

August 13, 2014

Nationals 3, Mets 2

Two weeks after being traded to Washington by the Cleveland Indians in exchange for Zach Walters, Asdrubal Cabrera hit his first home run as a Nat, which turned out to be the game-winner. Bryce Harper and Kevin Frandsen each hit sacrifice flies in the seventh inning. Pitcher Jordan Zimmermann didn't allow an earned run or a walk in six and one-third innings on the way to improving his record to 14–5.

August 14, 2014
Nationals 4, Mets 1
Adam LaRoche hit a two-run homer in the first inning, and Bryce Harper did the same in the fourth. Stephen Strasburg pitched seven strong innings, allowing only one run, two walks, and three hits while striking out eight. It was Washington's 11th straight win at New York's Citi Field, the worst home streak the Mets had experienced against any opponent.

August 15, 2014
Nationals 5, Pittsburgh Pirates 4
Sporting a 5–0 lead after three innings in their home park, the Nats surrendered three runs in the fourth and a fourth run in the ninth. For the second straight night, Adam LaRoche and Bryce Harper each knocked in two runs. Tanner Roark improved to 12–7 on the season, pitching five and two-thirds innings, allowing two walks and three runs on five hits.

August 16, 2014
Nationals 4, Pirates 3
Down 3–0 in the third inning, the Nats rallied in the bottom of the eighth with a Kevin Frandsen single to right that scored Michael A. Taylor from third. With two outs and one swing of the bat, Adam LaRoche tied the game, scoring Denard Span and himself with his 18th homer of the year. Bryce Harper walked to lead off the top of the ninth. Wilson Ramos then hit a ground-rule double into the Nats' bullpen, which was caught by Drew Storen. Harper rounded home to give the Nats their fifth straight Curly W.

August 17, 2014

Nationals 6, Pirates 5 (11 innings)

The Nats took a 4–2 lead after a three-run seventh inning. After surrendering three runs in the ninth, Jayson Werth came off the bench, walked, and scored the tying run on an Asdrubal Cabrera single. Two innings later, Werth doubled to lead off, advanced to third on a Denard Span ground-out, and then was sent home on a Scott Hairston sacrifice fly to left.

August 18, 2014

Nationals 5, Arizona Diamondbacks 4 (11 innings)

Jordan Zimmermann pitched efficiently into the eighth inning for the home team until he gave up a two-run home run with no outs to give Arizona the 3–2 lead. The Nats responded in the bottom of the inning with an Anthony Rendon triple that plated Denard Span and a Jayson Werth sacrifice fly that scored Rendon to regain the lead. Tyler Clippard gave up the game-tying homer to David Peralta, and the game went into extras. Still riding a hot streak at the plate, Adam LaRoche came up big yet again, sending a 3–1 delivery from Will Harris into the Nats bullpen.

August 19, 2014

Nationals 8, Diamondbacks 1

Fueled by a six-run third inning, the Nats backed up Stephen Strasburg's strong outing. After giving up a solo home run in the first inning, Strasburg's final line was eight innings pitched, allowing only three hits, one run, and one walk while striking out four. The performance improved his record to 10–10. Singles from Jayson Werth and Ian Desmond and an Asdrubal Cabrera double gave the Nats a comfortable 6–1 lead. Desmond singled again in the eighth, bringing home two and putting the nail in Arizona's coffin.

August 20, 2014

Nationals 3, Diamondbacks 2

Tyler Clippard squandered a two-run lead in the eighth after Tanner Roark pitched a gem—seven innings, five hits, one walk, and no runs. Taking another tied ballgame into the bottom of the ninth, Bryce Harper led off with a single and advanced to third on a Kevin Frandsen single. Rendon then knocked him home with a single to left. Yet again, Harper scored the winning run and described the streak as "absolutely epic."

August 21, 2014

Nationals 1, Diamondbacks 0

The epic streak concluded with the wildest ending of all following a pitchers' duel between Gio Gonzalez and Arizona's Wade Miley. Gonzalez pitched seven innings, striking out six and surrendering only four hits and three walks. With Denard Span at second, Anthony Rendon grounded to Arizona third baseman Jordan Pacheco, who threw the ball past first baseman Mark Trumbo and into the camera well next to the Nats dugout. With a cracked Jayson Werth rally gnome looking on from atop a Gatorade bucket in the team's dugout, Denard Span casually rounded third and home to a raucous ovation from the Nationals Park crowd. Rendon then turned his batting helmet around backward in celebratory fashion as the team congratulated each other on the field.

The streak ended when the Nats dropped the first of a three-game home series to the San Francisco Giants 10–3. That game was memorable in its own right. Starting pitcher Doug Fister pitched six innings, allowing four earned runs, including two home runs just a couple days after undergoing a minor procedure to remove skin cancer from his neck. Fister said that had no bearing on his performance, simply stating "I just wasn't sharp. I left too many balls over the plate."

Giants slugger Michael Morse, a fan favorite during his Nats tenure, returned to Nationals Park for the first time since being traded to the Seattle Mariners in January 2013. Fans gave Morse a standing ovation in his first at-bat with some singing an impromptu version of "Take On Me," his popular walk-up song while in D.C.

42 When Owen Wilson Played for the Nationals

How Do You Know, the 2010 romantic comedy starring Reese Witherspoon, Owen Wilson, Paul Rudd, and Jack Nicholson is a movie that prominently features the Nationals. One highlight of the film is undoubtedly the scene featuring Owen Wilson playing a Nationals reliever sitting in the Nationals Park visiting bullpen (it's much more photogenic than the actual home bullpen) and daydreaming while a Nats outfielder saves a home run ball from making its way over the fence. Wilson's character, Matty Reynolds, who wears No. 33 and boasts a $14 million annual salary, is oblivious to the catch and asks his teammates around him: "When do you know you're in love?" One of his teammates, played by Domenick Lombardozzi (not to be confused with former Nat Steve Lombardozzi), chimed in with an answer.

The movie centers around Reese Witherspoon, who portrays a softball player cut from the USA team and trying to find herself. She meets Wilson's character, who is a philandering playboy with pink Nats garb stashed in his fancy apartment to give women after overnight trysts.

The stadium scenes were filmed over a 36-hour period. Hundreds of Nats fans gathered early on the morning of June 12, 2009, to sit in the left-field seats surrounding the bullpen. This was just hours after the real team defeated the Cincinnati Reds at home 3–2 and embarked on a road trip to face the Tampa Bay Rays.

Carol Flaisher, the film's location manager, is used to bringing films to D.C. She grew up a Senators fan and was thrilled to highlight Nationals Park and the team itself on the big screen. One qualm she did have with the film was the lack of baseball. "I wanted more, more, more," Flaisher said.

Nats pitcher Drew Storen made it out to the movie's Hollywood premiere and walked the same red carpet as the stars of the film. Not surprisingly, Storen enjoyed the event in relative anonymity. The team hosted a screening of the movie in December 2010 to benefit the Washington Nationals Dream Foundation. Want to get an idea of how zoned in Major League Baseball managers are? Nats skipper Jim Riggleman had no idea the movie was even filmed at Nationals Park until a few days prior to that screening.

Unfortunately for those involved in the production, *How Do You Know* was a dud at the box office, costing a reported $120 million while reeling in less than $49 million in theaters worldwide. For a fledgling franchise that finished 69–93 that season, though, 2010 sure resulted in a lot of camera time for the three-year-old Nationals Park. The Bravo reality show, *Top Chef*, filmed an episode at the stadium that May with Adam Dunn, John Lannan, and Matt Capps serving as taste testers.

Mickey Vernon

From 1939 into the early 1950s, first baseman James Barton Vernon, more commonly known as "Mickey," was one of the lone bright spots amidst a lackluster Washington Senators franchise.

Only twice did he experience a winning season in D.C. A good mix of defensive savvy and offensive production, Vernon was an easy choice as a fan favorite. "He is the only man in baseball who could play first base in a tuxedo, appear perfectly comfortable, and never wrinkle his suit," said Jack Dunn, an executive with the Baltimore Orioles in the 1950s.

Vernon served in the Navy for two years during World War II. He returned with a vengeance, winning the first of two American League batting titles with a .353 average in 1946. He also led the league in doubles that season, a feat he'd accomplish two more times in his career.

Before the 1948 season, Vernon was involved in one of the worst trades in Senators history. Owner Clark Griffith sent Vernon and future Hall of Famer Early Wynn to the Cleveland Indians for Joe Haynes, Ed Klieman, and Eddie Robinson. Known as "Thelma's Deal," Griffith made the trade to accommodate his niece and adopted daughter Thelma, who was married to Haynes. Vernon returned to Washington in a trade for Dick Weik during the 1950 season. The seven-time All-Star went on to win his second batting crown by hitting .337 in 1953.

Perhaps Vernon's most gratifying game came against the New York Yankees on Opening Day 1954 with President Dwight D. Eisenhower in attendance at RFK Stadium. On this day Vernon decided to save his best (and only) hit for last. With the game tied at 3–3 with one out and a man on in the bottom of the 10th inning, he approached the plate 0-for-4 on the day. Vernon hit a walk-off home run to give the Senators the 5–3 win.

The president was so excited that he tried to storm the field to greet Vernon as he touched home plate. Vernon recalled the experience in Donald Honig's book *Baseball Between the Lines*. "As I rounded third, I saw some of the players waiting at the plate to congratulate me, and there was one civilian there," Vernon said. "As I crossed the plate, he grabbed my arm. 'It's okay,' he said. 'I'm a Secret Service man. The president wants to see you over at his box.' Mr. Eisenhower was standing up with a big grin on his face and his hand outstretched. 'Nice going,' he said."

In late May the commander in chief returned to present his favorite player with a silver bat in honor of his 1953 batting title. Vernon is the only player in D.C. baseball history to win two batting titles.

Vernon retired from baseball after spending the 1960 season with the World Series champion Pittsburgh Pirates as a player and coach. He's one of a select group to have played in four different decades. He finished his career with 2,495 hits, 172 home runs, 1,311 RBIs, and a .286 average in 2,409 games with the Senators, Indians, Boston Red Sox, Milwaukee Braves, and Pirates. He left the sport having played more games at first base than any player in history. Eddie Murray later broke that record.

In 1961 Vernon was tasked with managing the expansion Senators after the previous regime moved to Minnesota. Provided with a hodgepodge of young ballplayers and second-rate talent acquired in the expansion draft, Vernon failed to produce as a manager. He was fired in 1963 after 40 games, having gone 135–227 (.373) as a manager. He went on to manage at the Triple A and Double A levels and coach in six different organizations.

44 The Homestead Grays

From 1940 to 1950, the most successful baseball team residing in Griffith Stadium wasn't the Senators. It was the Negro Leagues' Homestead Grays, who originated from Homestead, Pennsylvania, and split time between Pittsburgh's Forbes Field and Griffith

Stadium for years. The Grays competed at Griffith Stadium when the Senators were on road trips.

Led by power-hitting catcher Josh Gibson and steady first baseman Buck Leonard, also known as the "Thunder Twins," the Grays won nine Negro National League championships from 1937 to 1948, including Negro World Series titles in 1943, 1944, and 1948. Gibson was referred to as the "black Babe Ruth" and Leonard, the only Gray to play all 11 seasons in D.C., was known as the "black Lou Gehrig." "Not only are the Grays champions of Negro baseball, but they are a cocky bunch of ballplayers," wrote sportswriter Wendell Smith in 1938. "They do not believe that any team can beat them. They don't give a hoot for umpires, fans, newspaper men, or anything else. Baseball is all they care about—it is their life."

Elite black D.C. residents were initially partial to Major League Baseball and the Senators when the Grays arrived. However, the beginning of World War II facilitated the Grays' popularity in the nation's capital. The Nats were hit badly in terms of losing prominent players to military service. With an aging roster, the Grays were not as affected as other teams, losing only six players to war service. Leonard was 35 with a bad back, and Gibson was 32 with bad knees. Both were deemed unfit to serve in the war, a major boon for the Grays.

Griffith Stadium's location in the heart of an African American neighborhood, where Howard University Hospital now stands, gave the Grays a prime opportunity to thrive. Being a winning franchise with top-notch talent didn't hurt either. Beginning in the 1942 season, it gave local fans, both black and white, a better chance to see the Negro League talent playing right in their back yard. On May 31, 1942, legendary pitcher Satchel Paige pitched for the Grays at Griffith Stadium against the Dizzy Dean All-Stars, a team of former major leaguers led by the former St. Louis Cardinals star. No matchup between the lowly Senators and the Grays ever took place, but fans were able to watch Nats fan favorite Cecil Travis play in the exhibition. Travis, who batted .359 and finished second to Ted Williams' .406 in 1941, was given a weeklong furlough by the Army to play with Dean's team. Paige, wearing his Kansas City Monarchs uniform, allowed a single to Travis in the second inning but struck him out in the fifth. The exhibition drew more than 22,000 fans, quadrupling the Senators' 1942 average attendance.

On June 18, Paige returned to Griffith Stadium with his Monarchs, the class of the Negro American League, to take on the Grays, the class of the Negro National League, in an evening battle for the ages that drew around 28,000 fans. Grays pitcher Roy Partlow tossed nine scoreless innings but surrendered a run in the top of the 10th inning. Tied in the bottom of the 10th, Partlow knocked in the game-winning RBI with a triple into the left-field corner. That game further established the Grays' presence in D.C.

Sportswriter Sam Lacy was a huge proponent of integrating Major League Baseball and giving Negro League players a chance to compete against some of the majors' best players. Two powerful opponents to Lacy's ideals were Grays owner Cumberland Posey and Senators owner Clark Griffith. Posey, a former Grays player and manager who developed into a merciless entrepreneur, built the Grays into a Negro League dynasty and didn't want to see his team (and his profits) picked apart. Griffith also didn't want to diminish the pretty penny he made from renting out his stadium to Posey.

During their Grays career, Gibson and Leonard met with Griffith and discussed the possibility of becoming trailblazers and joining the Senators, but nothing came about. Over the years Griffith claimed he didn't want to exploit the Negro Leagues or take away from their success by signing their best players and biggest draws.

Several factors contributed to the end of the Grays and the Negro Leagues. Gibson suffered a fatal stroke in 1947 at the age of 35 after years of drinking problems and battling mental illness. Just a few months later, Jackie Robinson broke MLB's color barrier with the Brooklyn Dodgers. Shortly after, integration began to gain steam. Paige and Larry Doby, the first black player in American League history, returned to Griffith Stadium as members of the Cleveland Indians from 1948 to 1949. Doby received loud cheers from the segment of African American fans who sat in Griffith Stadium's segregated right-field area. Leonard, while still producing enough to garner a roster spot, was aging, and the team was in a rebuilding mode. Those issues translated to smaller amounts of fans watching one of baseball's great dynasties.

The Grays played their final game at Griffith Stadium in September of 1950 during a Sunday doubleheader against Paige and the Philadelphia Stars. Paige was in between stints with Major League Baseball's Cleveland Indians and St. Louis Browns. Grays fans saw a familiar name step up to the plate when 19-year-old Josh Gibson Jr. faced Paige. Before the game, the third baseman declared, "I'll hit Satch just like my dad did." As it turned out, Paige hit Gibson, but the latter went two-for-three with a triple that day.

When you head to Nationals Park, you will see the names of six Grays legends memorialized behind home plate in the Ring of Honor. The list consists of charismatic and speedy center fielder James "Cool Papa" Bell, pitcher Ray Brown, Gibson, Leonard, Posey, and heavy-hitting third baseman Jud Wilson. All are members of the National Baseball Hall of Fame.

45 Get Ready for the 2018 All-Star Game

Not since Baltimore's Oriole Park at Camden Yards hosted the 1993 MLB All-Star Game have D.C. area baseball fans been able to witness the best ballplayers in the world convene in their backyard.

Fans around the country still remember Ken Griffey Jr.'s monster shot that bounced off the famous warehouse during the Home Run Derby, eliciting a raucous standing ovation.

They also remember Seattle Mariners fireballer Randy Johnson blazing a fastball a couple feet over the head of Philadelphia Phillies batter John Kruk, causing the latter to reevaluate what he's doing with his life. Visibly scared, Kruk played to the crowd and smiled nervously at Johnson's intimidation factor. After cooling himself off by pulling the collar of his jersey back and forth, he then stepped toward first base as he missed swinging and then struck out spinning like a top. "When I stepped in the box, I said, 'All I want to do is make contact,'" he said. "Then after the first pitch, I said, 'All I want to do is live.' And I lived. So I had a good at-bat."

Fast forward 22 years to Opening Day 2015 in Southeast D.C. One of the worst kept secrets—in a city chock full of them—became official when a banner was unveiled in a pregame ceremony to celebrate Nationals Park being named the host of the 2018 All-Star Game.

For the first time since 1969, the nation's capital will play host to the best collection of baseball players on planet Earth. It will be the fifth time the city has hosted the Midsummer Classic. Griffith Stadium played host in 1937 and 1956, and D.C. Stadium held the game in 1962 and in 1969 when it was renamed RFK Stadium.

Fans in D.C. should take advantage of this opportunity and enjoy all of the festivities of this week. Be sure to go to the All-Star Futures Game the day before the big boys play. This game features every team's best prospects, many of whom you'll see in big league parks in a year or two. Check out the Home Run Derby and buy outfield seats. It would be quite the story to tell if you caught a Home Run Derby ball from Bryce Harper in his home park. Also make sure to take the kids to FanFest and give them the full baseball experience. In what is called "the largest interactive baseball event in the world," fans can meet baseball legends, take part in training and batting drills, and enjoy giveaways. The festivities wouldn't be complete without going to the All-Star Legends & Celebrity Softball Game, where celebrities and legends show off their competitive side.

By the time 2018 rolls around, Half Street and the areas surrounding the Nationals Park will be further developed, giving fans more dining and entertainment options. The festivities will benefit the city as well, which is expected to generate $50 to $60 million during that time.

The 31,391 spectators at the 1937 All-Star Game witnessed President Franklin Roosevelt's first pitch and Lou Gehrig's two-run homer off Dizzy Dean to lead the American League to an 8–3 win against the National League. The Washington Senators representatives were brothers Rick and Wes Farrell, Buddy Myer, and Cecil Travis.

The 1956 All-Star Game was the first to be dedicated to a baseball figure and was renamed the "Clark Griffith Memorial All-Star Game." That name appeared on the cover of the game program, which featured an illustration of the former Senators owner who had died on October 27, 1955. More than 28,000 fans attended the game and witnessed home runs from legends such as Willie Mays, Stan Musial, Mickey Mantle, and future Senators manager Ted Williams. The lone Senators representative at that game was first baseman Roy Sievers.

D.C. Stadium, later renamed RFK Stadium, played host to one of two 1962 All-Star Games; the other took place at Chicago's Wrigley Field. President John F. Kennedy threw out the first pitch. Senators pitcher Dave Stenhouse, who was the team's representative, did not play. But a native of the projects of Northeast D.C. and a graduate of Cardozo High School took the game over. Maury Wills, the Los Angeles Dodgers' speedy shortstop, pinch ran for Stan Musial in the sixth inning and immediately stole second base. He then scored the game's first run. After getting a single in the eighth inning, he eventually rounded his way home and was named the game's MVP following the NL's 3–1 victory.

Detroit Tigers pitcher (and future Washington Senator) Denny McLain was the American League's starting pitcher for the 1969 All-Star Game at RFK Stadium, but he arrived too late to make the start. In the second inning, Senators legend Frank Howard gave the hometown crowd a thrill when he homered to deep center field off of Steve Carlton. Senators pitcher Darold Knowles tossed two-thirds sof an inning in the bottom of the third, forcing two groundouts and surrendering no runs or walks.

46 Senators No-Hitters

Nationals fans may not realize how lucky they are to have experienced three no-hitters in a year.

Jordan Zimmermann's no-no on September 28, 2014 and Max Scherzer's impeccable performances on June 20, 2015 and October 3, 2015 helped further cement the excitement of baseball in the nation's capital.

Jordan Zimmermann douses Max Scherzer with chocolate syrup after he throws a no-hitter on June 20, 2015, the first of two no-hitters Scherzer would throw during that season.

During the Washington Senators' existence from 1901 to 1971, the feat only happened twice. The first no-hitter occurred on July 1, 1920, fittingly from the best pitcher in D.C. baseball history—Walter Johnson. Strangely enough, Johnson only pitched in 21 games that season—the third fewest of his career—after suffering a severe cold in spring training that resulted in lasting arm soreness. He finished the year with just eight wins, the second fewest of his career.

Johnson arrived at Boston's Fenway Park on July 1 about an hour before first pitch after tending to his ill son, Walter Jr., who turned five years old that day. His no-hitter almost didn't even happen. Red Sox player/manager Harry Hooper reached base with two outs in the seventh inning on a soft grounder that was mishandled by rookie second baseman Bucky Harris, who was given the error. In the ninth inning, Hooper subbed in Benn Karr and Hack Eibel as pinch hitters. After Johnson struck out Karr and Eibel, Hooper approached the plate as the final barrier between "The Big Train" and a no-hitter.

Hooper connected on a Johnson delivery and sent it down the first-base line. First baseman Joe Judge dove to knock the ball down and corralled it. Unable to reach first on his own, Judge tossed the ball to Johnson, who made the bare-handed snare and touched first to secure his only Major League Baseball no-hitter. He finished the masterful performance with 10 strikeouts and no walks.

The second and final no-hitter in Senators history occurred on August 8, 1931, courtesy of Bobby Burke. The opponent? Who else? The Boston Red Sox. This time, Senators fans got to witness history live at Griffith Stadium with Johnson as manager. Before the game Johnson and team owner Clark Griffith told the 24-year-old to take advantage of his fastball, and that's exactly what he did. Burke struck out eight batters and walked five in a 5–0 Washington victory. "He was throwing the last pitch over there as if it was the first one," Johnson said after the game, "and he soon found out he was getting away with it, like we told him he would."

Burke was an unexpected candidate to toss a no-hitter. He wasn't a regular starter, often pitching in relief. Harris called him "the kid who got an 11-year tryout." During Washington's 1933 American League championship season, Burke was called the team's unsung hero by manager Joe Cronin for his ability to use spot starts to snap losing streaks. Burke's no-hitter was one of 27 complete games in a 10-year career that included nine seasons with the Senators from 1927 to 1935. He finished his career with a record of 38–46.

# The Chief

If the Nationals reaching an astonishing 19 games above .500 before the All-Star break in their maiden voyage in D.C. was the most surprising team storyline, the top individual plot of the year belonged to the unforeseen rise of 23-year-old closer Chad Cordero. Like most of the roster in 2005, Cordero was a relative unknown to Nats fans, but it didn't take long for him to make an impact.

Heading into that season, fans in Washington didn't know what to expect from their new team, and they didn't care. They were just happy that the national pastime had returned after a 34-year hiatus. It didn't take Cordero long to contribute to their joy and become a fan favorite, seemingly coming out of nowhere to emerge as the most reliable closer in all of baseball.

Cordero was nicknamed "the Chief" by college teammate Jon Smith, who thought he was Native American. Cordero is actually a Mexican American, though he has Cherokee relatives. Selected by the Montreal Expos in the first round (20th overall) of the 2003 draft out of Cal-State Fullerton, Cordero made his debut that season, appearing in 12 games, saving one and finishing with a 1.64 ERA. His workload increased to 82⅔ innings in 69 games the following season, which ended with 14 saves, a 2.94 ERA, and the distinction as the winning pitcher in the final victory in Expos history.

On the mound the Chief led by example, and his stoic demeanor concealed a steadily racing heart with each pitch. As the Nats rocketed toward the top of the National League East standings in the early stages of 2005, Cordero was the man the team relied on to secure tight victories. The Chief entered the All-Star break with 31 saves, including 15 in June, which tied a Major League Baseball record and earned him NL Pitcher of the Month.

Along with ace Livan Hernandez, he was selected to represent the Nationals in the All-Star Game. Cordero faced one batter in the bottom of the eighth inning, striking out future Nationals catcher Ivan Rodriguez. Cordero finished the 2005 season with a 1.82 ERA and 47 saves, the most in baseball at the time and still a Nationals single-season record. His amazing 2005 campaign earned him the National League Rolaids Relief Man of the Year Award. He was also named the 2005 Washington Nationals Player of the Year.

In 2006 he pitched 68 games and saved 29, but his ERA ballooned to 3.19. He saved 37 games in a career-high 76 appearances in 2007, but his ERA climbed to 3.36. On June 12, 2007, at 25 years and 86 days old, he became the second-youngest player in baseball history to reach 100 saves when he secured the 7–4 victory against the Baltimore Orioles.

Cordero pitched in just six games in 2008, failing to record a save. He tore a labrum in his right shoulder. Weeks after undergoing surgery, he found out general manager Jim Bowden revealed in a radio interview that he intended to non-tender him, making him a free agent after the season. The Chief wasn't pleased that this decision was made months before the non-tender deadline arrived and that he found out about it after Bowden had disclosed it on the air. He did not re-sign with the Nats after the season. Having earned saves in the first and last Nationals games at RFK Stadium, he finished his career in Washington. He is still the Nats' all-time leader in saves with 113.

Cordero signed a minor league deal with the Seattle Mariners in 2009 and re-upped with them for the 2010 season, appearing in nine games that year. He was granted free agency in mid-July of that year and joined the New York Mets minor league system.

In December of 2010, Cordero and his wife, Jamie, suffered a terrible loss. Their 11-week-old daughter, Tehya, was spending the night at his parents' house 40 miles away along with her sister,

Riley. Tehya was put to bed in her crib and was checked on an hour later. She wasn't breathing. She had died of Sudden Infant Death Syndrome, commonly referred to as SIDS. Still struggling with the tragedy, Cordero signed with the Toronto Blue Jays on a minor league deal in January 2011 and was released in May. He retired the next month.

After two years away from the game, Cordero attempted a comeback in 2013, signing a minor league deal with the Los Angeles Angels of Anaheim. He split time between the Single A Inland Empire 66ers and the Triple A Salt Lake City Bees, but he never made it back to the bigs.

48 The Mysterious Demise of D.C.'s First Batting Champion

The circumstances that resulted in the beginning and end of Hall of Famer and former Washington Senator Ed Delahanty's career are quite amazing and symbolic of the time period in which he lived. "Big Ed" made his debut in 1888 as a 20-year-old with the Philadelphia Phillies after star pitcher Charlie Ferguson died of typhoid fever. Delahanty went on to play 13 years in Philadelphia and played the final two seasons of his career for the Senators in 1902 and 1903. He led the newly formed American League with a batting average of .376 in his first and only full season in D.C.

After signing a three-year deal with the New York Giants, he experienced gambling and drinking problems. The contract, which included a large advance, was voided before the 1903 season. Unable to repay the advance to the Giants after spending most of it at a race track in New Orleans, he begrudgingly returned to the Senators.

His career came to an abrupt end on July 2, 1903, when he fell 25 feet to his death from the International Bridge into the Niagara River at Niagara Falls. His body was found one week later, sans a leg that was assumed to have been torn off by the propeller of the Maid of the Mist, the boat that ferries tourists as close to the falls as safely possible.

Delahanty had gone missing from the Oriental Hotel in Detroit, where the Senators were staying during a road trip. He had ditched the team to catch a train from Detroit to New York to reconcile with his wife after his marriage fell apart. Delahanty had consumed five shots of whiskey, continuously rang the alarm bell, pulled a razor on a conductor, broke a glass case with a firefighting axe, smoked in the sleeper car, and pulled on the ankles of a woman in the upper bunk of a sleeper car. His belligerence led him to be removed from the train.

Instead of delivering Delahanty to the Canadian police, the conductor, John Cole, kicked him off at a station in Bridgeburg, Ontario. Delahanty ventured across the International Bridge while part of it was open to let a boat pass through. He was stopped by a night watchman named Sam Kingston, who was holding a lantern. What happened after is not clearly known. How did Delahanty fall to his death? Was it foul play? Was it suicide? Was it an accident? The circumstances have been debated for more than a century.

Kingston changed his story about the incident multiple times. One claimed he was threatened by Delahanty. Another involved a scuffle in which Delahanty got away, and Kingston later heard a splash. Kingston later recanted those and said there was no scuffle, and Delahanty simply ignored him and walked off the bridge.

What isn't debatable is that Delahanty's death at the age of 35 cut short one of the best careers in Major League Baseball history. A testament to his skill, his career ended in the middle of a 16-game hitting streak. He was the first player to hit .400 three times, a feat matched only by Rogers Hornsby. He's third all time in Major

League Baseball history with a .346 batting average over a 16-year career that spanned 1888–1903. He only trails Hornsby (.358) and Ty Cobb (.367).

He is the only player in baseball history to win a batting title in the National League and American League. Delahanty led the NL in triples in 1892 with 21 and is still 13th all-time on Major League Baseball's triples list with 185 over the course of 1,835 career games. That equals a triple once every 9.92 games. In comparison the all-time triples leader, Sam Crawford, hit 309 three-baggers in 2,517 games, a rate of one triple every 8.15 games. Crawford is a Hall of Famer and was one of the most decorated hitters of his era, batting .309 over a 19-year career with the Cincinnati Reds and Detroit Tigers. Even he appreciated Delahanty's skill at the plate. "Ed was the best right-handed hitter I ever saw," Crawford said.

Delahanty's 31-game hitting streak in 1899 was the longest in Phillies history until Jimmy Rollins knocked 38 in a row over the course of the 2005 and 2006 seasons and Chase Utley hit safely in 35 straight games in 2006. Delahanty's offensive proficiency lent itself well to stealing bases, leading the National League with 58 thefts in 1898. He's 52nd on the all-time list with 455.

Delahanty was a part of one of the largest group of brothers to play in the major leagues. Along with Ed were Frank, Jim, Joe, and Thomas. Jim played with the Senators from 1907 to 1909, batting .278 with four home runs and 105 RBIs in 281 games in the nation's capital. A sixth brother, Willie, played minor league ball.

"Big Ed" was inducted into the Baseball Hall of Fame in 1945 by the Old Timers Committee, but no official ceremony was held until 2013. His Cooperstown plaque reads: "One of the game's greatest sluggers. Led National League hitters in 1899 with an average of .408 for Philadelphia; American League batters in 1902 with a mark of .376 for Washington. Made 6 hits in 6 times at bat twice during career and once hit 4 home runs in a game."

49 World Series or Bust

Fresh off the best record in baseball, the franchise's first division title, and a heartbreaking Game 5 National League Division Series loss to the St. Louis Cardinals, Nationals manager Davey Johnson decided to go all in and raise the stakes for 2013. A month after being bounced out of the playoffs, Johnson, who was turning 70 in January 2013 and heading into his final season as skipper, had just been named NL Manager of the Year. Prompted by MLB Network analyst Larry Bowa for a 2013 season prediction, Johnson made this proclamation: "World Series or bust. It's going to be my last year anyway." Just a few weeks later at the annual Baseball Winter Meetings, he doubled down on his remarks. "World Series or bust," Johnson said. "That's probably the slogan this year. But I'm comfortable with that."

Johnson didn't want the Nats to mortgage their future and go all in for a one-year stretch. He thought long term and wanted his replacement to have a roster to be proud of. "If we don't win, it'll be my fault," Johnson said. "I want it to be a solid base for a long time. I'm not trying to hold on to all the chips to protect my ass. I don't worry about my ass. I think we can win with whoever we got." This was coming from the same guy who said before the 2012 season that "they can fire me" if the Nationals missed the playoffs.

The acquisitions of center fielder Denard Span, starting pitcher Dan Haren, closer Rafael Soriano, and re-signing of first baseman Adam LaRoche were expected to bolster that 98-win roster. The pressure and lofty expectations mounted when the team's top two stars appeared on the cover of *Sports Illustrated* in about a one-month span. Bryce Harper, Washington's 20-year-old phenom, graced the cover of the February 25 edition standing on the Lincoln

Nationals manager Davey Johnson acknowledges the crowd at the last home game of the 2013 season, during which the team fell short of his lofty World Series aspirations.

Memorial with the National Mall's reflecting pool, Washington Monument, and Capitol building in the background. For those who believe in the infamous *SI* jinx, the April 1 issue presented the final nail in the season's coffin before the first pitch was even thrown. With Stephen Strasburg on his second *SI* cover, the magazine called the Nats ace "Mr. October" followed by the statement: "The Nationals Will Break Through and Win the World Series." With such high hopes enveloping the team that revitalized a fanbase just a year prior, D.C. die-hards must have experienced some sort of subconscious sense of gloom and doom upon seeing that cover.

The Nats began the 2013 campaign with a 2–0 Opening Day victory against the Miami Marlins—thanks to two solo blasts from Harper. The team started out hot, going 4–1 in its first five games and spending four of those tied with the Atlanta Braves for first in the NL East and one in sole possession of the lead. The Braves then sprinted to a 12–1 record and never looked back. From that point on, the Nats fluctuated between second and third place.

Harper battled through injuries all year. He collided with the Dodger Stadium outfield wall in May, which required him to get 11 stitches on his chin. He missed all of June with a knee injury but appeared in his second All-Star Game in July and even finished in second place in the Home Run Derby with his father pitching to him. He ended up with 20 home runs and 58 RBIs on the year.

Span's presence in the lineup and in center field paid dividends. The 29-year-old led all of baseball with a 29-game hitting streak and 11 triples. Outfielder Jayson Werth led the team with a .318 average and 82 RBIs. Shortstop Ian Desmond played in a team-high 158 games and completed his second straight season with 20 home runs, 20 doubles, and 20 stolen bases, earning his second consecutive Silver Slugger.

Jordan Zimmermann emerged as the team's top pitcher, going 19–9 on the season and tossing 213⅓ innings with a 3.25 ERA. He was nominated for his first All-Star Game but didn't play due to neck soreness. The team also witnessed the rise of 26-year-old rookie Tanner Roark, who pitched in 14 games, started five, and ended up 7–1 with a 1.51 ERA. Soriano tied for fifth in the majors with 43 saves.

The team was 15 games behind the Braves entering September and went on a hot streak of sorts, winning 12 of 14 games early in the month but eventually petered out. Washington never came within eight games of Atlanta the rest of the way and placed second in the division with an 86–76 record. What would have been a dream season just a couple years before morphed into utter disappointment given the numerous preseason World Series predictions.

50 Brad Wilkerson and the Nats' Cycles

For newfound Washington Nationals fans who were casual observers of baseball during the sport's 34-year absence in the city, aside from ace Livan Hernandez, outfielder Brad Wilkerson was perhaps the most recognizable member of the Montreal Expos who made the move to Washington, D.C.

It didn't take the converted first baseman long to make an impression as the team's leadoff hitter. In the franchise's second game on April 6, 2005, a road contest against the Philadelphia Phillies, Wilkerson made history. On the way to the franchise's first victory, a 7–3 triumph at Citizens Bank Park, he notched the first cycle in team history.

Wilkerson walked to lead off the game but was then caught stealing second. In the third inning, he homered to right to put the Nats up 1–0. Two innings later he singled to right and was then thrown out at second after Cristian Guzman grounded into a fielder's choice. In the seventh inning, he tripled on a hit to center field. He was stranded when Guzman popped out to second. In the eighth inning, he finished the job by bouncing a ground-rule double to deep center, scoring Terrmel Sledge and advancing Brian Schneider to third.

With the feat, he finished 4-for-4 with a walk and two RBIs, accounting for 25 percent of the team's 16 hits on a momentous night. The cycle was the second of Wilkerson's career. He hit a natural cycle (a single, double, triple, and home run in order) with the Expos against the Pittsburgh Pirates on June 24, 2003, at Montreal's Olympic Stadium. It was the first cycle in D.C. baseball history since Senators outfielder Jim King did it against the Boston Red Sox on May 26, 1964.

The 2004 Expos Player of the Year as voted by the Baseball Writers' Association of America, Wilkerson was a man of many firsts for the Nats. He was the team's first batter and got its first hit (a single) on the fifth pitch of its first game against Phillies pitcher Jon Lieber. His triple of the cycle was the first three-bagger in franchise history. He also hit the team's first grand slam on August 4, 2005, against the Los Angeles Dodgers off of Duaner Sanchez.

Wilkerson hit .248 with 11 home runs, 57 RBIs, and a career-high 42 doubles in 148 games in his only season in Washington. He was traded to the Texas Rangers along with Sledge and pitcher Armando Galarraga for All-Star outfielder Alfonso Soriano in December 2005.

Three years later, on August 28, 2008, against the Dodgers, Guzman became the second player in Nats history to hit for the cycle. After a two-run home run from Manny Ramirez put the Dodgers up 2–0 in the first inning, Guzman began a five-run scoring barrage in the bottom half of that inning with a solo homer to left off of rookie Clayton Kershaw. The next inning Guzman singled but was thrown out trying to extend the play into a double. He grounded into a fielder's choice in the fourth and then doubled to deep left center in the sixth, scoring Anderson Hernandez. At this point, Guzman had only three triples in 487 at-bats during his All-Star season, but he belted a hit to deep center, chugging his way around the base path as teammate Aaron Boone scored. As soon as he connected with the ball, the Nationals dugout erupted with teammates yelling at him to "Go three!" Guzman slid into third before a relay throw could be made from center field. "As soon as I hit the ball, I knew I was going to third," he said.

His cycle put a stamp on an 11–2 victory that clinched a series sweep against Los Angeles. Guzman finished the 2008 season batting .316 with career highs in hits (183) and doubles (35). During his five seasons in D.C., he hit .282 with 23 home runs and 177 RBIs in 550 games. On July 31, 2010, the Nationals traded

Guzman to the Texas Rangers for right-handed pitchers Tanner Roark and Ryan Tatusko.

51 Bryce's Benching

Sixteen-year-old Bryce Harper graced the cover of *Sports Illustrated* for the first time in June of 2009. He told the publication that he wanted to "be considered the greatest baseball player who ever lived." And this came after he was labeled as "possibly the country's best 12-year-old hitter" by *Baseball America* in 2005.

The focus, tenacity, and energy with which he played was apparent long before he stepped on a Major League Baseball diamond. In his pro debut at Dodger Stadium on April 28, 2012, at the age of 19, Harper smacked a double to center field in the seventh inning. As he made his way to second base, he flipped his batting helmet off his head, revealing the free-flowing mohawk he had grown out.

The son of a blue-collar ironworker has always been known for his all-out style of play reminiscent of Pete Rose. He played hard, he played fast, and he sometimes played with reckless abandon. That's why it was so surprising that, on April 19, 2014, against the St. Louis Cardinals, Harper failed to run out a comebacker that led off the sixth inning. Even more surprising, Matt Williams, in just his 18th game as Nationals manager, benched him for a "lack of hustle" and "the inability to run 90 feet." The Nats lost 4–3. "He and I made an agreement," Williams said following the game. "This team made an agreement that when we play the game that we hustle at all times, that we play the game with intensity and the willingness to win."

"I respect what he did," Harper said about Williams' decision. "That's part of the game." Nationals general manager Mike Rizzo also picked a side. "I unequivocally support the manager's decision 100 percent," Rizzo said.

Ironically, the program handled out at the gates during the homestead featured Harper with the phrase: "Nothing but hustle."

Williams made his modus operandi clear during his introductory press conference five months earlier. "I will be aggressive. My natural tendency is to go," Williams said on his first day as the Nationals' manager. "I want to steal second base, I want to hit and run, I want to go first-to-third. Those are important to me. I think we've seen that if we can score that extra run, we can be really special. So yes, aggressiveness is key."

The 21-year-old didn't reach base in three at-bats that night. His average dropped from .310 to .295. Kevin Frandsen supplanted Harper, and with the Nats down 4–2 in the bottom of the ninth, grounded out to third, scoring Zach Walters and advancing Denard Span to third. The next batter, Jayson Werth, struck out to end the game. "It's too bad that it came down to that situation in the ninth inning, when he could have been at the plate," Williams said. "For the sake of his teammates and the sake of the organization, he needs to play with aggression…He's an exciting player. People come to pay money and watch him play and watch him play the way he can play. And it's pretty exciting. It's pretty dynamic. But there's another side to it. The other side is, regardless of how the ball comes off the bat or regardless of how he's feeling about an at-bat, he must maintain that intensity and that aggressiveness. And that means running all the way to first base and touching the base."

Harper has not been benched since.

52 The Senators' Spy

In what seems like the most D.C. thing ever, a former Washington athlete transformed from an unremarkable ballplayer to one of America's key gatherers of foreign intelligence.

Moe Berg was a reserve catcher for the Senators and had a lifetime batting average of .243. In his three seasons in Washington, Berg batted .228 and only managed 79 hits. He hit .185 during the Senators' 1933 American League pennant run.

A graduate of Princeton University and Columbia Law School, he studied philosophy at the Sorbonne in Paris. For Berg, an exceptional mathematician and linguist who read at least six newspapers a day, the running joke was that Berg could speak 12 languages but couldn't hit in any of them. He spent 15 years in the majors primarily because of his intellect and defensive prowess.

Berg, a lifelong bachelor who neither learned to drive a car nor owned a house, was called "the strangest man ever to play baseball" by the legendary Casey Stengel, Berg's manager with the Boston Braves from 1938 to 1939. His brains and charisma made him popular during his stint in D.C. He was often invited to embassy dinners and parties and caught the attention of the Roosevelt administration.

Those who watched him play had to be surprised when they saw him selected to join legends like Babe Ruth, Lou Gehrig, and Jimmie Foxx during a 1934 Major League All-Star tour in Japan just a few months after being released by the Senators and signing with the Cleveland Indians.

Berg arrived at St. Luke's Hospital on November 29, 1934, while his teammates were playing in Omiya. Wearing a black kimono and holding a bouquet of flowers, Berg claimed to be a friend of ambassador Joseph Clark Grew, whose daughter Cecil Burton had just had a baby. He got off the elevator but never visited Burton. He instead headed up the stairs to the roof. "[Berg] bluffs his way up onto the roof of the hospital, the tallest building in Tokyo at the time, and from underneath his kimono he pulls out a movie camera," Berg biographer Nicholas Dawidoff said. "He proceeds to take a series of photos panning the whole setting before him, which includes the harbor, the industrial sections of Tokyo, possibly munitions factories and things like that. Then he puts the camera back under his kimono and leaves the hospital with these films."

The footage he captured on top of the hospital was intended to be used by General Jimmy Doolittle's pilots during the World War II bombing raids in Tokyo in 1942—just months after the attack on Pearl Harbor.

In January of 1942, Berg left baseball and worked under Nelson A. Rockefeller in the Office of Inter-American Affairs (OIAA) to study the health and fitness of the populations of Central and South America. In 1943 Berg was recruited by the Office of Strategic Services (OSS)—the forerunner of the CIA.

In late 1944 he was sent to Switzerland to attend a lecture by German physicist Werner Heisenberg to gather intelligence on Nazi Germany's efforts to develop an atomic bomb. If Heisenberg revealed that an atomic bomb was in fact being made, Berg was instructed to assassinate the physicist and take cyanide to avoid capture. Luckily for both men, Heisenberg stated in the lecture that Germany had already lost the war. Berg interpreted that statement to mean Germany was not close to developing nuclear weapons. President Franklin D. Roosevelt remarked: "Fine, just fine. Let us pray Heisenberg is right. And my regards to the catcher."

Berg was awarded the Medal of Freedom in 1946 but declined the honor. His sister accepted the award on his behalf after his death. He's the only major leaguer to have his trading cards on display at CIA headquarters. The rights to Dawidoff's 1994 Berg biography titled *The Catcher Was a Spy* were bought by George Clooney for him to produce and star in, and the motion picture is tentatively slated for a 2016 release.

Berg died on May 29, 1972. It's said his sister, Ethel, took his ashes to Israel, but the exact location of his remains is still unknown. Just as he lived, Berg is still mysterious long after death.

53 Scott Boras' Ties to the Nationals

Deemed the most powerful agent in sports, Scott Boras has negotiated $2.3 billion in active Major League Baseball player contracts and clocked more than $117 million in commissions as of late 2015, according to *Forbes*. Although he brokered two 10-year deals exceeding $250 million for Alex Rodriguez and a $242 million deal for Prince Fielder, his biggest impact with a single organization has occurred with the Washington Nationals. The Nationals have more players represented by Boras than any team in baseball. Bryce Harper, Stephen Strasburg, Max Scherzer (seven years, $210 million), Jayson Werth (seven years, $126 million), Anthony Rendon, Danny Espinosa, 2014 first-round pick Erick Fedde, and Gio Gonzalez (who switched to Boras in 2015) all let Boras handle their financial dirty work.

Boras, the man who spent his early 20s as a farmhand in the St. Louis Cardinals and Chicago Cubs systems in the mid-1970s, is notorious for playing hardball, as evidenced by having Strasburg and Harper literally wait until the last minute to dot the i's on their rookie contracts with the Nationals. Strasburg's deal was completed just more than one minute before his 2009 deadline and Harper's

2010 deal was finished with 26 seconds to go. The common criticism regarding Washington's relationship with Boras is that general manager Mike Rizzo kowtows to Boras and signs his clients to keep up a positive rapport with him for future negotiations. Fuel was added to that fire when Boras was asked about Strasburg's shutdown by *The Washington Post* in 2012. "Everyone was given

Bryce Harper: MLB's First $400 Million Man?

D.C. sports fans, who have been opining for Oklahoma City Thunder superstar and Prince George's County native Kevin Durant to join the Washington Wizards, got a taste of their own medicine when New York Yankees fans gawked over Bryce Harper during the Nationals' two-game series in the Bronx in June 2015.

Harper, a noted Yankees fan growing up, idolized Mickey Mantle and said in his 2009 *Sports Illustrated* cover story that one of his career goals was to play in the pinstripes. As far back as Harper's rookie season in 2012, it's been predicted that the young phenom is in line for $400 million when he becomes a free agent after the 2018 season.

Giancarlo Stanton set the bar when he signed the richest athlete contract in American history by inking a 13-year, $325 million contract with the Miami Marlins in November 2014. Many, including ESPN's Buster Olney, consider it an inevitability that Harper will land with the Yankees. Among those who also consider it a given are Yankees fans, who chanted "Twenty-Nineteen!" and "Fu-ture Yankee!" during Harper's first career series in New York last season. Harper embraced the moment, hitting .375 with a home run in his two games at Yankee Stadium in 2015.

Nats fans will certainly want the Lerners to pony up and give the Yanks a run for their money. One benefit on the side of the Nationals is a quote from Harper in June 2012, stating his desire to spend his whole career with one franchise. "You look at Cal Ripken. You look at Derek Jeter. You look at all the greats that played for one team their whole career," Harper said. "I want to be like that. I've always wanted to be like that. I've always wanted to play with that same team." Whether Harper re-signs with the Nationals or not, sit back, relax, and enjoy the next few seasons with him.

notice by Rizzo and everyone else that this was going to be what the format was," Boras said, "that Stephen is going to, hopefully, pitch the Nationals into position [to win the division]. [Strasburg's situation coming off surgery influenced how] Rizzo and I put this team together. I got eight or nine guys on the team. I got another whole group in the minor leagues."

Using the phrase "Rizzo and I put this team together" in any context raised red flags and for good reason. For an agent to have that much influence on a team's makeup is unusual, if not out of this world. One week later, Boras recanted his statement, denying he had any influence in front office and team decisions. "I don't make the decisions," Boras told *The Post*. "I don't even know when they're shutting down Strasburg and I don't need to. They're following expert medical opinion, and that's all I care about."

When explaining how so many of his clients are on the same roster, Boras broke it down in layman's terms years later. "Usually how this happens is that when a club is losing, they have high draft picks," Boras told *The Post* in 2015. "We represent a lot of high draft picks and we have three or four of them here. Now those high draft picks are very talented. They develop a core and now they start seeking our free agents. So you get this period of time where you have a culmination of draft and free agency, and then it creates a volume of players on the team."

Past Boras clients signed by the Nationals include Edwin Jackson (one year, $11 million in 2012), Rafael Soriano (two years, $28 million in 2013), Jesus Flores, and Rick Ankiel. After the 2008 season, the Nationals were courting Boras client Mark Teixeira, who grew up about 45 minutes from Nationals Park in Severna Park, Maryland. Despite Washington offering more money, both Boras and Teixeira told the Nationals he wanted to win immediately and sign with a contender. Teixeira eventually signed an eight-year, $180 million deal with the New York Yankees.

Many Nationals fans are concerned that Boras' influence could lead Harper down the same path as Teixeira when his contract runs out after the 2018 season. It's unlikely the 2018 Nationals will be as bad as the 2008 Nationals, but there is always the possibility the Yankees could outbid the Nationals for his services should he hit free agency. Harper made his childhood love of the Yankees well-known when coming up through the baseball ranks, and Boras loves getting his client top dollar.

54 An Owner Sells Off His Relatives

If you ever have gotten so angry at a relative, especially an in-law, that you wanted to just ship them off far away, you can live vicariously through the tale of Washington Senators owner Clark Griffith. The only difference is he didn't want to do it. He had to.

In dire financial straits in 1934, the Old Fox received an offer he couldn't refuse—except that he did initially. From 1928 to 1934, Joe Cronin was Washington's top shortstop and was named player/manager in 1933, leading the Senators to their final World Series appearance, where they fell to the New York Giants in five games.

Griffith, who was known to be wrong from time to time, expected nothing from Cronin when he signed him to a $7,500 contract in 1928. The owner told reporters he purchased a "young shortstop, name of Cronin." When asked for a first name, Griffith quipped, "It don't make no difference, and I don't even know if he's got a first name. He's only gonna be around long enough to give [shortstop] Bob Reeves a rest, then we'll ship him to Birmingham. Don't you fellows go writin' your heads off about him now—he's only a fair to middlin' busher."

Sure enough, Cronin developed into a Hall of Famer. And after the 1934 season, he married Griffith's secretary, who also happened to be his niece and adopted daughter, Mildred Robertson. She was adopted by Griffith along with her six siblings when they were kids.

In debt and needing to cut costs to help keep Washington afloat financially, Griffith was approached by 31-year-old Boston Red Sox owner Tom Yawkey, who was looking to make a deal. During the 1934 World Series, Yawkey met with Griffith in his hotel room and offered him $250,000 for Cronin, an astonishing figure at the time. "Tom, you had better leave," Griffith bristled. The persistent Yawkey called Griffith on his home line after the series and said, "How about that deal?"

Griffith responded by saying: "To hell with you!" and hanging up the phone.

The concept of nepotism gradually gnawed at the loyal Griffith, who read the criticism surrounding Cronin's relationship with the owner and the job status that came along with it. Griffith relented and eventually agreed to Yawkey's proposal on two stipulations— the first being that Boston include shortstop Lyn Lary and the second that Griffith can call Cronin to okay the deal. Cronin, who had completed his San Francisco honeymoon through the Panama Canal, gave his blessing to the move. Griffith looked at Cronin as a son and saw to it that he received a secure five-year deal with an annual rate of $50,000 as the Red Sox player/manager.

Another of Griffith's nieces and adopted daughters, Thelma, married pitcher Joe Haynes in 1941, the same year he was sold to the Chicago White Sox. Haynes only appeared in 11 games with the Senators in 1939 and 1940 before the move. Haynes spent eight seasons with Chicago before being traded to the Cleveland Indians in November of 1948. Thelma had made it clear to Griffith that she preferred to live in Washington, D.C. What she wanted, she got.

After the 1948 season, the Cleveland Indians traded Haynes, Ed Klieman, and Eddie Robinson to the Senators for Mickey

Vernon and Early Wynn in what is known as "Thelma's Deal." The deal was a theft for Cleveland. Wynn went on to become a Hall of Famer, winning 300 games and pitching 289 complete games, while Haynes' ERA was never better than 4.50 over his final four seasons, and he only won 10 games over the next four seasons.

Haynes went on to serve as Washington's pitching coach from 1953 to 1955 and later became vice president and general manager. Sherry Robertson, brother of Mildred and Thelma, spent most of 10 mediocre seasons with the Senators from 1940 to 1952. He never hit above .260 or more than 11 home runs in a season. He may best be known for his errant 1943 throw that went into the crowd and hit a fan in the head. The fan died the next day from a fractured skull and concussion.

55 "Hammering" Grand Slams in Consective Innings

On a relatively unremarkable Monday night on July, 27, 2009, in Milwaukee, the Nationals began a four-game road series against the 49–49 Brewers. Going into the series opener, the Nats were sitting at 31–67 and on the fast track to their worst season in franchise history. (They finished the season 59–103.) But on this night, an outfielder by the name of Josh Willingham, affectionately known as "the Hammer" for his Herculean build and power hitting style, spiced up a season most fans of the Curly W's would like to forget.

Willingham was acquired from the Florida Marlins in 2008, along with starting pitcher Scott Olsen, in exchange for second baseman Emilio Bonifacio, minor league second baseman Jake Smolinski, and minor league right-hander P.J. Dean. Willingham eventually became a Washington fan favorite. He had hit 14 homers prior to the Milwaukee series, but those came with an asterisk. Of those home runs, 12 had been solo shots, making him last in RBIs among the 91 players with at least 12 bombs on the season.

In the top of the second inning, Willingham doubled to deep left on a 1–1 count and grounded out to pitcher Jeff Suppan on a full count in the fourth. One inning later, with the Nats down 2–0 to Milwaukee, Alberto Gonzalez doubled and was advanced to third on a sacrifice by pitcher Craig Stammen. Nyjer Morgan singled and scored Gonzalez to cut the lead in half.

Next, Cristian Guzman singled. Ryan Zimmerman was then hit by a pitch to load the bases. Power hitter Adam Dunn was at the plate for a prime situation. But on eight pitches, he walked, scoring Morgan and tying the game. Nick Johnson couldn't capitalize,

Lucky 13

Willingham became the 13th player in Major League Baseball history with at least two grand slams in a game. He is only the third player in National League history to do it.

Here are the 12 before him who accomplished the feat:

1936: Tony Lazzeri—New York Yankees
1939: Jim Tabor—Boston Red Sox
1946: Rudy York—Boston Red Sox
1961: Jim Gentile—Baltimore Orioles
1966: Tony Cloninger—Atlanta Braves
(Note: Cloninger is the only pitcher in MLB history to hit two grand slams in one game)
1968: Jim Northrup—Detroit Tigers
1970: Frank Robinson—Baltimore Orioles
1995: Robin Ventura—Chicago White Sox
1998: Chris Hoiles—Baltimore Orioles
1999: Fernando Tatis—St. Louis Cardinals
(Note: Tatis is the only player to hit two grand slams in the same inning)
1999: Nomar Garciaparra—Boston Red Sox
2003: Bill Mueller—Boston Red Sox

striking out looking on the fourth pitch. Now it was Willingham's turn. On the first pitch, he took Suppan deep to left to score Guzman, Zimmerman, and Dunn to give the Nats a 6–2 lead.

One inning later the assault on Suppan continued. Gonzalez walked and again was advanced to second on a sacrifice—this time by pitcher Jason Bergmann. Morgan singled and advanced to second on a throw. Gonzalez was now at third. Guzman doubled to send Gonzalez and Morgan home. Zimmerman was intentionally walked, and Suppan was replaced by Mitch Stetter. Dunn then hit a ground-rule double to send Guzman home and Zimmerman to third. Johnson was walked to load the bases, prompting Mark DiFelice to replace Stetter.

The stage was set for Willingham yet again. The bases were loaded with only one out.

He swung and missed on the first delivery. But on the second pitch, he got all of it, sending the ball to center field and giving the Nats a 13–5 lead on the way to a convincing 14–6 victory.

Willingham struck out to close the top of the eighth but finished the night 3-for-5 with eight RBIs, tying a Nats franchise record. "That was a special night, and one I will never forget," Willingham said. "You don't get the opportunity to do that many times, much less come through in both situations."

"The Hammer" Willingham's efforts earned him National League Player of the Week for the week of July 27–August 2 as he hit .435 with three home runs and 11 RBIs in that time frame.

Willingham finished the season with a .260 average, 24 home runs, 61 RBIs, and 61 walks in 133 games. He finished his Nats career in 2010 batting .268 with 16 home runs, 56 RBIs, and 67 walks in 114 games. Washington traded him to the Oakland Athletics in December 2010 for right-handed reliever Henry Rodriguez and outfielder Corey Brown.

Rodriguez threw 100 mph fastballs like it was second nature but struggled with control, which led to his trade to the Chicago

Cubs on June 11, 2013, for minor league pitcher Ian Dickson. Brown only played in 36 games with the Nationals from 2011–2013, managing only seven hits in 40 at-bats.

Willingham retired after the 2014 season despite a substantial contract offer from a contender to play in 2015, finishing his career with a lifetime average of .253 with 195 home runs, 632 RBIs, and 988 hits. That career was, of course, highlighted by that grand game in July.

56 Visit Cooperstown

A trip down memory lane is a must for any baseball fan. The best place to take that trip is 380 miles northeast of Nationals Park at the National Baseball Hall of Fame and Museum nestled in Cooperstown, New York's historic Main Street and just south of Otsego Lake. On the outside the three-story brick building, much like the game itself, can be understated, blending in with the rest of its surroundings. But on the inside, the sport is brought to life, rejuvenating fans' love of the game with the sport's greatest collection of artifacts.

Upon entrance of the museum, fans enter the main lobby and decide to either make their way to the museum store on the right or the grand atrium with the shrine of new inductees on the left. From there visitors make their way through the Hall of Fame plaque gallery detailing the careers of every Hall of Fame member beginning with the inaugural 1936 class. Head up the ramp behind the gallery and browse the exhibit profiling baseball in the movies and the "Sandlot Kids' Clubhouse," a spot for kids to take pictures and interact with film clips.

The second floor contains the Cooperstown Room, which explains the town's important and permanent tie to baseball. There is also the "Baseball Experience," a 13-minute multimedia presentation that examines the history of the sport in the Grandstand Theater, a setup of 191 classic stadium seats. "Today's Game" is an exhibit designed like a clubhouse with lockers containing jerseys and memorabilia from every current team. While you're on the second floor, browse the exhibits dedicated to the influence of African Americans, Latin Americans, and women on the game of baseball.

The third floor features "Sacred Ground," an examination of the stadium experience; "One for the Books," a gallery dedicated to Hank Aaron and other record-breaking legends; and "Autumn Glory," a collection of artifacts from the most recent World Series.

D.C. Hall of Famers

Washington Potomacs: Ben Taylor (first baseman)

Washington Nationals: Connie Mack (catcher) and Frank Robinson (manager)

Washington Senators: Roger Bresnahan (catcher), Stan Coveleski (pitcher), Joe Cronin (shortstop/manager), Ed Delahanty (left fielder), Rick Ferrell (catcher), Goose Goslin (left fielder), Clark Griffith (pitcher/manager/owner), Vernon "Lefty" Gomez (pitcher), Bucky Harris (second baseman/manager), Whitey Herzog (outfielder), Walter Johnson (pitcher/manager), Harmon Killebrew (first baseman), Heinie Manush (left fielder), Jim O'Rourke (left fielder), Sam Rice (right fielder), Al Simmons (left fielder), George Sisler (first baseman), Tris Speaker (center fielder), Ted Williams (manager), and Early Wynn (pitcher)

Homestead Grays: James "Cool Papa" Bell (center fielder), Ray Brown (pitcher), Leon Day (pitcher), Martín Dihigo (second baseman), Bill Foster (pitcher), Josh Gibson (catcher), Judy Johnson (third baseman), Buck Leonard (first baseman), Biz Mackey (catcher), Cumberland Posey (outfielder/manager/owner), and Ernest "Jud" Wilson (third baseman)

Hall of Fame Weekend 2016 will take place July 22–25 with the induction ceremony on Sunday, July 24, just a mile south of the Hall of Fame on the grounds of the picturesque Clark Sports Center. There, the Hall's newest members become immortalized forever. This is the prime week for fans to attend, especially if your favorite player is being inducted. The week is filled with interactive events catered to fans, including "Legends of the Game Roundtable" (for museum members only) and the "Parade of Legends." The museum is open seven days a week but is closed on Thanksgiving, Christmas, and New Year's Day.

57 The Big Donkey

The signing of Adam Dunn prior to the 2009 season represented a much-needed boost at the plate. Acquiring one of the best power hitters in the game represented a form of legitimacy for a team that won just 59 games the year before. The Nationals' offense was putrid in 2008. They finished tied for 26th in batting average, 27th in hits, 28th in runs and home runs, and 29th in RBIs.

Dunn, 6'6" and 285 pounds, was the stereotypical boom or bust hitter. Whenever he stepped to the dish, fans braced for either a strikeout or one of his patented monstrous home runs. He made a name for himself with the Cincinnati Reds from 2001 to 2008. He hit 46 home runs in 2004 but also struck out 195 times in 568 at-bats. Then "the Big Donkey," as he was so eloquently nicknamed, went on to do something amazing. He went on to hit exactly 40 home runs a season for the next four years. He had also walked more than 100 times from 2004 to 2008. After blasting 270 home runs, 646 RBIs, and striking out 1,212 times in eight seasons in Cincinnati, Dunn was traded to the Arizona Diamondbacks in 2008, where he closed out the season, hitting eight home runs, 26 RBIs, and striking out 44 times in 44 games in the desert.

Dunn signed a two-year, $20 million deal with Washington before the 2009 season. The former University of Texas quarterback quickly became a fan favorite in D.C. and endeared himself to teammates with his likable personality. One embarrassing snafu Dunn may be remembered for came in 2009, when he and Ryan Zimmerman, the two most identifiable Nationals, took the field in a mid-April game donning jerseys with the word "Natinals" across the front. The next month a fan bought Dunn's jersey for $8,000 at the team's charity auction.

Dunn's home run numbers in D.C. dropped off slightly, but he was still the model of consistency. He led the team with 38 home runs in both of his two seasons with the team. He also knocked in 105 and 103 RBIs in 2009 and 2010, respectively. He struck out 177 times in 2009, his highest mark since leading the league in 2006, and set the Nationals' single-season record with 199 in 2010.

He was as advertised, finishing in the top five in strikeouts and in the top 10 in home runs in both seasons he was in D.C. When the time came for a new deal, Washington didn't want to pony up to keep the first baseman/outfielder. Dunn ended up signing a four-year, $56 million deal with the Chicago White Sox, struggling mightily in 2011, setting career lows in batting average (.159), home runs (11), and RBIs (42). He won the American League Comeback Player of the Year Award the next season with an All-Star campaign highlighted by his 41 home runs. In true Adam Dunn fashion, he batted just .204 and struck out a career-high 222 times that season. The Nats received Chicago's 2011 first-round pick as compensation for losing Dunn. Washington selected Kentucky pitcher Alex Meyer with that pick (23rd overall). The next year they traded Meyer to the Minnesota Twins for center fielder Denard Span.

Dunn retired after spending the 2014 season with the Oakland Athletics, finishing third all time on Major League Baseball's strikeout list behind Reggie Jackson and Jim Thome. With 462 career home runs, Dunn is tied with Jose Canseco for 35th on the all-time list. His 2,001 career games are 14th all time among players who have never appeared in a playoff game.

The former Longhorn made his big screen debut when he played a bartender in Texas graduate Matthew McConaughey's 2013 Oscar-winning movie, *Dallas Buyers Club*.

58 The Origins of the Senators Name

In 1859 the same year a group of government clerks founded a baseball team known as the "Potomacs," a collection of government employees created the National Base Ball Club of Washington, D.C., commonly referred to as the "Nationals." Those Nationals became the Senators from 1891 to 1899 when former pitcher Arthur Pue Gorman went on to become a U.S. senator and the leader of the Senate Democrats.

The Senators were bought out by the National League, and there was no professional baseball in D.C. in 1900. The first stable professional baseball franchise in the city formed when the American League debuted in 1901. The team was named the Nationals to prevent fans from mixing up that club with the previous Senators squad. We all see how well that worked out.

Following a miserable 1904 season that saw the club finish 38–113 (.252), team owners offered fans a chance to replace the Senators name. After reviewing thousands of submissions, "Nationals" was chosen. That didn't matter. Fans and media referred to the team as the Senators, Nationals, and Nats interchangeably for decades.

That was until the team hired Charlie Brotman in 1956. He was brought on to be the team's announcer at Griffith Stadium. He was also tasked as the editor and publisher of the team's media guide, yearbook, and programs for the 1957 season. To that, he replied: "Terrific. Now I have a question: who are we?"

Team owner Calvin Griffith, nephew and adopted son of Clark Griffith, told Brotman: "Just work it out." Brotman worked with graphic artist Zang Auerbach, brother of Boston Celtics coaching legend Red Auerbach. They struggled to come up with any kind of design for a team called the Nationals. "Nothing," Auerbach said. "It just lays there." But Senators? Now that really popped.

Ultimately, the caricature that ended up on the cover of the yearbook and press guide was a man in a Colonial frock and hat winding up to throw a pitch with one leg planted, one leg held high, and his right hand inside his left-handed glove. Above his head on the yearbook was "Washington" in blue and "Senators" in red. Griffith signed off on the idea, and thus, a new (old) identity was born. "It sounds so outrageous that someone could come up with the name for a major league team that way," Brotman told *The Washington Post* in 2012.

When the Expos' move was made official in late 2004, many locals clamored for the Senators name to return. Major League Baseball commissioner Bud Selig was in favor of the moniker, but D.C. Mayor Anthony Williams pined for the Grays as a tribute to the Negro League club that dominated Griffith Stadium for a decade. Eventually, the Nationals became the happy medium.

59 Great Trades

After moving to Washington from Montreal in 2004 with an average roster, then-general manager Jim Bowden had only so many bargaining chips to work with when it came to making deals. The farm system was a mess, and the few veterans that the team could attract through free agency were either past their prime or not good enough to make other major league rosters. Losing accompanied an undesirable roster, but with losing came better draft placement and a chance to replenish their depleted minor league system.

But when current Nationals general manager Mike Rizzo eventually took over the team, he was then able to watch the talent grow and transform one of the top minor league systems into trade bait. He also made a habit of trading with Oakland Athletics GM Billy Beane. The two clubs have made nine deals from December 2010 through the end of the 2015 season, including five swaps in the 2013 calendar year.

Here are some of the most memorable deals the Nats have made through the end of the 2015 season.

1. Pitcher Tyler Clippard from the New York Yankees for pitcher Jonathan Albaladejo
December 4, 2007
This one was a pure steal for the Curly W's and may go down as the best trade in the team's first decade of existence. In exchange for a pitcher who would only throw in 49 games for New York from 2008 to 2010, the Nats received a two-time All-Star who would play seven seasons in Washington and develop from a starter into the best set-up man in baseball.

Going into the 2015 season, Clippard's tenure in D.C. (2008–2014) was tied for the second longest behind Ryan Zimmerman, who has played at least one game every year since the 2005 inaugural season. Clippard pitched at least 70 games a season in his last five years with the club before being traded to the Athletics in January 2015.

2. Shortstop Trea Turner and pitcher Joe Ross in three-team trade

December 19. 2014

In this three-team deal, the Nats netted themselves a shortstop of the future in speedster Trea Turner—the 13th overall pick in the 2014 draft—and a reliable young pitcher in Joe Ross—the 25th overall pick in 2011—who revealed himself to be a steady mound presence composed beyond his years. All Washington gave up was reserve outfielder Steven Souza Jr., the savior of Jordan Zimmermann's 2014 no-hitter, and minor league pitcher Travis Ott, a former 25th round pick.

In a weird quirk, Turner couldn't join the Nats until June 14, 2015, one year after signing his rookie deal with San Diego. The Padres received Jose Castillo, Gerardo Reyes, Ryan Hanigan, and Wil Myers from the Tampa Bay Rays. Along wuth Souza Jr. and Ott, the Rays received Jake Bauers, Rene Rivera, and Bruce Smith from the Padres. Ross debuted in June 2015 and was impressive enough to earn a spot in the rotation despite being on an innings limit. Turner made his debut in August 2015. It may be early to call this trade a win for the Nats, but it looks promising.

3. Left fielder Alfonso Soriano from the Texas Rangers for outfielders Brad Wilkerson and Terrmel Sledge and pitcher Armando Galarraga

December 8, 2005

The Nats needed some pop in their lineup, and that's exactly what they got with Soriano, who had 46 home runs, 41 doubles, and 41 stolen bases in 2006, his only season with the club. In Washington he became the only 40-40-40 player in baseball history and then signed a whopping eight-year, $136 million deal with the Chicago Cubs after the season.

Wilkerson spent his first four seasons in Montreal but became one of the faces of the Nats during his only season in D.C. He appeared in 148 games and hit .248 in 2005. Sledge was an Expos prospect who never developed in Washington. Galarraga may best be remembered for his 2010 near-perfect game that was taken away by a missed call from umpire Jim Joyce at first base with one out to go.

4. Pitcher Doug Fister from the Detroit Tigers for infielder Steve Lombardozzi and pitchers Ian Krol and Robbie Ray
December 2, 2013

The Tigers originally wanted to swap Fister and reliever Phil Coke for Lombardozzi and pitching prospects Krol, Ray, and Taylor Jordan. Rizzo did not want Coke, nor did he want to rid himself of both Ray and Jordan, so both teams compromised on the three-for-one deal. Nats ownership killed the deal, not wanting to part with Ray. Incensed, Rizzo threatened to quit, forcing ownership to eventually relent, allowing the deal to be made.

The Nats easily won the deal. Lombardozzi was traded less than four months later to the Baltimore Orioles. Krol had a 4.96 ERA in 45 games for Detroit in 2014. His ERA ballooned in 2015, and he was traded to the Atlanta Braves in November of 2015. Ray was traded to the Arizona Diamondbacks a year later after pitching nine games for Detroit in 2014, going 1–4 with an 8.16 ERA.

Fister was dominant in his first year with the Nats. He went 16–6 with a 2.41 ERA on the way to the Nats' 2014 National League East Championship. He struggled with injuries and control in 2015 and was moved to the bullpen in early August.

5. Center fielder Denard Span from the Minnesota Twins for pitcher Alex Meyer

November 29, 2012

The Nats needed a true center fielder and they found one by giving up Meyer, the 23rd overall pick in the 2011 draft and their top pitching prospect. Span made an immediate impact in Washington, leading baseball with a 29-game hitting streak and 11 triples in 2013. He also provided athleticism and range at center field to complement corner outfielders Bryce Harper and Jayson Werth. He led the NL with 184 hits in 2014, but injuries derailed his 2015 season, forcing the 31-year-old to play a career-low 61 games.

Meyer spent the 2014 season in Triple A Rochester and was moved to the bullpen in 2015. He struggled mightily in his first two MLB games in June 2015, tossing two and two-thirds innings and allowing five earned runs for a paltry 16.88 ERA.

6. Pitchers Gio Gonzalez and Robert Gilliam from the Oakland Athletics for pitchers A.J. Cole, Tommy Milone, Brad Peacock, and catcher Derek Norris

December 23, 2011

The Nats were looking to complement Jordan Zimmermann and Stephen Strasburg and fortified their starting pitching rotation by acquiring Gonzalez, who won 21 games in his first season in D.C. and earned his second straight All-Star honor. Gonzalez hasn't matched his 2012 consistency, but when he's on his game, he can be compared to the best pitchers in the sport.

The Oakland Athletics sent Cole back to Washington 13 months later, moved Peacock to the Houston Astros less than a month later, traded Milone to the Minnesota Twins in July 2014, and shipped Norris to the San Diego Padres in December 2014.

Other notable deals:
Catcher Wilson Ramos and minor league pitcher Joe Testa from the Minnesota Twins for closer Matt Capps
July 29, 2010

Outfielder Jose Guillen from the Los Angeles Angels of Anaheim for infielder Maicer Izturis and outfielder/first baseman Juan Rivera
November 19, 2004

Closer Jonathan Papelbon and cash from the Philadelphia Phillies for minor league pitcher Nick Pivetta
July 28, 2015

Outfielder/first baseman Michael Morse from the Seattle Mariners for outfielder Ryan Langerhans
June 28, 2009

Pitchers Tanner Roark and Ryan Tatusko from the Texas Rangers for shortstop/second baseman Cristian Guzman
July 30, 2010

60 The Amputee Pitcher

Bert Shepard wasn't your ordinary southpaw pitcher. His right leg had been amputated.

A minor leaguer in the Chicago White Sox system in 1940 and St. Louis Cardinals system in 1941, he was drafted into the Army in 1942 for World War II after the bombing of Pearl Harbor. He later signed up for the Army Air Forces.

On May 21, 1944, Shepard was bombarding a truck convoy about 70 miles northwest of Berlin on his 34th mission in a P-38 Lightning fighter plane with the 55th Fighter Group. He planned to return to pitch for his air base team that afternoon. Chatter over the radio caught Shepard's attention. There was warning of enemy antiaircraft fire as he was flying low over a cluster of trees. He then took a hit to his right ankle that he described as sledgehammer-like. Another bullet struck his chin, and then he lost consciousness. His plane crashed at a speed estimated at 380 mph.

A German military doctor, later identified as Austrian Ladislaus Loidl, pulled Shepard from the wreckage, even saving him from pitchfork-wielding farmers by holding them back at gunpoint. Shepard woke up as a prisoner of war in a German hospital with his right leg amputated below the knee. A Canadian detainee crafted an artificial leg made from scrap metal.

He didn't return to the United States until February 1945 on a prisoner exchange swap. He was fitted for a prosthetic at Walter Reed Army Medical Center in Bethesda, Maryland. There, he met Undersecretary of War Robert Patterson, who asked him what he wanted to do in life. Shepard said he wanted to play baseball again. "This is the thing I dreamed about in that prison camp for months—the day I could get back on a diamond," Shepard said in an interview with *The Washington Post*.

Patterson called Washington Senators owner Clark Griffith and asked if he would give Shepard a tryout during spring training at the University of Maryland, College Park. Wartime travel restrictions forced the team to stay local rather than prepare for the season down south.

Griffith obliged out of sympathy, signing Shepard as a coach under manager Ossie Bluege and then placed him on the team's active player roster after Shepard performed well in an exhibition game against the Brooklyn Dodgers.

On August 4 against the Boston Red Sox at Griffith Stadium, Shepard got his chance.

Trailing 14–2 after three and two-thirds innings, Shepard became Washington's third pitcher of the game, replacing Joe Cleary, who replaced Sandy Ulrich during George Metkovich's first

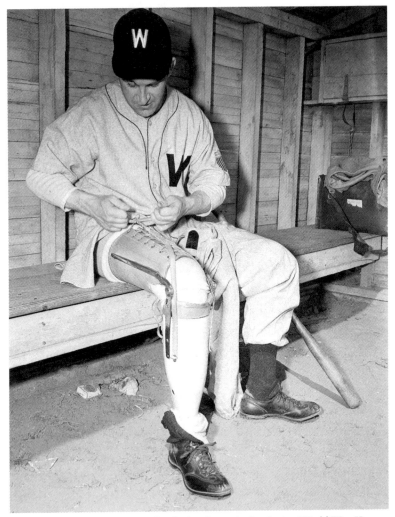

Nationals pitcher Bert Shepard, who lost his right leg during World War II, attaches his artificial limb on March 30, 1945.

at-bat of the inning. Shepard made his major league debut with the bases loaded, facing Metkovich for his second at-bat of the inning. He struck him out to end the inning.

He faced four batters in the fifth inning, allowing base runners because of an error from the first baseman and by hitting a batter. A double play ensued and was followed by a fly out. Shepard allowed his only run of the game in the sixth inning on a single by Tim McBride that brought home Eddie Lake from second base. Lake was walked by Shepard two batters earlier.

Shepard forced two fly outs and a ground-out in both the seventh and eighth innings, only surrendering a hit in the latter inning. He closed out the top of the ninth inning with a ground-out, a single, and a ground ball double play.

Washington lost 15–4, but Shepard's line was impressive. He allowed just three hits, one run, one walk, and struck out two in five and one-third innings for a 1.69 ERA. It was the only major league game Shepard ever played.

61 The Combustible Jose Guillen

The Nationals arrived in D.C. bereft of offense. General Manager Jim Bowden was a risk taker, so when the chance to acquire heavy hitting, though hotheaded, Jose Guillen arose, he took it. Guillen had a falling out with the Anaheim Angels in 2004. With eight games left in the season and in the middle of a pennant race, Angels manager Mike Scioscia and Angels general manager Bill Stoneman suspended Guillen because the fiery batter raised his hands up in disgust and tossed his helmet in the manager's direction after being pulled for a pinch runner. "I'm telling you," Bowden, who attended that game, said in *National Pastime*, "it wasn't that bad."

Guillen's services were no longer needed in Anaheim, so on November 19, 2004, Bowden swung a deal to send shortstop Maicer Izturis and right fielder Juan Rivera 3,000 miles west for the eight-year veteran outfielder. Before his feud with Scioscia, Guillen had put up his first 100-RBI-season and batted .294 with 27 home runs in his only season with the Angels. His acquisition brought a needed kick to the lineup and helped establish a team identity. In February 2005, at the team's uniform unveiling, Guillen delivered a great quip to indicate that he would try to toe the company line in his new environment. "I just have to be a political man," he said. "I'm in the right town to start learning that."

Guillen made an immediate impact at the plate, collecting eight hits in his first six games as a National. In mid-June of that season, Guillen made his first trip back to Anaheim on the heels of a memorable 10-game winning streak. He knew from his time there that pitcher Brendan Donnelly used pine tar to alter the direction of his pitches. He fed that information to Nats manager Frank Robinson, and it came in handy during the second game of the series.

With the Angels up 3–1 in the seventh inning, Donnelly approached the mound in relief of starter Ervin Santana. Robinson alerted the home-plate umpire to check Donnelly's glove. The umpires inspected the glove and ejected the reliever, setting off a firestorm. Scioscia threatened Robinson that he'd have every Nats pitcher inspected for pine tar, a gesture Robinson didn't appreciate. The two skippers argued virtually face to face, and Guillen erupted as his feelings toward Scioscia boiled back to the surface. The veteran slugger had to be restrained by teammates. Guillen went on to hit the game-tying home run on the way to a 6–3 victory.

After the game Guillen and Robinson said they knew Donnelly had pine tar on his glove after watching film, which was a lie.

Guillen was asked if he feared retaliation from his former club. "I've never been afraid of anyone," he said. "I will never be afraid of anyone. I hope that happens. I swear to God, I hope that happens."

The next night, Guillen was asked about Scioscia. He couldn't restrain himself anymore. He didn't take kindly to how Robinson was treated. "That's the stuff that pissed me off," Guillen said. "All I know is, Mike should show more respect...[He] talks about respect, leadership. I don't think he showed anything right there at all. That's it. Simple...I don't got truly no respect for [Scioscia] anymore because I'm still hurt from what happened last year. I don't want to make all these comments, but Mike Scioscia, to me is like a piece of garbage. I don't really care. I don't care if I get in trouble. He can go to hell. We've got to move on. I don't got no respect for him...I want to beat this team so bad. I can never get over about what happened last year. It's something I'm never going to forget. Any time I play that team, Mike Scioscia's managing, it's always going to be personal to me."

He finished his first season in D.C., batting .283 with 24 home runs and 76 RBIs. He was hit by a pitch 19 times in 2005, which tied for the National League lead. This came one season after being hit 15 times, third most in the American League. On April 6, 2006, during the Nats' third game of the season, Guillen was hit by a pitch delivered by New York Mets starter Pedro Martinez in the fifth inning. It was the second time Martinez hit Guillen that night, and the latter had enough. He pointed his bat at Martinez and charged the mound halfway until he was held back by Mets catcher Paul Lo Duca and the home-plate umpire. It was the third time in two nights Guillen was hit by a pitch. Cooler heads eventually prevailed.

Guillen played his final game in a Nationals uniform against the Florida Marlins on July 18, 2006, when he left the game with right elbow soreness. He underwent season-ending Tommy John surgery a week later and missed the rest of the season. He was a free agent after the season and wasn't retained by Washington. His 217-game Nationals career ended with 33 home runs, 116 RBIs, and a .263 average.

He returned to form the next season, playing in 153 games for the Seattle Mariners and batting .290 with 23 home runs and 99 RBIs. After the 2007 season, he was suspended by Major League Baseball for the first 15 days of the 2008 season for violating the league's drug policy.

He played the next two and a half seasons with the Kansas City Royals until he was traded to the San Francisco Giants in August 2010. Guillen was left off San Francisco's playoff roster due to a federal investigation into shipments of human growth hormone (HGH) addressed to his home. The Giants went on to win the World Series.

62 D.C. Baseball Stadium History

Baseball in Washington, D.C., predates Abraham Lincoln's tenure as president. In the 1860s groups of government clerks formed a team called the "Potomacs," and other government workers formed "The National Base Ball Club of Washington, D.C.," or "Nationals" for short.

The squads played their games on the White Lot, a field that sits in front of the White House that is now known as the Ellipse, where recreational softball games still take place. The Olympic Grounds—located at 16th Street NW, 17th Street NW, and S Street NW—played host to the Washington Olympics in 1871 and 1872, the Washington Blue Legs in 1873, and the 1875 Washington Nationals.

Athletic Park played host to the 1884 Washington Nationals, also known as the Statesmen, in their only season as a member of the Athletic Association in the National League of Professional Base Ball Clubs. Athletic Park was located at S Street NW, T Street NW, and 9th Street NW. The Capitol Grounds, also known as Union Association Park, was home to the Washington Nationals of the Union Association in 1884 and was located on C Street NE, Delaware Avenue NE, B Street (now Constitution Avenue) NE, and First Street NE. The location is now home to the Russell Senate Office Building. From 1886 to 1889, the Senators/Statesman of the National League played their games at Swampoodle Grounds or Capital Grounds II. The venue had a capacity of 6,000. The Nats finished last in three of those four seasons. Union Station and the National Postal Museum now stand in this location.

Boundary Field, which also went by National Park or Beyer's Seventh Street Park, was home of the future Griffith Stadium. It hosted the Senators of the American Association in 1891 and the Senators/Nationals of the National League from 1892 to 1899.

The American League's Washington Senators played at American League Park (aka National League Park II), located at Florida Avenue NE and Trinidad Avenue NE, from 1901 to 1903. In 1904 the Senators moved to the Boundary Field location, naming their wooden stadium American League Park II (aka National League Park III). It stood until it burned down (thanks to a plumber's torch in 1911) while the team was in spring training. After it was rebuilt, it was called National Park until it was renamed Griffith Stadium in the early 1920s to honor the team's owner, Clark Griffith. The stadium was home to three World Series (1924, 1925, and 1933).

Griffith Stadium had massive field dimensions and a large green wall in right field, serving as almost a mirror image of Boston's Fenway Park. In 1945 Washington's only home run at Griffith Stadium was of the inside-the-park variety by first baseman

Joe Kuhel. The stadium's center-field wall was notorious for its sharp, right-angle jut around houses and a large tree belonging to owners who were unwilling to sell their land to the team. The Negro Leagues' Homestead Grays played there from 1940 to 1950 and routinely drew large crowds.

After the 1960 season, the Senators moved to Minnesota to become the Twins. In their place were the lowly 1961 expansion Senators. The new Senators closed out Griffith Stadium in depressing fashion, taking on the old Senators (Minnesota) on September 21, 1961. The Senators lost to the Twins 6–3, dropping to 56–96 on the year in front of a measly 1,498 fans. "A stadium was laid to rest yesterday," declared Shirley Povich, *The Washington Post*'s legendary sportswriter. "Not many showed up for the services, and the deceased was not much of a draw."

Griffith Stadium was demolished in 1965 to make way for Howard University Hospital, which pays homage to the memorable facility with a home plate and batter's box in a hallway near a bank of elevators and a sign commemorating the stadium's history.

In 1962 the expansion Senators moved to D.C. Stadium, which was renamed RFK Stadium in 1969. The team stayed there until playing their final game on September 30, 1971, before becoming the Texas Rangers. Appropriately enough, the game ended in a riot—thanks to heartbroken and frustrated Senators fans storming the field to collect their own piece of history.

It would be 34 years before another D.C. baseball team stepped foot in RFK.

63 Why Getting Swept by the Padres Was a Good Thing

Other than Ryan Zimmerman's electric walk-off on the Opening Night unveiling of Nationals Park, there wasn't much to get excited about when it came to the 2008 Washington Nationals. A roster filled with names like Austin Kearns, Felipe Lopez, Lastings Milledge, Cristian Guzman, Ronnie Belliard, Elijah Dukes, Willy Mo Pena, Tim Redding, Odalis Perez, and Jason Bergmann didn't exactly scream "contender."

The team was a mess. Heading into the final month of the season, the Nats were a woeful 52–85—the worst record in baseball. However, there was competition for the basement. The Seattle Mariners were in a tailspin. They fired general manager Bill Bavasi and manager John McLaren, replacing the latter with bench coach Jim Riggleman on an interim basis less than a week after Washington had swept them in Seattle.

It also didn't take long for the Mariners to realize their swap of Adam Jones, George Sherrill, Chris Tillman, Tony Butler, and Kam Mickolio to the Baltimore Orioles for pitcher Erik Bedard prior to the season had become a bust. Bedard experienced multiple stints on the disabled list, and Jones developed into a superstar in Charm City. At 53–83 the M's weren't far behind the Nats heading into September. Washington's strongest competition for worst record in the National League at that time was the San Diego Padres, who also sported a 53–83 record when August was over.

The prize at the end of the misery maze was San Diego State fireballer Stephen Strasburg, who dominated the competition in his sophomore season with an 8–3 record, 1.57 ERA, 133 strikeouts, and 16 walks. As a junior in 2009, he upped the ante with a 13–1 record, 1.32 ERA, 195 strikeouts, and 19 walks, cementing his spot as the consensus No. 1 overall pick in the 2009 Major League Baseball Draft.

As the 2008 season came to a close, the question became who would win the Strasburg sweepstakes. Playing out the string, Washington, Seattle, and San Diego had long been out of the playoff race, but with enough losses, they'd have themselves a future ace to build their franchise around.

Nats Top Draft Picks

Since being placed annually in the depths of Major League Baseball's farm system rankings during their first several seasons, the Washington Nationals have vastly improved their minor league health through strong scouting.

Here is who the franchise selected first in each of its drafts:

2005: first round—fourth overall—Ryan Zimmerman—Third baseman—Virginia

2006: first round—15th overall—Chris Marrero—Outfielder— Monsignor Edward Pace (Florida) High School

2007: first round—sixth overall—Ross Detwiler—Pitcher— Missouri State

2008: first round—eighth overall—Aaron Crow—Pitcher— Missouri

2009: first round—first overall—Stephen Strasburg—Pitcher— San Diego State

2010: first round—first overall—Bryce Harper—Outfielder— College of Southern Nevada

2011: first round—sixth overall—Anthony Rendon—Shortstop— Rice

2012: first round—16th overall—Lucas Giolito—Pitcher— Harvard-Westlake (California) High School

2013: second round—68th overall—Jake Johansen—Pitcher— Dallas Baptist

2014: first round—18th overall—Erick Fedde—Pitcher—UNLV

2015: first round—58th overall—Andrew Stevenson— Outfielder—LSU

With less than two weeks left in the season, the Nationals (58–95) took on the Padres (58–95) in a three-game series with the Mariners looming at 57–95 with an eight-game losing streak. The Nationals weren't trying to lose, but Washington dropped the first

The futility of the 2008 Nationals worked out in the long run, as it allowed Washington to finish with a bad enough record to select Stephen Strasburg No. 1 overall in the draft the following season.

game of the series 11–6 in 14 innings, the second game 6–1, and the final game of the series 6–2.

Seattle went on to lose four more games to extend their losing streak to 12 but finished on a hot streak, winning four of their last six, including a three-game sweep of the Oakland Athletics to close the season. San Diego's sweep swung the balance of power in the ace race, costing the city the chance to see their favorite son play professional baseball in their backyard.

The Padres went 5–4 down the stretch while the Nats finished the year with one win in their final 10 games, etching their place as the worst team in baseball but the biggest winners in the draft, securing the top overall pick and a pitching phenom.

The Nationals, of course, took Strasburg, the hottest prospect in the sport, first overall. With the second pick, the Mariners selected center fielder Dustin Ackley. The Padres took center fielder Donavan Tate third overall.

Baseball is a funny game. The sport has thousands of moving parts in the major and minor league levels with players and coaches continuously getting recycled. Riggleman joined the Nationals as bench coach in 2009 and replaced manager Manny Acta when he was ousted at midseason. Riggleman brought McLaren in as his bench coach after the 2009 season. When Riggleman resigned in 2011, McLaren took over as interim manager.

Riggleman experienced the ups and downs of the race to draft Strasburg, the Strasmas of his rookie year, and the start of his 2011 shutdown season. Had it not been for Seattle's sweep of Oakland and San Diego's sweep of the Nationals, none of that would have happened.

The Six Aces

The 2014 pitching staff of Stephen Strasburg, Jordan Zimmermann, Gio Gonzalez, Doug Fister, and Tanner Roark worked wonders, combining for a Major League Baseball-best 2.94 ERA. Three of the five starters had an ERA under three. Adding two-time All-Star and reigning two-time American League wins leader Max Scherzer to the rotation in 2015 seemingly gave the Nats an embarrassment of riches. "To be able to have a guy like Scherzer come in," Bryce Harper said in spring training just weeks after the arrival of Washington's newest ace, "I just started laughing. I was like, 'Where's my ring?' You know what I mean? It's stupid. It's absolutely stupid how good our staff is."

The new-look staff drew comparisons to the 2011 Philadelphia Phillies rotation that boasted Roy Halladay, Cliff Lee, Cole Hamels, Roy Oswalt, and Vance Worley and the Atlanta Braves staff featuring Hall of Famers Greg Maddux, John Smoltz, and Tom Glavine in the mid-to-late 1990s. Welcoming Scherzer aboard meant moving Tanner Roark to the bullpen for long relief situations and spot starts after going 15–10 with a 2.85 ERA in a 2014 season that showed flashes of future promise. One wildcard that no one saw coming was the unpredictable emergence of 22-year-old Joe Ross, whom Washington acquired from the San Diego Padres in December 2014 and went 5–5 with a 3.64 ERA in 16 games in 2015.

Here's how the six aces fared during the 2015 season:

Max Scherzer

Scherzer's season was quite outstanding. He became just the sixth player in history to throw two no-hitters in one season, threw a Nats-record 276 strikeouts, pitched 11 games with at least 10 strikeouts, and won National League Pitcher of the Month in May and June. However, in the heat of a pennant race with the New York Mets, Scherzer faltered when he was needed the most. In seven starts from August 4 to September 7, he went 0–3, allowed 11 home runs, posted an ERA of 6.08, and allowed batters to hit .305 off of him. He had surrendered seven home runs in his first 15 games and then gave up 20 in his final 18. As a whole, though, Scherzer was amazing. His season featured a career-best 2.79 ERA, a league-high 33 games started, four complete games, and three shutouts.

Jordan Zimmermann

Mr. Consistency lived up to his name but not his usual numbers. After consecutive All-Star nods that included winning a league-high 19 games in 2013 with a 3.25 ERA and posting a 14–5 record, 2.66 ERA, and career-high 6.28 strikeout-to-walk ratio in 2014, Zimmermann's numbers appeared more human-like in 2015. He allowed at least six hits in 24 games, the most of his career, and went 13–10 with a 3.66 ERA as he approached free agency. He didn't pitch a shutout for the first time since 2012 and also allowed a career high in runs (89) and home runs (24). Zimmermann struck out 164 batters, the second most of his career, and also started a career-high 33 games, tying Scherzer for the NL lead.

Stephen Strasburg

Strasburg landed on the disabled list twice in 2015, battling through a left trapezius strain in the neck and a left oblique strain. Injuries forced him to play in only 23 games, his fewest in a season since pitching in five games at the end of the 2011 season. When he was healthy, he was as dominant as ever. He compiled an 11–7 record, 3.46 ERA, and a 5.96 strikeout-to-walk ratio. Strasburg faced 523 batters and allowed 14 home runs, 26 walks, and 56 runs, the lowest totals in his four full seasons in the majors. He appeared to get stronger and more confident as the season went on. He went 2–5 in April and May, 2–0 in June, and finished the season 6–2 in August through October. He threw five games with 10 or more strikeouts, and those contests all came in August and September. He tossed a one-hitter with 14 strikeouts in Philadelphia on September 15.

Gio Gonzalez

The lovable lefty again struggled with consistency and command, continuing his reputation of unpredictability night in and night out. Gonzalez ended the season with an 11–8 record for the second time in three years and a career-high 181 hits allowed. His 3.79 ERA was his highest since his second season in the big leagues when he posted a 5.75 ERA in 2009. On a positive note, July was the only month that Gonzalez didn't have a scoreless outing of six innings or more.

Doug Fister

Like Zimmermann, Fister was entering the final year of his Nationals contract. Like Zimmermann, he also saw his value drop when his season didn't go as planned. After leading the Nats with a 2.41 ERA in 2014, Fister saw it skyrocket to 4.19 in 2015, the highest in his seven-year career. He was placed on the disabled list in May with a flexor tendon strain in his right elbow and missed a month. He pitched twice in June, allowing five runs in one start and tossing a seven-inning shutout the next, but struggled mightily, giving up 21 runs in his next six starts. The Nationals had gone 5–11 in games started by Fister. Ross' 2.80 ERA in his first seven starts coupled with Strasburg's return from his second disabled list stint equated to Fister's move to the bullpen in early August, an unfathomable concept when the season started. Fister wasn't happy about the transition but handled the move like a pro. He pitched 10 games of relief, striking out 15 and allowing 16 hits, eight runs, and six walks in 17 innings. He earned his first career save on September 14.

Tanner Roark

Roark was a magician on the mound in 2014, striking out 138 batters and walking 39 in 31 starts. Scherzer's addition meant a move to the bullpen for Roark. Fister's injury meant five starts in which Roark went 3–0 from May to June. He started the second game of a doubleheader in late June against Philadelphia and started six games at the end of the season when Ross was moved to the bullpen due to his innings limit. Roark appeared in 40 games and went 4–4 in 12 starts. He notched his first career save and ended the year with a 4–7 record and 4.38 ERA.

65 Visit RFK Stadium

Robert F. Kennedy Memorial Stadium has been rapidly aging since its 1961 opening. Despite the tens of millions of dollars spent in renovations since baseball returned in 2005, paint still peels, concrete still chips off, and pipes still leak. However, its decrepit nature is part of why local sports fans love it so much.

The formerly named D.C. Stadium was the first of the cookie-cutter, multi-purpose stadiums built in the 1960s. The blueprint was a circular concrete slab with more than 50,000 seats inside that could host both football and baseball games. Gone are Philadelphia's Veterans Stadium, Cincinnati's Riverfront Stadium, Pittsburgh's Three Rivers Stadium, and St. Louis' old Busch Stadium. Yet, RFK still stands as the final remnant of that era.

The stadium hosted more than 1,000 combined games between MLB's Senators and Nationals, NFL's Redskins, MLS' D.C. United, USFL's Federals (football), and NASL's Diplomats (soccer). It was home to the 1962 and 1969 Major League Baseball All-Star Games and the 1972, 1983, 1984, 1987, and 1991 NFC Championship Games.

RFK is known for epic concerts, too. On July 4, 2015, the Foo Fighters performed there with frontman Dave Grohl riffing his guitar on a throne while nursing a broken leg. Other top musical acts to play at RFK include Elton John, the Rolling Stones, Stevie Wonder, U2, the Eagles, and the Grateful Dead. It also used to host the famous HFStival, a rock festival played every May in front of tens of thousands of high school and college-aged music fans.

In their 20-year existence, D.C. United has called RFK home since the MLS' inception in 1996 and has won four MLS Cups (1996, 1997, 1999, and 2004). The team will move into a new, soccer-only stadium at Buzzard Point just a handful of blocks down the Anacostia River from Nationals Park. The smaller venue is expected to open for the 2018 Major League Soccer season, so take advantage of D.C. United's final two years at the only home stadium the team has ever known.

When you head to RFK for a DCU match, make sure you tailgate with their top fan clubs—La Barra Brava, Screaming Eagles, and District Ultras—and make the walk through the tunnel that takes fans under Independence Avenue straight to the stadium. Once you get to your seat, take a look around the stadium and absorb the memories and the history that has taken place at that building.

Think back to the night baseball returned to D.C. on April 14, 2005, a 5–3 win against the Arizona Diamondbacks that made the stadium rock. George W. Bush tossed out the first pitch, Vinny Castilla went 3-for-3 with four RBIs and a home run, and Livan

Hernandez went into the ninth inning with a one-hitter until allowing a three-run home run.

Reminisce about the 5–3 win against the Philadelphia Phillies on September 23, 2007—their send-off to the 46-year-old park. "Without RFK, who knows where we would be? We might still be in Montreal," Nationals closer Chad Cordero said after the game. "We could be somewhere else. This place has treated us well. We have some great memories here. The whole '05 season was awesome."

The dugouts where the Senators, Nationals, and their opponents peered out onto the field on a nightly basis still remain. When you look up at the faded burgundy and gold upper deck seats on the east side of the stadium, you'll see three white seats. Much like the stadium itself, those seats are fragments of an older time. Section 535, Row 5, Seat 17; Section 538, Row 4, Seat 19; and Section 542, Row 3, Seat 3 are marked to indicate where several of the monstrous home runs of Washington Senators legend Frank Howard landed over the course of his seven-year tenure in Washington. Nationals players, as well as their opponents, were stunned when they were informed what those white seats meant. They couldn't believe anyone could actually hit a baseball that distance.

A Fan's Quest to Torment a Former Senators Owner

Have you ever disliked the owner of your favorite team so much that you vowed to make his life a living hell? (Don't get any ideas, Redskins fans.) Well, that's exactly what legendary Washington Senators fan Bill Holdforth did after Bob Short moved the Senators to Texas to become the Rangers.

Working as an usher at RFK Stadium, "Baseball Bill" took exception to the reality that he was going to lose his baseball team. In 1971, his third season on the job, he and a pal spotted a Bob Short dummy hanging in effigy from a noose in right field and decided to wear it through the stadium aisles. He was fired the next day.

He attended the final Senators game but chose to watch the ruckus of the fans rushing the field from the stands. When the 1972 Rangers schedule came out, he marked on his calendar when they would make their first appearance just up the road at Baltimore. It was in May.

Holdforth and his brother decided to make their own dummy this time around. They stuffed it with old articles from *The Sporting News* and put a shirt and tie on it. Holdforth and some buddies bought tickets in Short's section by the Rangers dugout and headed to Memorial Stadium.

Once there, Holdforth made an agreement with an usher at the stadium that he knew from his time with the Orioles, for whom he ushered when the Senators were on the road. Baseball Bill, holding the dummy, and a friend, holding a "Short Stinks" sign, made their way to the infamous owner for a couple minutes, lifting the items over his head with a great deal of pleasure, a small measure of revenge for taking their club away. A photographer for *The Washington Post* captured the moment, and the shot was featured in the next day's paper. "What's the matter, Bobby Baby? Is something bothering you?" Holdforth recalled asking Short. "Why don't you go fuck yourself?" the Rangers owner replied, spurring laughter from Holdforth.

After the taunting, a beer was poured on Short. Many believed Holdforth was the person responsible for it, but he was in the bathroom when it happened. It turns out a female culprit was being escorted out of the stadium. "I wouldn't waste a beer like that," Holdforth said.

Holdforth and company returned the next night, brought a Senators batting helmet, sat five rows behind Short, and screamed "Bobby Baby…we're back!" Holdforth brought the helmet to Short and said: "Here, you might need this for protection."

During the game Holdforth noticed Short's assistant, Joe Burke. "We saw big Joe Burke bringing hot dogs down to Short," Holdforth said. "So we yelled, 'Hey Joe, they finally found something for you to do.' Later, we told Short, 'We need a couple beers. Will you send Joe after 'em?' Even Short laughed at that." After the game Holdforth told Short he hoped they didn't spoil the game for him. "That's all right, you paid to get in," Short said.

"We figured you'd say that," Holdforth said in one final dig.

In 1978 Holdforth and Short's paths crossed again in an even more unconventional manner. The former Senators owner was actually running for U.S. Senate from his home state of Minnesota as a Democrat. Holdforth was having none of it. Holdforth and his friends formed "Baseball Bill's Committee to Keep Bob Short Out of D.C." and raised more than $3,000 in a beer bash fundraiser at his apartment. The money was used to fund a half-page ad in the Sunday *Minneapolis Star* before the Democratic primary. The ad warned the people of Minnesota: "Don't Be 'SHORT' Changed" with a paragraph explaining how Short stole the trust of Senators fans. That was followed by a list of comments from the former owner along with actions contradicting those statements.

Short won the primary, but Republican candidate Dave Durenberger caught wind of Holdforth's campaign and asked for permission to make copies of the ad to hand out at Minnesota Vikings football games. Holdforth, of course, had no problem with it. He just wanted to see Short lose. And lose he did. Durenberger defeated Short and credited Baseball Bill's efforts for his victory. "It was an easy way of saying folks in Washington don't want Bob Short any more than the people of Minnesota want him," Durenberger said.

67 The Kidnapped Catcher

For years Nationals catcher Wilson Ramos has crouched behind home plate and mastered the art of framing every throw delivered by his pitchers. On any given toss, he was prepared to master a lack of control.

But on the night of Wednesday, November 9, 2011, he faced the ultimate feeling of helplessness when he was abducted at gunpoint by three armed men in front of his family's home in Valencia, Venezuela. The act was quick and happened just seconds after his mother had walked inside her house.

Back home to play for the Aragua Tigers of the Venezuelan Winter League, Ramos was targeted by a Colombian informant who lived near his family. That informant, who was linked to paramilitary and kidnapping groups, was the mastermind behind the operation and had plotted out Ramos' movements and routine. He became the first known Major League Baseball player to be kidnapped.

Abductions for ransom in Venezuela are a frequent occurrence with hundreds happening every year. They're used to target high-profile or well-off residents in order to get something in return.

About 40 Nationals fans gathered for a candlelight vigil outside of Nationals Park's center-field gate on Friday, November 11, just before word of his rescue got out. Curly W supporters held signs, shared memories of Wilson, and offered words of encouragement amidst a hopeful and positive atmosphere. The team provided coffee and hot cocoa to the well-wishers.

Ramos was held captive for 51 hours until a gun battle between his captors and Venezuelan commandoes put an end to the terror. The rescue operation, which was authorized by Venezuelan president Hugo Chavez, took 12 hours, required 30 people, and occurred on foot after rescuers were dropped off by helicopter. Over the course of the two-day search, around 200 police and National Guard troops had become involved.

Ramos was found unharmed in a cabin in a remote mountainous area about 40 miles northwest of his family's home in the town of Montalban. Eight people were arrested for involvement in his kidnapping. Ramos said the captors laughed and joked about his ordeal and were going to work together to get a lot of money for him. However, no known ransom was requested nor paid. After the rescue Chavez invited Ramos for a friendly game of baseball and joked "get your glove ready because not even Wilson can catch the curveball that I throw."

Ramos returned to Nationals spring training in Vierra, Florida, in February 2012 with a new outlook. "I feel like I'm living again," Ramos said. "I've got a new life."

That new life included a renewed sense of humor. Baseball, a sport known to house some of the best jokesters around, gave Ramos a place to release some of the tension developed during his personal nightmare. As pitchers and catchers reported to spring training, Ramos bumped into pitching coach Steve McCatty. "So, how was your winter?" McCatty asked. "Anything goin' on?" Infielder Andres Blanco couldn't contain his laughter when he heard McCatty. Ramos was momentarily shocked but quickly got the joke, laughed and replied, "I see, I see."

The young catcher, who was acquired from the Minnesota Twins in 2010 along with minor league pitcher Joe Testa in exchange for All-Star closer Matt Capps, was so appreciative of his second chance, he memorialized the traumatic moment on his left arm in the form of a tattoo the week before reporting to spring training. The tattoo contains the Spanish translation of the Bible verse Philippians 4:13, which reads: "I put everything in Jesus because he has my back." Below the verse is the date "11-11-11," the day in which Ramos was rescued.

Ramos eventually replaced future Hall of Famer Ivan "Pudge" Rodriquez and has become a consistent and reliable force behind the plate for the Nats. He caught all three Nationals no-hitters in 2014 and 2015. That's just one behind the MLB record shared by Carlos Ruiz and Jason Varitek. In January of 2015, Ramos won the 25th Tony Conigliaro Award, which honors the player who most exemplifies spirit, determination, and courage. Ramos has overcome a torn ACL in his right knee, repeated hamstring strains, a broken hamate bone in his left hand, and, of course, one terrifying ordeal.

68 The Bryce Harper Timeline

Bryce Harper is only 23 years old, but in four seasons, he's already accomplished what some veterans do in their whole career.

June 7, 2010: Harper is selected by the Nationals with the first overall pick in the 2010 Major League Baseball Draft out of the College of Southern Nevada.

June 6, 2011: Playing with the Class A Hagerstown Suns, Harper blows a kiss, apparently in retaliation for pitcher Zachary Neal glaring into the Suns dugout after throwing strikeouts, toward the Greensboro Grasshoppers hurler after homering off him.

July 10, 2011: Harper plays in MLB Futures Game and goes 0-for-4.

December 25, 2011: Harper gets a chocolate lab puppy for Christmas and names him "Swag."

April 28, 2012: At 19 Harper makes his MLB debut in Los Angeles as the youngest player since 2005, going 1-for-3 with a seventh-inning double against the Dodgers.

May 6, 2012: Philadelphia Phillies pitcher Cole Hamels intentionally hits Harper on his first pitch to the rookie. Harper steals home two batters later.

May 11, 2012: Harper swings a bat at a wall in a dugout tunnel in frustration after one of his three strikeouts in Cincinnati. The bat breaks, ricochets off the wall, and opens a gash next to his left eye, requiring 10 stitches. He goes 0-for-5 on the night.

May 14, 2012: He hits his first career home run against the San Diego Padres at Nationals Park.

June 3, 2012: He is voted National League Rookie of the Month for May after hitting .271 with four home runs, 10 RBIs, four triples, and scoring 21 runs that month.

After Philadelphia Phillies pitcher Cole Hamels intentionally plunked him on May 6, 2012, Bryce Harper gets his revenge by stealing home.

June 12, 2012: A Canadian reporter asks Harper if he'll celebrate his monster home run against the Toronto Blue Jays with a beer. Harper replies: "That's a clown question, bro."

July 10, 2012: Harper makes his first MLB All-Star Game appearance as the youngest position player and the third-youngest of all time. He strikes out once and walks once.

July 15, 2012: After Miami Marlins manager Ozzie Guillen complained that the pine tar on Harper's bat was too high in the first inning, Harper brings out a new bat and holds it out toward the Marlins dugout in his next at-bat in the fourth inning, incensing Guillen, who yells from the dugout, causing the umpire to get involved. Harper goes 0-for-4.

October 2, 2012: Harper is voted NL Rookie of the Month for September after scoring 26 runs, totaling 69 bases with a .651 slugging percentage that month.

October 7, 2012: In St. Louis, Harper goes 0-for-5 in his postseason debut against the Cardinals.

November 12, 2012: Harper is named 2012 NL Rookie of the Year.

April 1, 2013: Harper hits two home runs on Opening Day against the Miami Marlins, becoming the youngest player ever to hit multiple homers in his team's season opener.

May 13, 2013: With a 6–0 lead in the fifth inning, Harper slams into the right-field wall at Dodger Stadium, jamming his left shoulder and cutting his chin, requiring 11 stitches.

July 15, 2013: Harper finishes second in the Home Run Derby and becomes the youngest player to make it to the final round. His father, Ron, pitches to him and even accidentally hits him with a pitch.

July 16, 2013: In his second All-Star Game appearance, Harper fails to get on base in two plate appearances.

March 31, 2014: *ESPN The Magazine*'s baseball preview issue has a poll of 143 players, asking them to name the most overrated player in the sport. Harper receives 24 percent of the vote.

April 19, 2014: Harper is benched by manager Matt Williams for failing to run out a comebacker that led off the sixth inning against the St. Louis Cardinals. The free program handed out at the Nationals Park gates features Harper on the cover with the phrase: "Nothing but hustle."

April 25, 2014: Harper tears the ulnar collateral ligament in his left thumb while sliding into third base against the San Diego Padres, causing him to miss games until June 30.

August 9, 2014: Harper drags his cleat across the Atlanta Braves "A" in the dirt behind home plate in his first three trips to the plate.

October 6, 2014: Harper walks and hits a ninth-inning home run to help lead Washington to its only win against the San Francisco Giants in the National League Division Series.

February 25, 2015: Before the team's first full-squad practice of spring training, Harper is asked about the acquisition of ace Max Scherzer. "I was like, 'Where's my ring?'" Harper said. "You know what I mean? It's stupid. It's absolutely stupid how good our staff is."

March 30, 2015: Harper is again named the most overrated player in baseball in *ESPN The Magazine*'s baseball preview issue, receiving 41 percent of the vote in a poll of 117 players.

April 6, 2015: In the fourth inning against the New York Mets on Opening Day, Harper walks up to the plate to Frank Sinatra's "The Best is Yet to Come." On the second pitch, he hits a home run, which represents his third career Opening Day home run.

May 6, 2015: Harper victimizes Marlins pitcher Tom Koehler by hitting three home runs in a game for the first time in his career.

May 30, 2015: Cincinnati Reds reliever Tony Cingrani hits Harper in the back with the first pitch of the seventh inning. Harper stared at Cingrani while taking his time going to first base. Reds first baseman Joey Votto takes exception. Both players exchange words, and an umpire steps in between them. "He should've jogged," Cingrani said. "Be a baseball player. Sorry I hit you. Run."

June 3, 2015: Harper is named NL Player of the Month for May after batting .360 with 13 home runs and 28 RBIs.

June 10, 2015: Harper faces a pitcher younger than him for the first time in his career when New York Yankees reliever Jacob Lindgren enters the game in the eighth inning. Harper flies out to left field on the second pitch. It marks Harper's 2,303rd plate appearance and 554th game in pro baseball.

July 4, 2015: Harper homers off of Giants ace Madison Bumgarner in the first inning with a patriotic bat featuring a paint scheme with the American flag and D.C. skyline.

July 14, 2015: Harper makes his third All-Star Game appearance in four years, grounding out in the first inning and striking out in the fourth and sixth innings.

September 3, 2015: Harper walks four times and scores four times without a recording a hit. He also records an RBI with a bases-loaded walk, becoming first player since the RBI became a recorded statistic in 1920 to walk four times, score four times, and record an RBI without getting a hit.

September 22, 2015: Harper walks three times against the Baltimore Orioles and breaks Adam Dunn's Nationals record of 116.

September 27, 2015: During a game against the Philadelphia Phillies, teammate Jonathan Papelbon yells at Harper after not running out a pop fly. Papelbon then chokes Harper in a dugout fight.

September 29, 2015: Harper sets a Nationals/Expos franchise record by recording his 124th walk of the season.

November 12, 2015: Bryce earns his first career Silver Slugger Award.

November 19, 2015: Harper wins National League MVP, becoming D.C.'s first baseball MVP since Roger Peckinpaugh in 1925.

69 The Only Player to Play in Both of the Senators' Last Games

Shortstop Ron Hansen may have only played 86 games as a member of the Washington Senators in 1968, but his short tenure remains one of the most interesting in D.C. baseball history. The first of the two-part feat occurred on October 2, 1960, when Hansen visited Griffith Stadium as a member of the Baltimore Orioles. That was the last game played by the original Washington Senators, who headed to Minnesota the next season to become the expansion Twins.

The 1960 AL Rookie of the Year went an undesirable 0-for-4 in a 2–1 Orioles victory. On September 30, 1971 at RFK Stadium, Hansen, playing third base for the New York Yankees, became the only player in Major League Baseball history to play in both of the final games in Senators history. (This second incarnation of the Senators had begun in 1961 before they moved to Texas a decade later.)

Just as he had in the original Senators finale, Hansen went 0-for-4. This one was a 9–0 Yankees victory despite the 7–5 Senators lead with two outs in the top of the ninth. With one out to go, frustrated Senators fans stormed the RFK field, causing both teams to head toward the dugout. That meant the Senators had to forfeit the game, and the score officially stood at 9–0 (the standard score of a forfeited game, according to the rules). It was perhaps a fitting end of the expansion Senators, who had experienced just one winning record in their 11-year run in D.C.

At 6'3", Hansen revolutionized the ideal frame for athletic short-stops. He proved his size wouldn't hinder his range or his ability to field the ball cleanly and consistently, paving the way for bigger shortstops like Cal Ripken Jr., Derek Jeter, and Alex Rodriguez.

The Senators acquired Hansen on February 13, 1968, from the Chicago White Sox along with Dennis Higgins and Steve Jones in exchange for Tim Cullen, Buster Narum, and Bob Priddy. On July 30, the new member of the Senators became just the eighth player in MLB history to pull off an unassisted triple play and the first in 41 years. In the first inning, facing the Cleveland Indians at Municipal Stadium, Hansen caught a line drive from Cleveland's Joe Azcue, stepped on second as the momentum of the play carried him to force out Dave Nelson, and ran toward first to tag out Russ Snyder. "The whole thing is instincts," Hansen told *The Washington Post* in 2007. "It wasn't something I thought about. It just all happened at once. I don't remember how far I had to go to tag the runner from first. And I've never seen a replay. I don't even think a tape of the game exists."

Only seven players had done it before him. Only seven have done it since.

Two days later, Hansen led the charge in a 9–3 romp against the Tigers in Detroit to start off the month of August. In the fourth inning, he blasted a grand slam off of pitcher Pat Dobson that scored Ken McMullen, Paul Casanova, and Bernie Allen. Hansen finished the game 1-for-2 with two walks and two runs.

As fate would have it, Hansen was traded back to the White Sox the very next day in exchange for Cullen, the same infielder the Senators originally sent to acquire Hansen. That move marked the first time the same two players were traded for each other twice in the same season.

Hansen's 86 games in Washington ended with a .185 batting average with just eight home runs, 28 RBIs, 51 hits, 35 walks, and 12 doubles. He finished his 15-year career with a .234 average, 1,007 hits, 106 home runs, and 501 RBIs in 1,384 games with the Senators, Orioles, White Sox, Yankees, and Kansas City Royals.

70 Watch the Nats' Minor League Teams

"You're going to the minors" is a phrase no baseball player dreaming of competing on a Major League Baseball diamond ever wants to hear. For fans, however, that's a different story.

Attending minor league games gives baseball fans a glimpse at future MLB stars at a very affordable rate in an intimate, family-friendly setting. If the children get bored, take them to the merry-go-round or have them test out their fastball at the kids section of the stadium. Mascots make their way around the ballpark and give kids a great photo op (if they're not terrified of the creatures). Minor league teams also do a good job of offering on-field contests for children. If they're into the sport, they can have their own personal Q&A with their favorite players while getting an autograph. Typical venues are so intimate that you can hear conversations between pitchers in the bullpen.

Here is the breakdown of the Nationals' minor league affiliates. Be sure to plan your road trips accordingly.

Syracuse Chiefs
AAA—International League
Stadium: NBT Bank Stadium—Syracuse, New York
Capacity: 11,071
Miles from Nationals Park: 376 miles (about five hours, 45 minutes)
Tickets: $4–$12 (free general admission seats for military)
Parking: $5
Triple A baseball gives fans a close-up look at prospects just one step away from the major league call-up. The players who make up Triple A rosters are typically the best of the best that the major

league team has in their farm system. Top Nats prospects who played in Syracuse in 2015 include pitchers Joe Ross, A.J. Cole, Taylor Hill, and Taylor Jordan; shortstop Emmanuel Burriss; and center fielder Tony Gwynn Jr.

Harrisburg Senators
AA—Eastern League
Stadium: Metro Bank Park—Harrisburg, Pennsylvania.
Capacity: 6,187
Miles from Nationals Park: 119 miles (about two hours)
Tickets: $9–$34
Parking: $3

Metro Bank Park is unique in many ways. For one, it's built on an island in the middle of the Susquehanna River and has survived several floods. Secondly, it hosts arguably the most popular of the Nats' minor league affiliates. The Nats frequently send their regular starters down to Harrisburg for rehab assignments. Stephen Strasburg, Anthony Rendon, Denard Span, and Doug Fister all worked their way through injuries while donning the Senators uniform in 2015.

For those of you who want to see the Senators but don't want to drive two hours, check them out when they take on the Bowie Baysox, the Baltimore Orioles' Double A affiliate, at Prince George's Stadium in Bowie, Maryland, just 20 miles from Nationals Park. Last summer, fans got to catch both Anthony Rendon and Orioles catcher Matt Wieters make rehab stints in Bowie in the same series. If you live in Virginia and want to catch the Senators, they head to Richmond to play the Flying Squirrels every year at The Diamond.

Potomac Nationals
A—Carolina League
Stadium: Pfitzner Stadium—Woodbridge, Virginia
Capacity: 6,000
Miles from Nationals Park: 29.6 miles (about 40 minutes)

Tickets: $8–$16

Parking: $5 per car, $7 per bus

Known locally as the "P-Nats," the Potomac Nationals are the closest minor league affiliate to D.C. and annually play host to the pro Nats on rehab assignments. Jayson Werth and Casey Janssen played at "The Pfitz" in 2015. Top prospects who played for Potomac include pitchers Lucas Giolito, Jake Johansen, and Reynaldo Lopez. Potomac has won the Carolina League three times since 2008. Seeing them on the road is easy as well. They take on the Frederick Keys, the Baltimore Orioles' Carolina League affiliate, every year.

Hagerstown Suns

A—South Atlantic League

Stadium: Municipal Stadium—Hagerstown, Maryland

Capacity: 5,000

Miles from Nationals Park: 72.1 miles (about one hour, 20 minutes)

Tickets: $9–$12

Parking: Free

The Suns truly play in a real throwback environment. Municipal Stadium, which hosted its first game in 1930, is one of the oldest in baseball. It has a manually operated scoreboard and even has a Hagerstown Suns Hall of Fame located under the first-base stands. Legendary outfielder Willie Mays played his first minor league game there in 1950. Bryce Harper's infamous blown kiss took place at Municipal Stadium in 2011. From 1993 to 1994, Redskins general manager Scot McCloughan hit .289 with three home runs and 37 RBIs in 69 games as a member of the Suns when they were a Toronto Blue Jays affiliate. Fans on Maryland's Eastern Shore can also see them play in Salisbury to face the Delmarva Shorebirds, the South Atlantic League affiliate of the Baltimore Orioles.

Auburn Doubledays

A—Short-Season New York-Penn League
Stadium: Falcon Park—Auburn, New York
Capacity: 2,800
Miles from Nationals Park: 380 miles (about six hours)
Tickets: $5–$9
Parking: Free

The team is named after Abner Doubleday, an Auburn native, who is rumored to have invented the game of baseball as a cadet in the United States Military Academy in 1839. What's not in dispute is that the squad, which plays from June to early September, has been affiliated with the Nats since 2011. Prospects such as Nationals 2014 first-round pick Erick Fedde, 2015 second-round pick Andrew Stevenson, and 2015 fourth-round pick Mariano Rivera Jr. laced it up for the Doubledays. The short-season squad also faces the Aberdeen IronBirds, who play in Ripken Park, located 80 miles northeast of Nationals Park.

The rookie-level **Gulf Coast League Nationals** play from June through August at the Washington Nationals Training Complex in Viera, Florida. While that may not fit into a road trip per se, it's a nice excuse to head out to a ballgame while on summer vacation.

71 The Deaf Center Fielder

Ever wonder how the use of hand signals in baseball developed? Why the umpire makes the quick whip and pointing motion to emphasize a strike? Why third-base coaches are willing to look silly by touching their ears, nose, shoulders, eyes, or elbow when looking at the batter?

Legend has it that those can be traced back to William "Dummy" Hoy, who played with the short-lived Washington Nationals in 1888 and 1889 and another failed D.C. baseball franchise, the Washington Senators, in 1892 and 1893. The former only existed from 1886–1889 while the latter operated from 1891–1899.

The 5'4" speedster made an impact in his debut major league season in 1888, stealing a National League-high 82 bases in 136 games. He led the team in hits with 138 and in batting, averaging .274 with the two closest teammates hitting .225. Not bad for a rookie. Not bad for a 26-year-old who lost all hearing at the age of three after battling meningitis. And not bad for the first deaf player in Major League Baseball history.

Hoy was given the horribly politically incorrect nickname "Dummy," a spin on the term "dumb," which was commonly used during those times to refer to a person who couldn't hear.

Prior to his 14-year major league career, Hoy graduated from the Ohio State School for the Deaf as class valedictorian. After graduation he opted to play semi-pro baseball while maintaining a job as a shoemaker. When Hoy joined the Nats for spring training in 1888, he posted a message of on-field guidelines on the clubhouse wall: "Being totally deaf as you know and some of my teammates being unacquainted with my play, I think it is timely to bring about an understanding between myself, the left fielder, the shortstop, and the second baseman and the right fielder.

"The main point is to avoid possible collisions with any of these four who surround me when in the field going for a fly ball. Whenever I take a fly ball, I always yell 'I'll take it!'—the same as I have been doing for many seasons, and, of course, the other fielders will let me take it. Whenever you don't hear me yell, it is understood I am not after the ball, and they govern themselves accordingly and take it. If a player hears the patter of my feet, pay no attention as I am only backing up. I watch both the player and the ball, and never have I had a collision."

Hoy is widely credited with the development of hand signals in the sport. Umpires began to use them to delineate balls and strikes rather than simply yelling out "Ball!" or "Strike!"

Not being able to trust the pitcher when he was at bat, he'd turn to his third-base coach, who'd use one finger for a strike and two for a ball. Umpires would also raise their right arm for a strike and left arm for a ball. Hoy allegedly also concocted the safe and out signals, though the National Baseball Hall of Fame plaque of umpire Bill Klem credits him as the creator of hand signals.

On June 19, 1889 against the Indianapolis Hoosiers in his second season with the Nats, Hoy threw out three runners at home, a remarkable feat. Hoy finished his first two seasons in D.C. with 277 hits, 117 stolen bases, 14 triples, and 144 walks in 263 games. His second stint in Washington, this time with the Senators of the National League, consisted of 282 games, 305 hits, 31 doubles, 14 triples, 120 RBIs, 152 walks, and 108 stolen bases. After the 1893 season, he was traded by the Washington Senators to the Cincinnati Reds for Mike Sullivan. In his career, Hoy spent time with the Nationals (two years), Buffalo Bisons (one year), St. Louis Browns (one year), Senators (two years), Reds (five years), Louisville Colonels (two years), and Chicago White Sox (one year).

On October 7, 1961, Hoy tossed the first pitch of Game 3 of the World Series between the New York Yankees and Cincinnati Reds in front of a crowd of 32,589 at Crosley Field. On December 15, he died of a stroke, just less than seven months shy of his 100th birthday. In 1986 Hoy's life was turned into a two-act comedic play titled *The Signal Season of Dummy Hoy* written by Allen Meyer and Michael Nowak. Hoy was inducted into the Reds Hall of Fame in 2003.

72 Nats Superfans

There are some fans whom you probably spot right away at Nationals Park or from your living room. When I would see the two guys sitting in the front row behind home plate every single game, my first thought always was, *Man, they're lucky.* My second thought was, *How do they make it to every game?*

The man who sits in the aisle seat with the black hat with the white bill and bald eagle design on it happens to be Henry Itkin, a retired Navy vet who moved to Las Vegas in the early 1990s to run an insurance company. The man who's almost always accompanying him is his 56-year-old brother Murray, who lives in McLean, Virginia. Henry sports a white No. 3 jersey (it's his favorite number) with Henry on the nameplate. Murray dons No. 88 with Itkin across the back. The brothers spend around $50,000 for those seats, including Henry's airfare. "Well, if you have one passion in life, you may as well spend a lot of money on it," Henry told *The Washington Post* in 2015. "I'm 72. I don't know how many more passions I'm going to have or how many more excitements I'm going to have. This is it."

The brothers are on TV so much that strangers recognize them around the country (and even in vacation spots like Fiji). Murray moved to Florida during high school and came back to the area to attend the University of Maryland. He filled the void of not having pro baseball in D.C. by investing in Bowie Baysox season tickets. When it was announced that the Montreal Expos would move to D.C., Henry called his younger sibling and said: "Get us season tickets right away!" The brothers didn't see each other much before the Nats arrived, but their time behind the plate has helped strengthen their bond.

Another easily recognizable fan with a Natitude problem spends his time along the first-base line in shiny fashion—literally and figuratively. That fellow with the white glove on his right hand with wacky suits, glasses, and hats dancing to every song at every

Famous Nats Fans

Any trip to a baseball game could bring the unbridled excitement of a chance encounter with a celebrity or public figure. Hey, they're sports fans, too.

The Nats, despite a short existence, have several celebrity fans of note. NBA superstar Kevin Durant (stomach) and Washington Redskins wide receiver DeSean Jackson (arm) have Curly W logos tattooed on them. Durant was born in Washington, D.C., and raised in Prince George's County, Maryland, so that easily explains his fandom. Jackson, who isn't necessarily a fan of the team, was born and raised in California and got the tattoo years before he joined the Redskins. Why he got the logo inked on his body is pretty inscrutable.

Former WWE superstar and actor Dave Bautista grew up on K Street SE near the Washington Navy Yard—just a hop, skip, and a jump from Nationals Park. He has been known to attend games.

Maury Povich, son of Shirley Povich, a legendary sportswriter for *The Washington Post* who covered most of baseball's D.C. tenure in the 20th century, is a noted Nats fan and was a Washington Senators batboy in the 1940s.

The political city regularly hosts pundits at Nats games. Political comedian Lewis Black, a Silver Spring, Maryland, native, is a Nationals fan. After the Texas Rangers lost the 2011 World Series to the St. Louis Cardinals, Black tweeted "Congrats to Ms. Madigan and her Cards. Sorry Texas fans. I am from the DC area. They should still be the Washington Senators. The pricks."

Pulitzer Prize-winning writer and noted baseball aficionado George Will is often seen at Nats Park when summer rolls around. Democratic strategist James Carville has season tickets. CNN reporter Wolf Blitzer attends games and even discussed "Natitude" on the airwaves the night the Nats clinched a playoff berth in 2012. Former host of NBC's *Meet the Press* David Gregory also supports the home team at Nationals Park.

game is Tripp Whitbeck, a 35-year-old Virginia sales consultant by day—and sequined superfan by night. Whitbeck earned the nickname of "the Mayor of Nats Town" from a vendor in his section (135) when the rows behind him were noticeably empty and he appeared to be the only one there.

The Mayor was born and raised in New York City and grew up as a die-hard Mets fan. He moved to Arlington, Virginia, in 2008 and bought a Nationals season ticket plan that August. In 2009 he made the decision to root for the Nats or Mets based on whoever "needed it more." Once he was embraced by the fans in his section—as well as ushers, vendors, and security at Nationals Park—he decided to go all in as a Nats fan.

The man who owns three sequin suits thrives on the attention his personality provides him. If he seems to have a flair for the dramatic, that's not by accident. He performed musical theatre for years and was the mascot at Amherst College. "I've always been a vigorous sports fan," he said. "I just love supporting my team, and if I can be colorful doing so, why not do it?"

Whitbeck recalled a moment from a few seasons ago when outfielder Jayson Werth whistled at him and told him to sit down when he was dancing. If you go to a game, chances are you'll see him there. He says he averages about 75 home games a season.

73 Meet the Lerners

It's not every day that dreams come true, but for Theodore "Ted" Lerner and his son Mark, that day came to fruition on July 24, 2006, when they finalized their $450 million purchase of the Washington Nationals. Ted had long loved the Senators, paying

25 cents to sit in the Griffith Stadium bleachers—including at the 1937 All-Star Game—and later working there as an usher selling programs. He was a high school classmate of Bowie Kuhn, a Hall of Fame executive who worked the Griffith Stadium scoreboard for $1 a game as a kid and went on to became Major League Baseball's fifth commissioner from 1969 to 1984.

Mark, the man pitcher Gio Gonzalez called "the pimp with the limp" after the team clinched the 2012 National League East title a few months removed from the owner's foot surgery, has been known to put on a Nats uniform and shag fly balls with players before games. He is also the family representative with Monumental Sports & Entertainment, the company that owns the Washington Capitals, Washington Wizards, Washington Mystics, and the Verizon Center. Fans can often see Mark sitting in his front row seat to the right of home plate wearing his red Nationals cap. A die-hard sports fan, he thrives on being close to the action.

At 26 the elder Lerner made a life-changing decision. He asked his wife if he could borrow $250. He used that money to found Lerner Enterprises in 1952 and then took the local real estate industry by storm. Since then he has built up quite the nest egg. He is the 86th richest person in the world, ninth richest American sports owner, and the richest person in the state of Maryland with a net worth of $5.4 billion, according to *Forbes'* 2015 calculations. The Nationals were valued at $1.28 billion, nearly triple the Lerners' purchase price nine years earlier and almost double its 2014 value of $700 million.

Lerner's interest in baseball never waned during his real estate success. He tried to buy the expansion Senators before Bob Short purchased the club in 1968 and moved them to Texas in 1971. For decades Ted worked to bring baseball back to D.C., when he saw the opportunity.

In 1975 Ted and his brother, Lawrence, wanted to buy the Baltimore Orioles when they found out they were for sale. So Ted called Orioles owner Jerold Hoffberger and asked his selling price to which the owner replied "$12.5 million." Lerner offered to pay it, but Hoffberger eventually sold the team to Edward Bennett Williams. Ted had considered splitting the team's time between Baltimore and D.C.

The next year he offered to buy the San Francisco Giants from Horace Stoneham for $10 million in an effort to move the fledgling franchise to Washington. Stoneham, the man who moved the Giants from New York, had a stadium contract in place and couldn't move the team again. He had to settle for an $8 million sale to local buyers. The Lerners even put in a bid to buy the Washington Redskins in 1998 before Daniel Snyder was named owner in 1999. Oh, what could have been. Sorry, Redskins fans.

Buying the Nationals was the culmination of a decades-long pursuit for Ted, who lives anonymously despite his business success. Rather than bask in the limelight, he lets Mark run the day-to-day operations and speak on behalf of ownership when the press needs a quote or two. The family model of ownership, which includes sons-in-laws Edward Cohen and Robert Tanenbaum, was a primary reason then-commissioner Bud Selig selected the Lerners over seven other bidders back in 2006.

The passion of the 90-year-old Lerner showed with the seven-year, $210 million contract he approved for pitcher Max Scherzer in January 2015. Ted wants to win a World Series sooner rather than later. "Mr. Lerner is a stud," Nationals general manager Mike Rizzo said after Scherzer's introductory press conference.

The Future

The Nationals' minor league system is a far cry from the barren wasteland that arrived in Washington in late 2004 when the 29 other major league teams owned the big club. Thorough scouting and an improved player development staff, the Nationals have become one of the most respected teams in baseball when it comes to talent evaluation. In recent years Washington has been able to furnish top picks into productive homegrown talent as well as valuable trade bait. The team has been able to use that talent to acquire needed pieces to their roster. Steve Lombardozzi, Ian Krol, and Robbie Ray were used to acquire Doug Fister; Alex Meyer, the 23rd overall pick in 2011, was used to bring in Denard Span; and A.J. Cole, Tommy Milone, Brad Peacock, and Derek Norris helped reel in Gio Gonzalez. Below are some of the top prospects expected to make an impact with the Nationals—some sooner rather than later.

Pitcher—Lucas Giolito

Selected 16th overall in the 2012 draft at age 17, Giolito possesses the size (6'6", 255 pounds), accuracy, and power of a workhorse ace. A sprained ulnar collateral ligament (UCL) that forced him to miss his senior season of high school ruined his chance of going first overall, which was a real possibility. He underwent Tommy John surgery less than three months after his selection and weeks after appearing in one game with the Gulf Coast League Nationals. Considered the top prospect in baseball by the end of the 2015 season, Giolito has worked himself through the minor league ranks, progressing to Double A Harrisburg in 2015. In 53 minor league appearances with five teams from 2012 to 2015, Giolito has accumulated a 19–10 record with a 2.63 ERA and 1.15 WHIP. He impressed in the 2015

All-Star Futures Game, pitching two scoreless innings on just 20 pitches. Giolito was reportedly considered by Nationals brass one of the "untouchable" prospects at the 2015 trade deadline.

Shortstop—Trea Turner

Another "untouchable" was Turner, whom the Nats officially acquired in June 2015 to complete a December 2014 trade. The heir apparent to fan favorite Ian Desmond, Turner has blazing speed and a knack for getting on base. Desmond labeled Turner "a fast little whippersnapper." Like Giolito, Turner put on a show at the Futures Game, collecting a two-run double and a triple in two at-bats. In 10 games with Harrisburg in 2015, Turner hit .359 and stole four bases. He batted .322 in 48 games with Triple A Syracuse, stealing 14 bases and hitting seven doubles and three triples. The Nationals called up Turner in late August 2015. He appeared in 27 games and logged one home run, one RBI, two stolen bases, nine hits, and a .225 batting average.

Pitcher—Joe Ross

Joe Ross was an added piece to the Turner trade and immediately made an impact while Stephen Strasburg was dealing with a neck injury in early June. Called up from Harrisburg, Ross impressed in his MLB debut, showing composure beyond his years. He retired the first nine Chicago Cubs batters but allowed three runs in the fourth and fifth innings in a 4–2 loss. His next two outings were even better, allowing just three runs total and pitching into the eighth inning in both of them. His third start consisted of 11 strike-outs and just one walk in a 4–1 win against the Pittsburgh Pirates. In his first seven games, Ross boasted a 2.80 ERA, struck out 47 batters, and walked just four for a staggering 11.75 strikeout-to-walk ratio. It was the highest rate produced by a rookie with at least 45 innings since 1900. He wore down a bit and regressed toward the mean as the season went on but finished with a 5–5 record and

3.64 ERA in 16 games. Ross' mound presence and ability to shake off adversity will suit him well in the pros.

Pitcher—A.J. Cole

Cole, reacquired from the Athletics in January 2013, was ranked by *Baseball Prospectus* as the sport's No. 30 prospect before the 2015 season. The team's 2010 fourth-round pick worked his way up through the Nationals system all the way to Syracuse, where he has played since the 2014 season. His MLB debut against the Atlanta Braves on April 28, 2015, was one he'd like to forget. He was roughed up for nine runs and lasted just two innings. Fortunately for Cole, he didn't take the loss because the Nats staged the biggest comeback in team history, winning 13–12. He pitched in relief twice in May, tossing three shutout innings and earning a save to cap a 10–0 win against the San Diego Padres and went four and a third innings with seven strikeouts and allowed two runs in an 8–1 loss to the Philadelphia Phillies. Cole's 2015 season with Syracuse went a bit smoother. He went 5–6 in 21 games, striking out 76 batters and posting a 3.15 ERA.

Pitcher—Erick Fedde

Fedde likely would have been a top 10 pick had he not suffered a torn right UCL while at UNLV. Before the injury he posted a 1.76 ERA and an 8–2 record in 11 starts during his junior campaign. He underwent Tommy John surgery in May 2014, but the Nationals still chose him 18th overall the next month. Like Giolito, his potential was too enticing to pass up. He made his minor league debut in late June 2015 with Class A Auburn, striking out four, walking three, and allowing two hits and one run in three innings. He seemed to grasp the New York-Penn League, earning a 2.57 ERA in eight games with the Doubledays but had trouble adjusting to Class A Hagerstown, where he ended his season with a 4.34 ERA in six games with the Suns. With both teams he completed his first season with a 5–3 record, 3.38 ERA, 59 strikeouts, and 18 walks. Fedde is a prospect to keep an eye on as he climbs up the ranks in 2016.

Second baseman/shortstop—Wilmer Difo

The young Dominican prospect had played in just 14 games at the Double A level when he was called up for his first action in the majors in May 2015 and got a hit in his first at-bat. The utility infielder progressed very well in 2014 and 2015 after years of trying to find himself as a player. He stole 49 bases and hit .315 with 90 RBIs in 136 games with Hagerstown in 2014, earning South Atlantic League MVP. Splitting time between Harrisburg and Class A Potomac in 2015, Difo stole 30 bases and hit 28 doubles and six triples with a .286 average. Difo played in 11 games with the Nats in 2015.

Pitcher—Reynaldo Lopez

After missing most of 2013 with an arm injury, Lopez made a name for himself with an eye-opening 1.08 ERA and 0.82 WHIP in 16 games between Auburn and Hagerstown in 2014. He came back to Earth a bit in 2015, allowing 47 runs in 99 innings over 19 starts with Potomac. He allowed five home runs—almost twice as many as he had allowed in 23 games from 2012 to 2014. His 2015 season consisted of a 6–7 record, 4.09 ERA, and a career-high 93 strikeouts.

Outfielder—Victor Robles

At just 18 years of age, Robles has rapidly ascended the Nationals' minor league ranks to such an extent that the club considered him among the untouchable prospects during 2015–2016 offseason trade talks. Robles has hit .300 at every level and stole 46 bases in two seasons with the Dominican Summer League Nationals, Gulf Coast League Nationals, and Auburn Doubledays. In 108 minor league games, Robles compiled a .334 average and .924 OPS. MLB.com listed the speedy outfielder as Washington's seventh best prospect in 2015.

The Natinals

After starting 0–7, the 2009 Washington Nationals embarrassed themselves even more on their path to the worst season in franchise history (59–103), one more loss than the season before. On April 17 the most recognizable stars and top hitters for the 1–7 Nationals—third baseman Ryan Zimmerman and right fielder Adam Dunn—took the field at Nationals Park against the Florida Marlins wearing their standard home white uniforms. But instead of the standard red lettering saying "Nationals," the jersey scripts read "Natinals." Missing was the "O" directly in the middle of their uniform, causing a wardrobe malfunction heard 'round Major League Baseball and shining an even more unflattering spotlight on the team than their play on the field already had.

For three innings Zimmerman and Dunn sported the misspellings, much to the amusement of rival fans and Nats fans as well. They then changed into jerseys with the proper nickname emblazoned across the front. The Marlins went on to win the game 3–2 in 10 innings to improve to 9–1, their best start in franchise history. Zimmerman went 2-for-5, and Dunn went 0-for-3 with a walk.

Majestic, the official jersey manufacturer of MLB, issued an apology the next week. "All of us at Majestic Athletic want to apologize to both the Washington Nationals and Major League Baseball for accidentally omitting the 'o' in two Nationals jerseys," Majestic Athletic president Jim Pisani said in a statement. "We take 100 percent responsibility for this event and we regret any embarrassment for the Nationals organization, players, and fans."

The Baltimore Orioles' unofficial program *Outside Pitch* even took a playful jab at Washington's jersey foul and Majestic's apology in the "Fair or Foul?" section of their June/July issue.

Wearing the infamous misspelled jersey, Ryan Zimmerman runs to first base after hitting a single against the Florida Marlins on April 17, 2009.

"Recenly, we were responsible for a a typogrficle error on to jersies of the Nationals," the sidebar read. "We take 100 percent responsibly for this. We are proud of all the thins we get right, having never mispelded Mets and DC."

In early May, a fan bought Dunn's "Natinals" jersey for $8,000 at the team's fourth annual Dream Gala in an effort to help raise money for the Washington Nationals Dream Foundation. The jersey was the highest-priced item of the night.

76 Is Killebrew MLB's Logo?

Before Harmon "Killer" Killebrew went on to have a Hall of Fame career as a member of the Minnesota Twins, the Idaho native began his path as a pro baseball player in 1954 as a 17-year-old prodigy with the Washington Senators.

He played sparsely in his first five seasons in D.C., appearing in just 113 games with only 11 home runs and 30 RBIs. In 1959 he broke out with an All-Star performance, hitting an American League-leading 42 home runs with 105 RBIs, 132 hits, and 90 walks in 153 games.

That was the first of eight seasons in his 22-year career that he hit at least 40 home runs and the first of nine seasons with at least 100 RBIs. He followed that up with 31 home runs and 80 RBIs in 124 games during the original Senators' final season in Washington in 1960. Those numbers were pedestrian by his standards.

Killebrew, along with the Senators, moved to Minnesota to create the expansion franchise known as the Twins. This news was devastating to Senators fans, who, despite not seeing a winning season since 1952, saw gradual improvement in a squad led by young hitters like Killebrew and Bob Allison along with veterans Roy Sievers and Jim Lemon. During Killebrew's last four seasons in Washington, the Senators had experienced a win increase every year, going 55–99 (.357) in 1957, 61–93–2 (.396) in 1958, 63–91 (.409) in 1959, and 73–81 (.474) in 1960.

D.C. baseball fans, while grateful they had received an expansion franchise in 1961 to replace the departed Twins, certainly missed their rising star. Killebrew hit 46 home runs and 122 RBIs and walked 107 times in his first year in Minnesota. To add insult to injury, Killebrew helped lead the Twins to a 6–3 victory against the expansion Senators in the last game at Griffith Stadium on September 21, 1961. He went 2-for-5 with two RBIs and scored the final run in to the stadium's history on a double from Minnesota's Joe Altobelli off of Washington pitcher Marty Kutyna. Only 1,498 fans were in attendance to witness it.

Killebrew went on to become the Senators/Twins all-time franchise leader in games (2,329), total bases (4,026), home runs (559), RBIs (1,540), and walks (1,505). He's second in at-bats (7,835) and runs (1,258) and sixth in hits (2,024). Killebrew was inducted into the National Baseball Hall of Fame in 1984, choosing the Minnesota Twins as his primary team.

Although those facts can't be disputed, a common misconception is that Killebrew was the inspiration for the Major League Baseball logo—much like Jerry West was for the National Basketball Association logo. Even Killebrew himself mistakenly thought that the iconic MLB silhouette was based off of a 1967 photo of him taken by the Associated Press' Bob Wand. The black and white image showed Killebrew with an almost mirrored stance to that of the league logo. The hand placement, stance, hunch, the outline of the nose, the chin buried into the shoulder, overhang of the sleeve, and pointed batting helmet were all strikingly similar to that picture. The primary change was the angle of the bat.

"The Killer" stated in a 2008 interview with ESPN.com's Paul Lukas that he was in the MLB commissioner's office when he saw a man sitting on a table toward the back, working on a design with his picture in front of him. "He had a photograph of me in a hitting position and he had one of those grease pencils that you see at a newspaper and he was marking that thing up," Killebrew said. "I said, 'What are you doing with that?' and he said they were going to make a new Major League Baseball logo. I never thought any more about it. And then the logo came out, and it did look like me. The only change was the angle of the bat. They changed that to kind of make it fit more into the design."

However, in a 2009 interview with MLB.com, the league's logo creator, Jerry Dior, disputed that. "People have said my design was based on Harmon Killebrew, but it wasn't," Dior said. "Mine wasn't based on anyone—just a nondescript figure with a bat…It was intentionally ambiguous in every way, including righty vs. lefty. I was only told to create a nondescript figure, and that's what I did."

Following Killebrew's death in 2011, Dior said in an interview with the Associated Press that he eventually had a conversation with the 13-time All-Star and 1969 American League MVP and broke the news that the logo was not modeled after him. "I told him he wasn't the figure in the design. It was nondescript. He asked me if I was sure, and I said yes," Dior said. "It was a great phone call. It was really, really nice. He seemed like a nice person."

Dior admitted to using many pictures to create the logo but was never fully sure if a Killebrew image subconsciously inspired his design. "I had a bunch of photographs," Dior said. "I can't swear that it wasn't Harmon."

As it turns out, Killebrew was the source of the Major League Baseball Players Alumni Association's logo. Formed in 1982, the organization uses a three-person silhouette of a batter pre-swing, mid-swing, and connecting on a ball.

77 Tony Plush

In the middle of the 2009 season, the Nationals decided to acquire Nyjer Morgan from the Pittsburgh Pirates along with pitcher Sean Burnett in exchange for pitcher Joel Hanrahan and outfielder Lastings Milledge. That move brought speed on the base path and an infusion of energy and personality to a team destined for the worst record in franchise history. That personality included Morgan's alter ego, Tony Plush, who helped make him a fan favorite.

The scrawny hockey player turned center fielder was known in D.C. for his impact—both the good and the bad. As part of the good, he batted .351 and stole 24 bases in 49 games during his first season with the Nats. As part of the bad, he allowed an inside-the-park home run to Baltimore Orioles outfielder Adam Jones in May of 2010 after slamming his glove down in frustration, thinking the hit had gone over the wall. Morgan, though, batted .253, stole 34 bases, scored 60 runs, and hit 17 doubles and seven triples in 136 games. He also introduced the club to the famous silver Elvis wig for the player of the game to wear during postgame interviews.

Weeks after his arrival to D.C., Morgan described his need for an alter ego. "I'm an entertainer," Morgan said. "I've got to go out there and entertain every night, so I figure everybody needs a stage name…I'm not crazy, just out there having fun, just enjoying the game, just trying to make it exciting, trying to put a little different twist to it."

Inside Pitch, the program handed out at Nationals Park, delineated the difference between Morgan and Plush in a feature story during a homestand against the Florida Marlins and Arizona Diamondbacks in early August 2009. "The speed and stolen bases, that's Tony Plush," the story read. "Getting caught stealing, that's Nyjer Morgan. The diving catches and home run robbing grabs, that's Tony Plush. The mental mistakes, that's Nyjer Morgan."

Morgan's emotions were known to get the best of him. No time frame better depicts that than the whirlwind two-week span he experienced late in the 2010 season. On August 21 he had been heckled by fans in Philadelphia's Citizens Bank Park in what was described as friendly banter. After warming up between innings, he tossed a ball into the stands, striking an unsuspecting fan in the head. Four days later he was suspended seven games. A Phillies fan emailed *The Washington Post* to defend Morgan, saying he threw the ball "rainbow-style" to a young fan who called for the ball but that Morgan's aim was off and inadvertently hit another fan. Morgan appealed the suspension and won.

On August 28 he was dropped to eighth in the lineup and in the eighth inning of the Nationals' 14–5 win against the St. Louis Cardinals, he ran over catcher Bryan Anderson at the plate, then missed home plate, and was called out when teammate Ivan Rodriguez helped to push him back to touch home plate. Manager Jim Riggleman benched Morgan the next day, saying that he would be hit by Cardinals pitchers in retaliation for his "unprofessional" move.

On August 31 Morgan collided with Marlins catcher Brett Hayes at home plate in the 10th inning, separating Hayes' shoulder. Florida won 1–0 in the bottom of the 10th. The next night Morgan was hit by a pitch from Florida's Chris Volstad. Down 14–3 at the time, Morgan then stole two bases. Not feeling like Morgan got the message, Volstad threw behind Morgan in the sixth inning. The 5'10" Morgan charged the mound and hit the 6'8" Volstad with a left hook to the face, clearing both benches. Marlins first baseman Gaby Sanchez immediately clotheslined Morgan to the ground, and Morgan was suspended eight games. "I thought it was over after [the fourth inning], but once I saw the ball go right behind me, it's time to go," Morgan said. "Once is good enough, but twice, no, it's time to go."

In spring training of 2011, Morgan and newly signed Jayson Werth reportedly engaged in a verbal altercation after Werth called him out for not fully running out wind sprints in the outfield. "Man, you don't know me," Morgan reportedly told Werth. "You've been here two weeks." The two almost came to blows but were separated by teammates.

The Nats eventually grew tired of Morgan's antics and traded him a few weeks later to the Milwaukee Brewers for minor leaguer Cutter Dykstra. Morgan developed another cult following in Milwaukee, helping them to the 2011 National League Championship Series and playing 122 games in 2012. He spent 2013 with the Yokohama BayStars of Japan's Central League, hitting a career-high 11 home runs and 50 RBIs in 108 games. He appeared in 15 games with the Cleveland Indians in 2014 and then signed with the Hanwha Eagles of the Korea Baseball Organization in December 2014 but was kicked out of preseason camp in February 2015 and was released three months later.

78 Sit in the Lexus Presidents Seats

If you're a true baseball fan, you owe it to yourself to treat yourself to an ultimate fan experience and the best seat in the house at least once. For Nationals fans, that means sitting in the Lexus Presidents Seats directly behind home plate.

The face value of the tickets is steep, ranging between $200 and $400 a seat. Their actual price depends on the opponent and whether the game is considered a diamond game, marquee game, prime game, or regular game. The best bet is to find the seats on StubHub.com. There they can sometimes run in the low to mid-$200 range, cutting a good percentage off the top ticket cost.

The Lexus Presidents Seats give fans access to a gourmet buffet, the aptly named Oval Office Bar, complimentary in-seat food and beverage service, and access to the Lexus Presidents Club, PNC Diamond Club, and Norfolk Southern Club. The seats are cushioned (an exclusivity reserved for locations such as directly behind home plate) and give fans more leg room than the average stadium seat.

In the Presidents Club, fans are offered a high-class dining experience with live music and can look into the press conference room after games and look down at the Nats practicing inside the batting cages and on makeshift pitching mounds. To be able to watch a live press conference just a few feet away from the reporters who cover the team is a very neat experience. The same goes with watching players practice their swings before a game.

The next best location is the PNC Diamond Club directly behind the Presidents Seats. Sitting there will cost well north of $100 a ticket but is more cost effective, considering you are only a few more rows back than the Lexus seats. Nationals owner Mark Lerner frequently sits in the front row just to the right of home plate. It's also very likely you can run into a star athlete or celebrity in those seats during a game.

If the opportunity to sit in those seats is not in your near future, it's never a bad thing to scour StubHub for $5 to $15 upper deck seats. Those prices are usually for games played early in the week. Weekend game prices are typically higher.

79 Frank Robinson's Showdown with Mike Scioscia

Whether during his 21-year Hall of Fame playing career or as a manager for four franchises, Frank Robinson was never one to back down. That was certainly evident when the 69-year-old went head-to-head with 46-year-old Los Angeles Angels of Anaheim manager Mike Scioscia.

Two months into their inaugural season, the Washington Nationals were on a roll heading into Anaheim for a three-game series. The first-place Nats had won 10 games in a row and 13 of their last 14 prior to their 11–1 series-opening loss on Monday, June 13. However, on Tuesday all hell broke loose. Outfielder Jose Guillen, who was unceremoniously shipped out of Anaheim to Washington that offseason, tipped off Robinson that Angels reliever Brendan Donnelly kept pine tar in his glove to alter the break of his pitches.

Up 3–1 with one out in the seventh inning, Donnelly came in to relieve starter Ervin Santana, who had struck out seven and allowed only four hits to that point. Robinson, who was still wearing his sunglasses after having laser surgery on his right eye earlier in the day, approached home plate umpire Tim Tschida before a warm-up pitch was thrown. The 43,874 fans in attendance were perplexed. At Robinson's urging umpires took a look at Donnelly's glove. They convened and agreed it was indeed pine tar on the glove and ejected the fourth-year pitcher. Scioscia, who had already made his way to the mound at this point, called for another reliever, Scot Shields.

Scioscia pointed at Robinson, who was still standing along the first-base line, and made his way over to him before Shields even arrived on the mound. The sixth-year Angels skipper said: "I'm going to have every one of your pitchers undressed," a threat to have each Nats pitcher checked for foreign substances.

Robinson—the stud athlete who won National League Rookie of the Year, a Triple Crown, World Series MVP, All-Star Game MVP, Manager of the Year, and is still the only player to win MVP in both leagues—was not some docile old man. When threatened or challenged, his inner fire sears hotter than ever. He followed Scioscia, and the two nearly came face to face before umpires separated the feisty skippers. Robinson wasn't going to knowingly let an opponent cheat and he damn sure wasn't going to be pushed around. "Let me tell you this," Robinson said the next day. "If people let me intimidate them, then I'll intimidate them. But I wasn't going to let him intimidate me. *I am the intimidator.*"

Benches cleared, and, on cue, Guillen was in the middle of the scrum. The next inning he exacted revenge by hitting a game-tying, two-run home run. The Nats went on to win 6–3 to improve to 38–27. After the game Guillen discussed his tumultuous relationship with Scioscia during the end of his reign with the Angels. "That's the stuff that pissed me off," he said. "All I know is, Mike should show more respect…[He] talks about respect, leadership. I don't think he showed anything right there at all." Guillen continued his rant the next night. "I don't got truly no respect for [Scioscia] anymore because I'm still hurt from what happened last year," he said. "I don't want to make all these comments, but Mike Scioscia to me is like a piece of garbage. I don't really care. I don't care if I get in trouble. He can go to hell. We've got to move on. I don't got no respect for him."

Donnelly was suspended 10 games, and the managers were suspended one game apiece and fined by Major League Baseball for what were deemed "aggressive and inappropriate actions."

80 The Midseason Parade "The Wondrous Nats"

These days, the idea of a parade taking place for any team other than a champion is unimaginable. But after experiencing eight losing seasons in the previous 10 years and no postseason appearance since the 1933 World Series, fans of the 1949 Senators were starving for something to get excited about.

When the Nats completed a 14-game May road trip that included a nine-game winning streak, they returned as hometown heroes despite only boasting a 12–12 record. They reached a mark of 12–11 but dropped the final game of the trip 2–1 to the Detroit Tigers. Thrilled by what had transpired on Washington's western swing—despite their team being in fourth place—5,000 fans greeted the team upon arrival at Union Station. The team continued on a motorcade down Pennsylvania Avenue. Fans flocked to see their squad and brought signs that read: "We'll win the pennant," "Drink a toast with Eddie Yost," "We'll win plenty with Sam Dente," and "No raspberries for our boy Sherry."

"We knew all along on the Hill that we had the best team in the American League," said Maryland senator Millard Tydings. The longtime legislator and esteemed Democrat was not alone in his excitement. The district commissioners gave manager Joe Kuhel the keys to the city. Fans were so eager for a winner that they called Griffith Stadium to reserve World Series tickets.

Dubbed "The Wondrous Nats," Washington peaked at 25–20. They went 25–84 over the final 109 games, finishing at 50–104, their worst record since 1909. The team had 16 losing streaks of at least three games. No regular batter on the Senators hit above .294, and no one in their regular pitching rotation had an ERA better than 4.21.

It shouldn't come as a surprise that Kuhel's second season was less successful than his first. Before the 1949 season, owner Clark Griffith traded two of the Senators' star players, Mickey Vernon and Early Wynn, to the Cleveland Indians for Joe Haynes, Ed Klieman, and Eddie Robinson. In what is known as "Thelma's Deal," Griffith made the move to bring his niece and adopted daughter, Thelma Robertson, back home after she spent the previous eight seasons in Chicago while her husband, Joe Haynes played for the White Sox. Just a few weeks before his return to Washington, Chicago traded Haynes to Cleveland.

After going 56–97–1 in 1948, Kuhel knew his firing would be imminent before 1949's last place finish had even concluded. He, however, refused to take all of the blame. "I'll probably be canned at the end of the season and I'm not griping," Kuhel said. "That's baseball. But in my defense, I'd like to say this: 'You can't make chicken salad out of chicken feathers.'" Odds are he didn't actually say "feathers." You can fill in the blank on that one.

Kuhel was replaced with Bucky Harris, who entered his third stint as Washington's manager.

Uniforms and Logos

On September 29, 2004, official word came that the Montreal Expos would move to Washington, D.C., and baseball's 33-year hiatus in the nation's capital would end the next April. It was only natural that the team would return to the classic red caps with the white Curly W that the Washington Senators wore in the late 1960s and early 1970s.

Washington, D.C., mayor Anthony Williams and other representatives around him on the podium during the press conference announcing baseball's return to the city were sporting those same caps before the unnamed team's identity had even been decided.

That was a big hint.

On Monday, November 22, 2004, Williams, team president Tony Tavares, and general manager Jim Bowden—while wearing those hats—helped unveil the team's name and logo at a lunchtime ceremony at Union Station in front of a few hundred spectators. The primary logo offered a presidential look of red, white, blue, and gold. "Washington" was displayed in white text on a red banner above white block letters with red outlines and gold shading that read "Nationals." The nickname curved over a baseball with nine white stars in a rounded blue border below it. The secondary logo was a roundel design featuring an interlocking "DC" in a field of red surrounded by a blue circle with white text that read "Washington" on top and "Nationals" on the bottom with gold stars on the left and right side.

Less than two weeks before pitchers and catchers reported to spring training, the team unveiled their home and road uniforms on February 2, 2005, at downtown D.C.'s ESPN Zone. Bowden, outfielder Jose Guillen, shortstop Cristian Guzman, starting pitcher Zach Day, and closer Chad Cordero wore the duds.

Guillen and Guzman sported the classic red hats with the white Curly W for the home uniform with Day and Cordero wearing solid blue hats with the same script W for the road uniforms. The home jerseys were white with "Nationals" in red lettering with gold shading and blue trim strewn across the front and the jersey number on the left side just below. The team logo served as the patch on the left sleeve. Two red stripes surrounding a blue stripe in the middle adorned the bottom of the sleeves and the collar.

The road grays had "Washington" displayed across the front in blue letters with gold shading and a red border for each letter. The secondary roundel logo served as the patch on the left sleeve. Two blue stripes with a red one in between made up the piping on the bottom of the sleeves and around the neck.

The Nats updated their roundel alternate logo with just the interlocking DC inside a blue circle that contained nine gold stars as opposed to the words "Washington Nationals." That replaced the home and road sleeve patch from 2006 to 2008. The team added a patch commemorating Nationals Park's inaugural season on the right sleeve of their home uniforms in 2008.

From 2006 to 2008, the team wore an alternate red jersey with the white interlocking DC logo on the upper left side and blue numbers with gold shading on the lower right side. The alternate red cap also sported the interlocking DC logo. The 2008 alternate also featured the Nationals Park patch.

The team altered its road jersey for the 2009 and 2010 seasons by replacing the blue, curved block lettering of "Washington" with a red, diagonal, and underlined script version of "Washington," which offered a more traditional look. The roundel sleeve patch was replaced with just the interlocking DC logo for both the home and road jerseys those seasons. The red alternate was replaced with a blue patriotic jersey featuring a stars and stripes DC logo on the jersey and hat and the team's primary logo as the left sleeve patch.

In November of 2010, with the help of third baseman Ryan Zimmerman, shortstop Ian Desmond, starting pitchers John Lannan and Jordan Zimmermann, reliever Tyler Clippard, and closer Drew Storen, the team showed off its overhauled logo and uniforms at Nationals Park.

The team removed gold from its color scheme and introduced a simpler, classic look. Washington replaced its primary logo with a red "W" inside a field of white surrounded by a blue circle encasing "Washington Nationals" and red stars on the left and right sides—essentially a cleaned-up version of their original alternate logo. After removing the gold treatment, the numbers and letters were no longer three-dimensional. The "W" replaced "DC" on the patriotic alternates. The left sleeve patches were replaced with the team's new primary logo. The red, white, and blue uniforms added piping that extended from the collar down the middle of the jersey, giving them a more upright appearance.

New for that season was a blue cap with a red bill to be used with their road and patriotic uniforms. In 2013 the team added a red alternate hat with a blue bill. The 2015 Nationals wore 10-year anniversary patches on their right sleeve.

The team wore '70s-style throwback Senators uniforms in 2010 against the Baltimore Orioles, 1936 Senators throwbacks in 2011 against the San Diego Padres, 1924 Senators throwbacks in 2012 against the San Francisco Giants, and have paid homage to the Homestead Grays by wearing their throwbacks several times over the years.

82 Nationals All-Stars

Nationals players have combined for 18 All-Star appearances since their inaugural 2005 season. Here's how each All-Star fared for the National League in the Midsummer Classic:

2005
Chad Cordero (pitcher)
The Chief led the league with 31 saves and a 1.13 ERA at the All-Star break. In his only All-Star appearance, he replaced Jake Peavy with two outs in the bottom of the eighth and struck out Ivan Rodriguez. The 23-year-old finished the season with a 1.82 ERA and 47 saves in 74 games.

Livan Hernandez (pitcher)
Livo helped lead Washington's amazing first half with a 12–3 record and a 3.48 ERA going into the break. He pitched the fourth inning and allowed a walk and a two-run single to Ichiro Suzuki to give the American League a 5–0 lead. The Nats went into a downward spiral in the second half, and Hernandez's final record was 15–10 with a 3.98 ERA.

2006
Alfonso Soriano (starting outfield)
The Nats' star left fielder joined the exclusive 40-40 Club in 2006 with 46 home runs and 41 steals. He created his own 40-40-40 Club by tacking on 41 doubles. Soriano hit leadoff in the All-Star Game, going 1-for-2 in the game. He flied out to right field off of Kenny Rogers in the first inning and singled to left field off Roy Halladay in the third inning.

2007
Dmitri Young (first base)
Young won National League Comeback Player of the Year in 2007, hitting .320 with 13 home runs and 74 RBIs. He pinch hit for pitcher Trevor Hoffman in the bottom of the ninth, getting on base with a single. Soriano, who signed with the Chicago Cubs that offseason, homered to score Young and himself. It was Young's only All-Star appearance.

2008
Cristian Guzman (shortstop)
Guzman pinch ran for Aramis Ramirez in the top of the ninth and batted three times in the 15-inning game. He didn't register a hit in three plate appearances in the only All-Star Game of his career. He finished the season batting .316 with 183 hits, the most of his career.

2009

Ryan Zimmerman (third base)

Mr. National made his first All-Star appearance during a season in which he had career highs in hits (178), home runs (33), and total bases (320). Zimmerman replaced future National Dan Haren in the lineup in the fifth inning and faced another future National, Edwin Jackson, and flied out against him. He stayed in the game and hit another fly ball out against Joe Nathan.

2010

Matt Capps (pitcher)

Capps replaced Halladay in the bottom of the sixth, striking out David Ortiz on five pitches to close the inning. The Washington closer earned the win on just five pitches thanks to Brian McCann's three-run double in the top of the seventh. Capps was traded 16 days later for catcher Wilson Ramos and minor league pitcher Joe Testa. In 47 games with the Nats, Capps registered 26 saves.

2011

Tyler Clippard (pitcher)

For the second straight year, a Nats pitcher replaced a Philadelphia Phillies pitcher to earn the win after facing one batter. Down 1–0 the Nats' set-up man replaced Cliff Lee in the fourth inning. He gave up a single to Adrian Beltre, but Jose Bautista was thrown out at home to end the top half of the inning. In the bottom half of the inning, Prince Fielder homered to score Carlos Beltran and Matt Kemp, eventually giving Clippard the win. Clippard finished the season with a 3–0 record and 1.83 ERA.

2012

Ian Desmond (shortstop)

Desi batted .292 in his first Silver Slugger season but chose to sit out the All-Star Game to avoid injury. He finished the year with 25 home runs and 73 RBIs.

Gio Gonzalez (pitcher)

Just 17 games into his Nats career, Gonzalez was an All-Star. He entered the game in the third inning, not allowing a hit. He finished the season with 21 wins, a 2.89 ERA, and 207 strikeouts.

Bryce Harper (outfield)

The 19-year-old rookie pinch hit for Carlos Beltran in the top of the fifth inning, earning a walk against Jered Weaver. The National League Rookie of the Year led off the seventh inning by striking out against Ryan Cook. Harper finished 2012 batting .270 with 22 home runs and 59 RBIs.

Stephen Strasburg (pitcher)

Strasburg replaced Gonzalez in the fourth inning and allowed one hit and one walk, surrendering no runs. He finished his first season since his 2011 Tommy John surgery with a 15–6 record and 3.16 ERA and 197 strikeouts.

2013

Bryce Harper (starting outfield)

The 20-year-old prodigy played center field and batted ninth. He closed out the third inning by lining out on a pitch from Chris Sale. His final appearance of the game came in the bottom of the sixth inning when he popped out against Grant Balfour. Harper finished his season with 20 home runs and 58 RBIs.

Senators All-Stars

The Major League Baseball All-Star Game debuted in 1933 at Chicago's Comiskey Park in what was dubbed "The Game of the Century." Legendary Senators shortstop/manager Joe Cronin and pitcher Al Crowder were the first to represent Washington, D.C., on the American League roster. Take a look at who else represented the two Senators franchises.

1933: Joe Cronin (SS), Al Crowder (P)

1934: Joe Cronin (SS/manager), Heinie Manush (OF), Jack Russell (P)

1935: Ossie Bluege (3B), Buddy Myer (2B)

1936: Ben Chapman (OF)

1937: Rick Ferrell (C), Wes Ferrell (P), Buddy Myer (2B), Cecil Travis (3B)

1938: Rick Ferrell (C), Buddy Lewis (3B)

1939: George Case (OF)

1940: Dutch Leonard (P), Cecil Travis (3B)

1941: Sid Hudson (P), Cecil Travis (3B)

1942: Sid Hudson (P), Stan Spence (OF)

1943: George Case (OF), Jake Early (C), Bob Johnson (OF), Dutch Leonard (P)

1944: George Case (OF), Rick Ferrell (C), Dutch Leonard (P), Stan Spence (OF)

1945: (Game not played due to World War II, but George Case, Dutch Leonard, and Rick Ferrell were listed on the proposed American League All-Star roster.)

1946: Stan Spence (OF), Mickey Vernon (1B)

1947: Buddy Lewis (OF), Walter Masterson (P), Stan Spence (OF), Early Wynn (P)

1948: Walter Masterson (P), Mickey Vernon (1B)

1949: Eddie Robinson (1B)

1950: Cass Michaels (2B)

1951: Connie Marrero (P)

1952: Jackie Jensen (OF), Ed Yost (3B)

1953: Mickey Vernon (1B)

1954: Bob Porterfield (P), Dean Stone (P), Mickey Vernon (1B)

1955: Mickey Vernon (1B)

1956: Roy Sievers (1B)

1957: Roy Sievers (1B)

1958: Rocky Bridges (SS)

1959: Bob Allison (OF), Harmon Killebrew (3B), Camilo Pascual (P), Pedro Ramos (P), Roy Sievers (1B)

1960: Jim Lemon (OF), Camilo Pascual (P)

1961: Dick Donovan (P)

1962: Dave Stenhouse (P)

1963: Don Leppert (C)

1964: Chuck Hinton (OF)

1965: Pete Richert (P)

1966: Pete Richert (P)

1967: Paul Casanova (C)

1968: Frank Howard (OF)

1969: Frank Howard (OF), Darold Knowles (P)

1970: Frank Howard (OF)

1971: Frank Howard (OF)

Jordan Zimmermann (pitcher)

Zimmermann did not pitch in the All-Star Game because of neck soreness and to save himself for the second half of the season. He finished the year with a 19–9 record, a 3.25 ERA, and 161 strikeouts in 213.1 innings pitched over 32 games.

2014

Tyler Clippard (pitcher)

A replacement for Julio Teheran, who pitched two days before, Clippard's second appearance did not go as swimmingly as his first. With two on and one out in the bottom of the fifth inning, he relieved Pat Neshek. Clippard gave up a run on a sacrifice fly from Jose Altuve and then forced Miguel Cabrera to fly out. He ended 2014 with a 2.18 ERA and 7–4 record in 70⅓ innings.

Jordan Zimmermann (pitcher)

Zimmermann yet again sat out the All-Star Game—this time with a bicep cramp. In 32 games he finished the 2014 season with a 14–5 record and 2.66 ERA.

2015

Bryce Harper (starting outfield)

Having a career year, Harper yet again started for the National League. He manned right field and batted third. Harper closed out the bottom of the first inning by grounding out on a full count against Dallas Keuchel and led off the bottom of the fourth inning, striking out on four pitches against David Price. Two innings later he struck out on five pitches against Zach Britton. Harper finished his breakout season with a league-leading 42 home runs and .460 on-base percentage.

Max Scherzer (pitcher)
One year after earning the win for the American League, Scherzer opted to pitch in Baltimore two days prior to the Midsummer Classic and did not pitch in the game as a result. Scherzer's season featured a career-low 2.79 ERA and two no-hitters.

Sam Rice's Secrets

If there was one thing Edgar "Sam" Rice could do better than play baseball, it was keep secrets. A 22-year-old aspiring ballplayer from Indiana, Rice ventured to Illinois to try out at a baseball camp in 1912. Little did he know what he had left behind. While pursuing his dream, a tornado ravaged his family's farm, killing his wife, two children, two sisters, and mother. Nine days later, his father passed away from injuries sustained during the storm. Other than an older sister who wasn't around during the storm, his entire immediate family was gone.

Everyone grieves in different ways, and Rice internalized the situation to the best of his ability. He remarried twice, and in the mid-1960s, a reporter traveled to Rice's home and asked him about the tornado that turned his life upside down more than 50 years earlier. That was the first his wife, Mary, had heard of that story.

Following the tragedy, Rice began soul searching and worked odd jobs to survive. His love for baseball began to blossom when he enlisted in the Navy in 1913 and joined the team housed aboard the USS New Hampshire. He was essentially sold to the Senators in 1915 because of a $600 debt that the owner of the Virginia League's Portsmouth baseball club owed Washington manager/part-owner Clark Griffith.

Though his first name was Edgar, Rice didn't correct the D.C. press when Griffith told them his name was Sam. For someone three years removed from an unthinkable tragedy, something like that didn't matter much to the modest Rice. From 1915 to 1934, Rice crafted a Hall of Fame resume as an outfielder but made his debut as a 25-year-old pitcher against the Chicago White Sox. He appeared on the mound in nine games through the middle of the 1916 season before making the career-altering shift to right field.

Rice played on all three of the Senators' World Series teams and reeled in one of the most controversial catches the Series has ever seen. In Game 3 of the 1925 World Series, Rice robbed Pittsburgh Pirates catcher Earl Smith of a home run. *Or did he?* In the top of the eighth inning, Rice pursued Smith's delivery to right-center field. As Rice approached the temporary bleachers, he caught

Rice's Records

Rice was more than just a player who may or may not have made a much-scrutinized catch. His stats still hold up in the Washington Senators/Minnesota Twins franchise record books. Here's where he stands among the club's all-time greats:

First: hits (2,889), runs (1,467), at-bats (8,934), doubles (478), triples (183)
Second: games played (2,307), total bases (3,833), stolen bases (346)
Third: batting average (.323)
Fourth: RBIs (1,045)
10th: walks (680)

He appears twice in the top 10 of both the franchise's single-season runs and hits records, is third in single-season stolen bases (63), and is tied for fifth all-time in single-season triples (18). Rice still holds the distinction for the most career hits (2,987) without being a member of the 3,000-hit club. He is the all-time leader in D.C. baseball history in games played and extra-base hits (695). He was added to the Nationals Park Ring of Honor in 2010.

the ball but disappeared from sight after falling head over heels into the crowd. Seconds later he emerged and hoisted the ball above his head in his glove for umpires to see.

To the dismay of Pirates manager Bill McKechnie and owner Barney Dreyfuss, who made his way onto the field from the stands, the umps ruled Smith out. The Pirates refused to believe Rice was able to hold on to the ball after a tumble like that. When pressed about whether he made the catch, Rice deferred to the umpire's ruling. He was inducted into the Hall of Fame in 1963 and, after continued pressure to disclose the truth about the catch, he penned a letter at the 1965 induction ceremony in Cooperstown, New York. He gave it to Hall of Fame president Paul Kerr and instructed him not to open the letter until after his death.

Rice died on October 13, 1974, and in a news conference on November 4, the letter was read. It detailed the sequence of events surrounding the catch and whether he actually caught the ball or not. Rice closed the letter by saying: "At no time did I lose possession of the ball."

84 Interesting Draft Picks and Minor Leaguers

The Nationals have had quite an interesting cast of characters who rolled through their minor league system or were drafted by the club.

Ryan Ripken

The Nationals drafted the son of the Iron Man, Cal Ripken Jr., in the 15th round (454th overall) of the 2014 Major League Baseball Draft. Ripken, a left-handed first baseman out of Indian River

State College in Florida, was also drafted by his father's Baltimore Orioles in the 20th round of the 2012 draft but chose to play collegiately at South Carolina before transferring to Indian River State College. He spent 2014 and 2015 with the Gulf Coast League Nationals, hitting .250 in 28 games during his second season.

Mariano Rivera Jr.

Like Ripken, Rivera Jr. was drafted by his father's team but did not sign with them. The New York Yankees selected the Sandman's son in the 29th round (872nd overall) of the 2014 MLB Draft. In 2015 the Nats selected the son of the last MLB player to wear No. 42 in the fourth round (134th overall). He posted a 1–2 record and 5.45 ERA in 19 games with the Class A Short Season Auburn Doubledays of the New York-Penn League during the 2015 season.

Tony Gwynn Jr.

The son of Mr. Padre began his major league career as a second-round pick (39th overall) in the 2003 MLB Draft by the Milwaukee Brewers. He spent 2006–2008 with Milwaukee and batted .238 in 130 games. As fate would have it, the outfielder was traded to San Diego in May 2009 for Jody Gerut. Gwynn played 236 games with the Padres through 2010, hitting .242 and gathering 165 hits. Following the 2010 campaign, he was granted free agency and joined the Los Angeles Dodgers, where he hit .245 in 239 games the next two seasons. Gwynn joined the Philadelphia Phillies in 2014 and appeared in 80 games before signing with the Washington Nationals in March 2015. He spent the 2015 season with the Triple A Syracuse Chiefs, batting .255 in 89 games. When you get the chance, be sure to check out the YouTube video from his Dodgers days where he deals with a heckling fan at Coors Field by mimicking him with his glove behind his back. It's quite amusing.

Cutter Dykstra

An infielder drafted in the second round (54ᵗʰ overall) by the Milwaukee Brewers, Dykstra was shipped to Washington just before the start of the 2011 season in exchange for outfielder Nyjer Morgan and cash. The son of former New York Mets and Phillies centerfielder Lenny Dykstra has spent the last five years working his way up through the ranks of the Nationals farm system, playing with the Potomac Nationals (2011, 2013), Hagerstown Suns (2012), Auburn Doubledays (2014), Harrisburg Senators (2014–2015), and Syracuse Chiefs (2015). Married to Jamie Lynn Sigler, best known for her role as Meadow Soprano in *The Sopranos*, Dykstra hit .229 with six home runs and 36 RBIs with Double A Harrisburg and Triple A Syracuse in 2015.

"El Duque" Orlando Hernandez

In July of 2010, the Nationals signed the 44-year-old "El Duque," the half-brother of former Washington pitcher Livan Hernandez, to a minor-league contract. He appeared in 11 games with the Gulf Coast League Nationals and the Harrisburg Senators, going 1–1 in 15 ⅔ innings of play, striking out 21 and allowing 10 hits and four runs. When Nationals general manager Mike Rizzo told Hernandez he would not be a September call-up, he left the Senators and hasn't pitched in the minors or majors since.

Bryan Harper

Bryce's older brother was actually drafted three times. In 2008 the Nationals selected him in the 31ˢᵗ round (931ˢᵗ overall) out of Las Vegas High School. The 6'6" left-handed pitcher chose to attend the College of Southern Nevada and played with his brother. He was then drafted by the Chicago Cubs in the 27ᵗʰ round (820ᵗʰ overall) in 2010, the same year his brother went first overall in the draft. In 2011 he opted to pitch for the University of South Carolina, appearing in 22 games for the college baseball powerhouse that won their second consecutive College World Series championship that season. Harper was drafted again by the Nats in 2011, going 907th overall in the 30th round. He signed with the team and has played for the Gulf Coast League Nationals (2011), Auburn Doubledays (2012), Hagerstown Suns (2013), Potomac Nationals (2014), Harrisburg Senators (2014–2015), and Syracuse Chiefs (2015). If you don't remember Harper for his minor league tenure, you may recall him sporting an epic handlebar mustache on ESPN while recording (via a GoPro affixed to his cap) his dad pitching to his brother during the 2013 Home Run Derby.

Aaron Crow

The Nats selected the highly touted right-handed pitcher out of the University of Missouri with the ninth overall pick in 2008, but he chose not to sign with the team because he wanted a major league contract and a premium signing bonus above the slotted $2.15 million for a ninth overall pick. He played independent ball that year and was then selected 12th overall in 2009 by the Kansas City Royals. Who was he drafted behind? First overall selection Stephen Strasburg and 10th overall pick Drew Storen. The 10th pick was awarded to Washington for not being able to sign Crow the year before. Crow toiled in the minors from 2008 to 2010 before making the American League All-Star team in 2011 with the Royals. After the 2014 season, he was traded to the Miami Marlins in exchange for pitchers Reid Redman and Brian Flynn. He suffered a partially torn ulnar collateral ligament in spring training and underwent Tommy John surgery in April, forcing him to miss the 2015 season.

Tim Raines Jr.

The son of the Montreal Expos' seven-time All-Star (1981–1987) and 23-year veteran Raines Jr. signed a minor league deal with the Nationals in 2006, spending the season with Double A Harrisburg and the Triple A New Orleans Zephyrs, batting .278 with 85 hits, seven home runs, and 28 RBIs in 91 games.

Skye Bolt

One of the leading members of the "cool name" division, Bolt was drafted by the Nationals in the 26th round (804th overall) in 2012. He never signed with the team, opting to play collegiately at North Carolina and improve his stock. Bolt was drafted by the Oakland Athletics in the fourth round of the 2015 draft and spent the year with the Vermont Lake Monsters. Whatever happens in his career, it will be tough to match the coolness of his name.

Burt Reynolds

No, Nats fans, the team did not select the *Smokey and the Bandit* star in the 30th round (901st overall) of the 2006 MLB Draft. The shortstop, drafted out of Bloomfield Tech in New Jersey, though, never signed with the Nationals. The cousin of Robinson Cano, Reynolds was in the Tampa Bay Rays farm system before joining his cousin and signing a minor league contract with the New York Yankees in 2012. He then signed a minor league deal with the Seattle Mariners in December 2013 shortly after Cano inked a 10-year, $240 million deal with the big club.

Seth Greene

As if the "e" at the end of his last name wasn't enough to give it away, the Nats did not draft Scott Evil from the *Austin Powers* movies. The Nationals selected the 6'3" right-handed pitcher in the 46th round (1,372nd overall) of the 2009 draft out of Deep Run High School in Virginia. He never signed with the team and played collegiately at VCU.

85 2005's 10-Game Winning Streak

The first half of the Nationals' 2005 season was magical for D.C.'s baseball-starved fans. The team was overachieving beyond belief with a record of 52–36 at the All-Star break, including winning 10 straight games in June to tie a Montreal Expos franchise mark.

Here's the game-by-game breakdown from the streak:

June 2, 2005

Nationals 8, Atlanta Braves 6

The Nats led 3–2 going into the eighth inning, but relief pitcher Gary Majewski gave up four runs to Atlanta in the top of the frame. Backup catcher Gary Bennett saved the day—first by hitting his first home run of the season to put the Nats up 2–0 and then by hitting a three-run double in the bottom of the eighth inning to give them an 8–6 lead and ultimately the home win.

June 3, 2005

Nationals 3, Florida Marlins 2 (11 innings)

The Nats were in a 2–0 hole after three innings but tied the game in the fourth inning with RBIs from Nick Johnson and Vinny Castilla. A Ryan Church single followed, but that would be Washington's last hit of the game. In the bottom of the 11th, Jamey Carroll walked and advanced to second on a throwing error after Jose Guillen singled on a fielder's choice. Johnson was walked to load the bases. Castilla popped out, but Church's sacrifice fly scored Carroll to give the Nats another home win.

June 4, 2005
Nationals 7, Florida Marlins 3
This home victory was overshadowed by Nats left fielder Marlon Byrd's run-in with second-base umpire Joe Brinkman after he was ruled to have swung around on a checked swing to close out the sixth inning. He had almost made it to first base, thinking he had drawn a walk. He glared at first-base umpire Bill Miller, who made the original call, uttered something, and was thrown out. Byrd was irate and went to argue with Miller. Brinkman intervened, saying he stuck out his arm to stop Byrd but ended up on the ground. Byrd was suspended two games by Major League Baseball for the outburst.

June 5, 2005
Nationals 6, Florida Marlins 3
Only managing four hits in the first six innings of the home contest, the Nats managed three runs apiece in the seventh and eighth innings to secure their fourth straight win. This was the deepest into a season that a D.C. baseball team was in first place since 1933.

June 7, 2005
Nationals 2, Oakland Athletics 1
Scott Hatteberg's first-inning double to center that scored Jason Kendall put the Athletics up 1–0. The Nats had three hits in the first five innings until Nick Johnson hit a two-run homer in the sixth inning of the home contest.

June 8, 2005
Nationals 7, Oakland Athletics 2
Esteban Loaiza gave up a two-run home run in the first inning of the home game but settled down to throw 123 pitches in seven innings, allowing just four hits. Thanks to homers from Ryan

Church, Brian Schneider, and Vinny Castilla, the Nats powered their way to seven runs.

June 9, 2005
Nationals 4, Oakland Athletics 3
Workhorse Livan Hernandez pitched seven scoreless innings for the Nats but allowed two runs in the eighth inning. He threw 127 pitches en route to his eighth straight win, tying the longest streak of his career. Nick Johnson's three-run double and Vinny Castilla's solo home run in the fourth were enough for another home win.

June 10, 2005
Nationals 9, Seattle Mariners 3
A trio of newcomers led the way to victory. Sun-Woo Kim found out he'd make his first start of the year just a few hours before the game. He pitched five innings, allowing two runs and five hits. Second baseman Junior Spivey was acquired from the Milwaukee Brewers that morning. He arrived after the game started and scored two runs, including the tying run in the bottom of the second as a pinch-runner. Rick Short spent more than a decade in the minors and got an RBI in his first major league at-bat. A six-run eighth inning cemented their eighth straight victory, which all came at home.

June 11, 2005
Nationals 2, Seattle Mariners 1
The pitchers' duel between Jamie Moyer and John Patterson resulted in just 10 hits and two runs allowed between the two. The deciding factor was Jose Guillen's game-winning single in the seventh inning. The 32nd home game of the year was attended by 39,108 fans, allowing the franchise to surpass one million on the season.

June 12, 2005

Nationals 3, Seattle Mariners 2

Junior Spivey hit a two-run homer in the second inning while Jamey Carrol hit an RBI single in the fourth. Tony Armas Jr. pitched five scoreless innings, but Gary Majewski allowed two runs over the sixth and seventh innings. Chad Cordero earned his 19th save with just seven pitches in the ninth inning. All 10 victories took place on home soil.

86 The Fan Who Died from a Wild Throw

Going to the ballpark is typically a laid-back, enjoyable experience. But despite its lax nature, baseball is very interactive with its fans. Every at-bat provides an opportunity to catch a foul ball, home run, errant throw, or even a bat that slipped out of the batter's hands. The need to be attentive is constant.

In April of 2015, a fan at a Chicago Cubs-Pittsburgh Pirates game was walking to her seat in the front row behind home plate when she was struck in the back of the head with a foul ball that pushed back the protective netting at PNC Park. She was released from the hospital within a day. In June of 2015, a woman sitting just to the left of the netting in Boston's Fenway Park was struck in the face with shards of a broken bat. She was sent to the hospital in life-threatening condition but was released one week later. Unfortunately, while the second-place Washington Senators took on the third-place Cleveland Indians on September 29, 1943, at Griffith Stadium, one fan suffered a similar experience but with a tragic ending.

Washington third baseman Sherry Robertson, nephew of owner Clark Griffith, wasn't known for his defensive acumen but started the first game of a twi-night doubleheader. In the top of the ninth, Robertson fielded a ground ball from Indians batter Ken Keltner, but what should've been a routine play turned into anything but. Robertson threw the ball to first baseman Mickey Vernon. It, however, sailed well past Vernon and into the crowd, striking the head of 32-year-old Alexandria, Virginia, resident Clarence D. Stagemyer, who was seated in the front row.

Stagemyer, the chief of the correspondence section at the Civil Aeronautics Administration, was dazed and shook his head a few times. He wanted to stay and watch the rest of the game but, after the urging of Senators physicians, he went to the hospital. He died early the next morning just hours after being hit.

The deputy coroner said Stagemyer suffered a concussion and a fractured skull. A native of York, Pennsylvania, Stagemyer was a big baseball fan who managed teams and umpired in softball leagues in his hometown. "Stagey," as he was called back home, suffered a knee injury as a boy and wasn't able to play the sport. Stagemyer was laid to rest at York's Greenmount Cemetery. He is the only fan at a Major League Baseball game to die from a throw into the stands.

87 Michael Morse's Phantom Grand Slam

In the movie *Major League*, Indians catcher Jake Taylor takes a swing with no pitch and no ball in sight and rounds the bases. Taylor was wearing jeans and a blazer; no one else was on the field. Then his teammates appeared from the dugout and jokingly cheered him on with Willie Mays Hayes putting his hand over his eyebrows, as if to gaze in the distance for the ball. Hayes said, "That was outta here!"

Michael Morse enjoyed a similar experience on September 29, 2012, when the Nationals were at Busch Stadium in St. Louis, just two wins away from clinching their first National League East title. In the top of the first inning, Morse faced Cardinals pitcher Kyle Lohse with Bryce Harper at third, Ryan Zimmerman at second, and Adam LaRoche at first base.

On the very first pitch, a 92-mph fastball low and away, Morse swung and took the ball to right field. The ball bounced off the top of the wall back into the field of play, but the game continued as if it was live. Harper scored easily. Zimmerman made it to third but hesitated to run home when Cardinals right fielder Carlos Beltran threw the ball to second baseman Skip Schumaker, who was playing the role of cutoff man in shallow right field between first and second base.

With LaRoche heading back to second, Morse made a beeline toward first to avoid a tag from Schumaker, but he was caught. Now there were two outs with only one run scoring on that play. That was until Nationals manager Davey Johnson contested the ruling on the field, saying the ball bounced off the top of the wall, making it an automatic home run and—in this case—a grand slam.

After a couple minutes of reviewing the play, the umpires came back out and awarded the grand slam. Morse was already past second after the announcement. LaRoche was in between second and third while Zimmerman was still on third base. The umpires made them return to their original bases before heading home in case any of them had passed each other amidst the chaos of the previous three minutes. Morse then headed back to first, stopped, and pointed to home as if to say, "should I go back and do this all over again?"

He trotted home and without a bat made a half-hearted swing in front of smiling Cardinals catcher Yadier Molina and jogged his way around the bases. "I guess I didn't have to do that," Morse said. "If I didn't do it and they were like, 'No, you're out,' I would

As part of a bizarre do-over scenario, Michael Morse pantomimes swinging the bat after a video review showed he had hit a grand slam against the St. Louis Cardinals on September 29, 2012.

never sleep again…It was pretty weird. I thought they were waiting for me to swing, and then everybody started running. It was such a crazy moment, might as well have some fun with it."

At first the St. Louis crowd chuckled at Morse's sense of humor of swinging without a bat, but by the time he reached first base, a chorus of boos grew louder at the reality that a one-run single-turned-out was changed to a grand slam. All in all, the sequence took three minutes, 52 seconds from Lohse's windup to Morse stepping on home plate.

It certainly livened up MASN's TV booth manned by play-by-play announcer Bob Carpenter and color analyst F.P. Santangelo. Carpenter even called the grand slam without the bat, saying, "There it goes!" Santangelo chimed in with laughter and added: "Are you kidding me?" Carpenter finished it with a home-run call: "Right field. It is deep. See you later! Grand slam! The Nationals are on top by four."

Santangelo chimed in with laughter and added: "That is the greatest thing I've *ever* seen in my life. I mean, right when you thought you've seen everything in a Major League Baseball game, they pressed rewind on the video, and Michael Morse went phantom grand slam. And that's how this one starts. Unbelievable."

That grand slam turned out to be Morse's only hit of the night. He finished the game 1-for-4 with two strikeouts. The Nats nursed that 4–0 lead until the bottom of the seventh when they surrendered three runs followed by a John Jay sacrifice fly to score Pete Kozma and tie the game at four in the bottom of the ninth.

In the top of the 10th inning, after LaRoche and Danny Espinosa were walked, Kurt Suzuki blasted a double, sending both baserunners home and giving the Nationals a 6–4 lead. Pitcher Craig Stammen closed the game and secured the two-run victory by facing just three batters in the bottom of the frame.

88 Did the Senators Nearly Sign Josh Gibson and Buck Leonard?

A tremendous opportunity presented itself when Washington Senators owner Clark Griffith met with Homestead Grays stars Josh Gibson and Buck Leonard, the Negro Leagues' Babe Ruth and Lou Gehrig, respectively. The Grays were a Negro League dynasty that won nine straight pennants from 1937 to 1945, and Gibson and Leonard were a big reason why.

Gibson played catcher and is credited by the National Baseball Hall of Fame with hitting almost 800 home runs in his 17 years in independent ball and in the Negro Leagues. Leonard, who played first base for the Grays, and Gibson formed the most fearsome batting duo in the league.

Leonard's first Major League Baseball game as a spectator was between the New York Yankees and Washington Senators on July 5, 1924, when he was a 16-year-old railroad worker. That was the same game Ruth knocked himself out running into a wall after chasing a foul ball. The famous photo capturing the moment shows Ruth lying on the ground unconscious as Griffith Stadium's right-field section of segregated black fans look on.

Legendary sportswriter Sam Lacy, a former Griffith Stadium food vendor, had lobbied Griffith for years to integrate, reiterating the talent the owner had right under his nose in his own stadium. The Grays alternated home games in Pittsburgh's Forbes Field and D.C.'s Griffith Stadium. Lacy stated in the August 3, 1935, edition of the *Washington Tribune* that: "Washington, D.C., seemed like the natural place for the twentieth century's first black major leaguer. It had a major league team that desperately needed players. It had an owner who seemed somewhat racially sympathetic, given his signing of Cubans and the way he permitted the black community to use his stadium. And it had a large and affluent black population that not only embraced the local major league team but also had the wherewithal to attack the city's racial segregation. All the city needed was an instigator."

After supporting the Negro Leagues and watching Gibson and Leonard play for years, Griffith met with them after a Grays game to discuss their interest in joining the Senators. According to Leonard, Griffith told them: "If we get you boys, we're going to get the best ones. It's going to break up your league. Now what do you think of that?'"

Both men said they would want to play for the Senators but wouldn't clamor for it. "We have seen some of you fellows play," Leonard recalled Griffith saying, "and we'd like to have you in the major leagues with us. But nobody wants to be the first one to hire black ballplayers."

They, though, never heard back from Griffith, eliminating the chance for the trio to break barriers. Accounts as to why Griffith passed over signing the Negro League legends vary. It's said MLB officials found out about the negotiations and ordered him to break them off. Griffith also made good money off of the Grays renting out Griffith Stadium. Grays games routinely outdrew Senators games, perhaps making him hesitant to take away from his cash cow. Griffith was also reluctant to be the first MLB owner to integrate, not wanting to accept any backlash the player(s) and he may face.

Whether one, two, or even all of those reasons were true, the end result was still the same. The opportunity to turn the Senators into a powerhouse was there but ultimately ignored. Imagine a lineup with Mickey Vernon, Cecil Travis, Early Wynn, George Case, Gibson, and Leonard. Revisionist history indicates had Griffith signed Gibson and Leonard, the Senators likely would have never left Washington.

89 Inviting Phillies Fans to Nationals Park

Supporting a team that finished 59–102 the previous season was bad enough. Seeing a rival win the World Series that year was even worse. Hearing your team president on that rival city's local radio station encouraging their already rowdy fans to continue their annual invasion of your ballpark? That's downright unacceptable and exactly what happened the day after Washington's 2009 season-opening loss to the Florida Marlins.

The Nats had finished with the worst record in baseball and struggled to fill seats. Team president Stan Kasten was interviewed on 950 ESPN Philadelphia and decided to invite Phillies fans down to Nationals Park when the two clubs faced each other in Washington's home opener the following week in an effort to sell tickets. "It will be fun, and I think Philly's our best, closest National League rival," Kasten said. "We always have great games with them here because there's so many Philly kids in college here. So we always have great, enthusiastic crowds and we hope you all come back again. We have an Opening Day here Monday. We'd love for all our Philly fans to come down because I know it's gonna be so hard to get tickets in Philadelphia this year. It'll be much easier if you drive down the road and come see us in Washington…We want to play you, we want to see you here, and we would *welcome* your fans here."

Already plagued with the distinction of having baseball's worst record two years running, Nationals fans were not okay with this. Kasten even went on to compare the nature of D.C. and Philly fanbases. "And I've got to tell you, I have gone to enough games in three different sports in Philly to tell you that I haven't always felt welcome in your parks," he said. "But you can root for whoever you want. You will be welcomed when you come to Nationals Park."

When asked about Opening Day giveaways, the president flaunted one of the signs of a losing ballclub: hawking enemy merchandise on your own turf. "Hey, you've got an Opening Day hat!" Kasten said. "It's a Nats hat, which is okay, but we do feature for sale many Philly hats in our store, so come on by."

Kasten quickly defended his desperate need to sell tickets during such a downtrodden period in the franchise's history. "For 30 years I've gone on radio in other towns to invite fans to our games," he said, "always have, always will. We want fans from everywhere to come to lovely Nationals Park."

A packed crowd of 40,386 observed a 9–8 Phillies victory in Washington's home opener on April 13. Washington ended its season with a 3–15 record against Philadelphia. At 59–103 the Nats finished last in the National League East for the fourth time in five seasons, and Philly went on to a second consecutive World Series appearance. Although this was a low point for the franchise, Kasten may have been the impetus for Washington's "Take Back the Park" campaign in 2012, the year the Nationals won their first division title.

90 Learn the Names on the Ring of Honor

On August 10, 2010, the Washington Nationals decided to pay tribute to D.C.'s unique baseball heritage by honoring 18 men who provided major contributions to the Washington Senators, Homestead Grays, and the Montreal Expos. The names, along with the logos of the team's they represented, are displayed above the Diamond Club behind home plate at Nationals Park.

The two Expos representatives, Gary Carter and Andre Dawson, were on hand for the ceremony.

The criteria, developed through a partnership between the Nationals and the Baseball Hall of Fame in Cooperstown, is:

- The player must be in the Baseball Hall of Fame.
- The player must have played with the Washington Nationals, Washington Senators, Homestead Grays, or Montreal Expos.
- The player must have played significant years with those franchises.

The first rule explains the notable absence of Senators legend Frank Howard.

Frank Robinson, who managed the Expos from 2002 to 2004 and the Nationals from 2005 to 2006, was the first member of the modern Nationals to be honored. On May 9, 2015, Robinson's name, placed next to the Nationals' Curly W, was unveiled between the signs for sections 233 and 235. There, he tossed out the first pitch to Ian Desmond, who switched jersey numbers from No. 6 to 20 to honor the Hall of Famer.

Here are the other members of the Nationals Ring of Honor:

James "Cool Papa" Bell—Homestead Grays center fielder (1932, 1943–1946)
Known for his speed and defensive acumen, Bell was elected to the Baseball Hall of Fame in 1974. Legendary pitcher Satchel Paige once said of Bell: "One time he hit a line drive right past my ear. I turned around and saw the ball hit him sliding into second."

Ray Brown—Homestead Grays pitcher (1932–1945, 1947–1948)
Brown won eight pennants with the Grays between 1937 and 1945 and also played in the outfield and pinch hit. He tossed a one-hitter

against the Birmingham Black Barons in the 1944 Negro League World Series.

Gary Carter—Montreal Expos catcher (1974–1984, 1992) "The Kid" led the Expos to their first playoff berth in 1981 and played a big role in the New York Mets' 1986 World Series title. He finished his career with 11 All-Star Game appearances, 324 home runs, and three Gold Gloves.

All-time Series Records

Since their inaugural 2005 season, the Nationals have played in 1,780 games with a cumulative record of 855–925 (.480). Washington is 468–421 (.526) at home and 387–504 (.434) on the road. The team is 760–793 (.489) against National League opponents and 95–106 (.473) against the American League. In 807 games against NL East opponents, the Nationals are 389–418 (.482). The Nats have 105 wins against the New York Mets, the most vs. any opponent. They have 113 losses against the Philadelphia Phillies, the most against any opponent. They are 23–33 against the crosstown rival Baltimore Orioles.

Here is the Nationals' record against every Major League Baseball opponent.

Arizona Diamondbacks: 42–30
Atlanta Braves: 101–101
Baltimore Orioles: 23–33
Boston Red Sox: 5–7
Chicago Cubs: 38–35
Chicago White Sox: 5–4
Cincinnati Reds: 33–39
Cleveland Indians: 4–5
Colorado Rockies: 31–44
Detroit Tigers: 2–8
Houston Astros: 34–26
Kansas City Royals: 4–2
Los Angeles Angels of Anaheim: 4–8
Los Angeles Dodgers: 26–39
Miami Marlins: 93–107

Milwaukee Brewers: 38–38
Minnesota Twins: 4–5
New York Mets: 105–97
New York Yankees: 7–6
Oakland Athletics: 3–3
Philadelphia Phillies: 90–113
Pittsburgh Pirates: 39–34
St. Louis Cardinals: 27–43
San Diego Padres: 31–38
San Francisco Giants: 36–35
Seattle Mariners: 11–1
Tampa Bay Rays: 5–8
Texas Rangers: 4–5
Toronto Blue Jays: 10–11

Joe Cronin—Washington Senators shortstop/manager (1928–1934)
A seven-time All-Star, he served as Senators player/manager in 1933 and 1934. He was traded by Senators owner Clark Griffith (also his father-in-law) to the Boston Red Sox for Lyn Lary and $250,000. He went on to become the general manager of the Red Sox and president of the American League.

Andre Dawson—Montreal Expos center fielder (1976–1986)
Dawson joined Carter as the only Hall of Famers to claim the Expos as their primary team. "The Hawk" became the second player in history to hit 400 homers and steal 300 bases. Dawson was the 1977 Rookie of the Year, 1987 National League MVP, and was an eight-time All-Star.

Rick Ferrell—Washington Senators catcher (1937–1941, 1944–1945, and 1947)
An eight-time All-Star, Ferrell retired with the American League record for most games caught until Carlton Fisk claimed the record in 1988. He played with his pitching brother, Wes, in Washington in 1937 and 1938.

Josh Gibson—Homestead Grays catcher (1930–1931, 1937–1940, and 1942–1946)
Known as the black Babe Ruth, Gibson is considered the greatest hitter in Negro Leagues history. It's said he hit almost 800 home runs in 16 Negro Leagues seasons. An athlete behind the dish, he was able to throw out runners in an instant.

Goose Goslin—Washington Senators left fielder (1921–1930, 1933, and 1938)
Goslin has the distinction of playing for all three Senators World Series teams. He won the 1928 American League batting title by hitting .379. He beat out Heinie Manush of the St. Louis Browns and was traded for him two years later.

Clark Griffith—Washington Senators pitcher/manager/owner
(1912–1955)
Griffith was a baseball lifer and had a large impact on the sport's roots in D.C. As a player with the Cincinnati Reds, he helped bring a team to D.C. as part of the newly formed American League at the turn of the 20th century. He pitched for the Senators from 1912–1914 and managed from 1912–1920 and owned the team until his death in 1955.

Bucky Harris—Washington Senators second baseman/manager
(1919–1928, 1935–1942, and 1950–1954)
As a player/manager at age 27, Harris led the Senators to the city's only World Series title in 1924 and managed the franchise during four different decades.

Walter Johnson—Washington Senators pitcher/manager
(1907–1932)
Johnson was the greatest pitcher in Senators history and his time period. His dominance was rivaled by no other. Johnson holds the MLB record with 110 career shutouts, won 12 strikeout titles, and tossed a no-hitter in 1920.

Harmon Killebrew—Washington Senators first baseman
(1954–1960)
Killebrew began his career in D.C. before the team moved to Minnesota, where he made a name for himself. He hit 573 home runs—good enough for 11th all time.

Buck Leonard—Homestead Grays first baseman (1934–1950)
His 17 years as a Gray is the longest single-team tenure in the Negro Leagues. Known as the black Lou Gehrig, Leonard played in a league-record 11 East-West All-Star games.

Heinie Manush—Washington Senators left fielder (1930–1935) Manush, who played on the Senators' 1933 World Series team, won the 1926 batting title with a .376 average with the Detroit Tigers. He finished his 17-year career with a .330 batting average in 2,009 games.

Hall of Fame pitcher Walter Johnson, who won 12 strikeout titles, is one of the greats listed in the ring of honor.

Cumberland Posey—Homestead Grays outfielder/manager/owner (1911–1946)
Posey was arguably the most influential figure in Negro League baseball. His ability to organize and manage talent made the Grays a league powerhouse.

Sam Rice—Washington Senators right fielder (1915–1933)
Rice is first in Senators/Twins history in hits, runs, doubles, triples, and at-bats. He's second in games played and third in batting average. He had six 200-hit seasons and, like Goslin, played on the Washington Senators' only three pennant-winning teams.

Frank Robinson—Montreal Expos/Washington Nationals manager (2002–2006)
Robinson ushered in a new era of baseball in D.C. by leading the Nationals for their first two seasons in the city. As a player he was the first to win MVP in both leagues and finished with 586 home runs.

Jud Wilson—Homestead Grays third baseman (1931–1932, 1940–1945)
Wilson hit over .400 multiple times and captained the 1931 Grays squad. A fiery competitor, he was considered the best hitter in the game by Josh Gibson and was one of the two toughest hitters to get out, according to Satchel Paige.

Early Wynn—Washington Senators pitcher (1939–1944, 1946–1948)
Wynn played 23 seasons, winning 300 games and leading the American League in innings three times. He won the 1959 Cy Young Award at age 39.

91 Hang Out with Screech

On April 17, 2005, at RFK Stadium—Washington's first Sunday home game in 34 years—the Nationals celebrated "Kids Opening Day" and unveiled their own friendly, fan-loving creature.

Here's how the Nationals' website described the buildup: "One day in January 2005, while working on the outfield walls, crews found a large egg nestled underneath the stands. And this was no ordinary egg. It took a crew of 10 men to carry the egg to safety behind home plate. Zoologists came from throughout the world to examine the egg, hoping to determine what magnificent creature waited inside. Throughout it all, the Nationals kept the egg a secret.

Teams of zoologists cared for the egg day and night, awaiting the day it would finally hatch. But the cold weather of D.C. didn't help. The zoologists and the Washington Nationals players anxiously waited 'til spring.

Finally, on a beautiful spring day—on April 17th, 2005—in front of a roaring home crowd at RFK, the egg began to move. Obviously ready to greet its team, the egg wandered into center field and began to tremble and crack. As stunned fans and nervous workers looked on, the egg slowly hatched, revealing the secret inside: a young (but enormous) eagle! The Nationals scrambled to name their newest fan—who wouldn't stop screeching about his favorite team."

The 6'2" bald eagle with a round physique, flappy brown wings, a fuzzy white head, and big yellow beak became known as Screech. He is the third eagle mascot in D.C. sports, following in the footsteps of D.C. United's Talon and the Washington Capitals' Slapshot. Screech was designed by fourth grader Glenda Gutierrez for a team-sanctioned contest. She said she decided to draw an eagle because "it's strong and it eats almost everything."

Here are some fun facts about Nationals Park's favorite mascot. Screech lists his favorite food as gummy worms, his favorite band as The Eagles, and his favorite song "Fly Like an Eagle." Screech lost weight and unveiled his new, sleek self in 2009. His new look included a trimmed down waist and arms...*ahem*...wings.

Now he's able to interact with the crowd more often than ever, making his way through the stadium every game. Be sure to get a picture of your child with Screech. And if you really want to be parent of the year, book Screech for your child's birthday party or special event. To do so send an email to mascot@nationals.com with the date and time of the appearance, location of the appearance, a brief description of the event, and any special requests you have of Screech.

92 Call Me Maybe

Mel Proctor, the Nationals' original TV play-by-play man, was hired by the Mid-Atlantic Sports Network three days before the Nationals' season opener and didn't meet his broadcast partner, Ron Darling, until the day of the first game. MASN, the Nats' broadcasting station, was 90 percent owned by Baltimore Orioles owner Peter Angelos as part of a deal to allow the Montreal Expos to move to D.C. in time for the 2005 season.

At the time Comcast aired Orioles games and provided cable service to two-thirds of the Washington-Baltimore region. Comcast refused to air Nationals games and sued the Orioles and Major League Baseball, claiming they denied a contractual right to match any third-party offer before the O's could move to another network when their deal ended in 2007.

That meant the majority of households in the area would not get to watch Nationals games on TV during their first season in D.C. It's a real shame, considering the team shot out of a cannon, reaching a shocking 51–32 record on July 5.

Prior to accepting the job, Proctor was unaware of the dispute that made the team invisible in most of the homes in the area. "They didn't tell us anything," Proctor said. "We found out by accident."

Proctor wanted to know for himself how bad the feud was and if he and Darling were in fact broadcasting to nobody. "I really wanted to find out if anyone was watching the games," Proctor said. So during a home broadcast early in the year, Proctor took it upon himself to find out. He said over the air, "We've heard nobody is watching these games. Here's my cell phone number… If anyone is watching, please call me."

Some time passed, and he got a call. It was a from a MASN employee in a production truck, who said "Go Nats!" That was it. No one watching at home took advantage of the opportunity to talk to the Nationals' first-ever play-by-play announcer.

MASN general manager Bob Whitelaw was not pleased with Proctor's request. "He called me up and just reamed me out," Proctor said. "'You're sabotaging the operation. This is insubordination!' I said, 'I didn't know I was in the army.'"

Whitelaw didn't want Orioles mentioned on the air either. Proctor, who was Baltimore's play-by-play announcer from 1984 to 1996, obliged…kind of. "Are you aware the Nationals are outdrawing that team north of here, you know, the team with the beak and the wings?" Proctor asked Darling during a game. "Mr. Whitelaw wants to know if you have a death wish," a producer said into Proctor's headphones.

While the Nats were having a banner first half during a dream inaugural season, times were trying for Proctor, a broadcast veteran who had been in the business for decades. "It was the worst year of broadcasting I ever had," he said. "Ronnie and I just tried to survive."

93 D.C. Baseball's Clowns

Long before Bryce Harper famously uttered the phrase "That's a clown question, bro," D.C. baseball had their own clowns. Sans a red nose and face paint, Nick Altrock and Al Schacht entertained baseball audiences for decades as players, coaches, and resident comedians.

Owner Clark Griffith hired Altrock in 1912 as a "comedy coacher" to amuse crowds with his array of shenanigans from the first-base coach's box. A natural physical comedian, Altrock boasted big, wide ears with a round nose and knew how to make a memorable expression. His first partner was Germany Schaefer until the latter left in 1915. Carl Sawyer joined in for the next two years. Altrock worked solo in 1917 and 1918 before the Washington Senators acquired pitcher Al Schacht in 1919. Schacht appeared in 53 games with an ERA of 4.48 from 1919 to 1921. He quickly found out his true calling was comedy and earned the title of "Clown Prince of Baseball."

Altrock and Schacht would put on shows before Senators games. Routines consisted of mocking pitchers' windups, juggling, rowing boats during rain delays, wrestling, imitating umpires, trick golfing, and boxing. They were such a hit they performed at the World Series, All-Star Games, and were regularly headlining vaudeville bills.

Altrock is one of two players to play in five different decades. The other is Chicago White Sox legend and former Senators player Minnie Minoso. Altrock made his debut in 1898 and on October 1, 1933, at the age of 57, played for Washington against the Philadelphia Athletics.

Schacht and Altrock had a falling out, as described by Altrock's Society for American Baseball Research bio: "In the midst of this success, Altrock and Schacht stopped speaking to each other in 1927. Although Altrock never spoke about the specific reasons for it, their rift was often attributed to a fake prizefight routine that got a little too real. The story is that Schacht thought it would be funnier if he actually hit Nick and so punched the older comic unexpectedly and knocked him to the ground. Altrock got revenge a few days later during a routine where he would normally fire a hard baseball at Schacht for him to dodge and follow it with a soft baseball that Schacht took on the head. Altrock switched the baseballs, and Schacht took a hard blow to the skull and hit the turf."

That wasn't a banner year for Altrock. In spring training star pitcher Walter Johnson took a line drive off his right leg while pitching to teammate Joe Judge in batting practice. Johnson collapsed on the mound, and Altrock sprang into action, counting to 10 like a boxing referee. What Altrock didn't know was that a less amusing result would ensue, as Johnson suffered a broken leg and wouldn't pitch again until the end of May. Johnson appeared in 26 games that season, which turned out to be his last. Those 26 games were Johnson's fewest since playing in 14 during his 1907 rookie season.

Despite their dispute Altrock and Schacht still performed together until Schacht joined the Boston Red Sox in 1934 to coach under Joe Cronin, who was sent there by the Senators in exchange for $250,000 and shortstop Lyn Lary.

On today's Nats, you'll see hijinks like rookie relievers walking from the dugout to the bullpen wearing pink backpacks.

Undoubtedly, the current title of clubhouse comedian extraordinaire belongs to ace Max Scherzer. Yes, the same Scherzer who zones out so much on days that he pitches that you'd be lucky to get a smirk out of him.

One of Scherzer's first public displays of humor for Nats fans came during the third inning of a 2015 spring training game against the Detroit Tigers. Scherzer was sitting in a chair in front of fellow funnyman Gio Gonzalez, who was being interviewed by MASN's Dan Kolko. Straight out of a scene from *Super Troopers*, Gonzalez managed to say the word "meow" 10 times during the interview. Scherzer was clearly in on the bit. He held out his hands and used his fingers to keep track of how many times Gonzalez said the magic word.

Just days after reporting to spring training, Scherzer pranked manager Matt Williams with a photo from *Dumb and Dumber* and Williams in an awkward pose. Scherzer even worked on a rap about new teammate Jayson Werth spending five days in jail following a reckless driving conviction. Scherzer's also the same guy who introduced the Nats to more chocolate syrup than ever expected, dousing teammates with bottles of the delicious substance after victories. Hershey's wanted to make sure the team didn't run out of syrup, so the company shipped 108 bottles to the team in late May.

94 The Origins of the Curly W

Despite the similarities between the baseball team and the pharmacy's Curly W, the Washington Nationals didn't actually steal the Walgreens logo. Before the 1963 campaign, Washington Senators owner Elwood Quesada sold the team to James Johnston, James

Lemon, and George Bunker. According to D.C. baseball historian Phil Wood, the new ownership group wanted to give the expansion Senators an original look and a fresh start after losing 201 games over the two previous seasons. "Quesada's GM was Ed Doherty, who'd had a longstanding relationship with the Boston Red Sox prior to the AL expansion," Wood recollected. "The 1961–62 Washington jerseys borrowed heavily from the Red Sox in terms of lettering and the new owners wanted a different look. [Senators equipment manager Fred Baxter] said they liked the idea of a scripted 'Senators' on both the home and road jerseys with a cap style that would be a departure from the previous block W."

The block W on the hat was derived from the thin W the original Senators wore on their sleeves and caps in the early 1900s. "The Wilson Sporting Goods rep that Fred dealt with came up with some samples," Baxter said, "and Fred chose a red script W with white trim (then referred to by some fans as a pretzel W) on a navy cap with red piping down the seams and a red button on top. They would wear that cap until 1968 when they went to a red cap with a white script W trimmed in navy. That's the cap they wore until they left town after the 1971 season."

Despite attempting to break away from the norm, the new look didn't bring the franchise any added luck from 1963 to 1968. Over that span, the club never won more than 76 games. When the Senators were sold to infamous owner Bob Short in December 1968, the team introduced not only a new manager in legendary hitter Ted Williams, but the more familiar red ball caps with white Curly W we all know and love now. The team went on to go 86–76 in 1969, the expansion club's only winning season.

95

Go to Nationals Park on Opening Day and Fourth of July

No matter the record the year before, Opening Day is a sellout. It represents a fresh start and a renewed hope that this could be the Nats' year. While taking in Opening Day, be sure to visit one of the new restaurants popping up around Nationals Park. The area surrounding the stadium has grown significantly since it opened in 2008. Pregame festivities outside the park keep fans occupied hours before the game begins, but make sure you're on time for the pregame ceremonies.

Players, coaches, and staff are given the red carpet treatment and are introduced individually. A giant American flag is then unfurled in the outfield for "the Star-Spangled Banner," which is topped off with a fly-over of fighter jets. At the 2015 Opening Day, the team unveiled its 2014 National League East Champions banner and officially announced Nationals Park would host the 2018 All-Star Game. While you're there for the opener, be sure to pick up a program and an Opening Day commemorative baseball. They're great keepsakes. The Nationals have a 4–7 record on home openers.

In addition to Opening Day, attending Nationals Park on the Fourth of July is a must. These games typically have an 11 AM start time, giving fans plenty of time to tour the city after the game or head home for their own celebrations. Nothing screams patriotism like wearing red, white, and blue while spending the Fourth of July in the nation's capital. The team also honors emergency personnel and those who have served the country on July 4 with giveaways and salutes as part of their Patriotic Series.

Typically the Nats sport their patriotic blue alternate jerseys with the American flag emblazoned on the Curly W, but in 2015 the team wore special Major League Baseball-issued white uniforms for the game. Bryce Harper put his own spin on the decorated holiday, stepping up to the plate with a special painted bat featuring the American flag and the Washington, D.C., skyline. On the third pitch he saw, Harper took reigning World Series MVP Madison Bumgarner deep to give the Nationals a 3–0 lead against the San Francisco Giants in the first inning. Harper added two more hits and a walk as the Nats went on to beat the Giants 9–3.

Washington is 7–3 at home and 7–4 overall on July 4. The team's lone road game on the nation's birthday was a 3–0 loss to the Cincinnati Reds in 2008, which was highlighted by a two-run home run from Ken Griffey Jr.

After the Independence Day game, stay for the fireworks on the National Mall. Enjoy lunch at a local restaurant and find a friend who has access to a rooftop in the city. That way, you get a 360-degree view of the fireworks going off at the Washington Monument and those going off in Maryland and Virginia. There's nothing like it.

96 Jayson Werth Goes to Jail

Jayson Werth isn't known for his hustle on the base path, but in 2014 he took to the highway to test out his speed in his Porsche GT3 RS. At 9:36 AM on July 6, the 35-year-old outfielder decided to race north onto the Capital Beltway in Virginia's Fairfax County and push his expensive ride to the limit. The man, who has been caught stealing on the diamond at least once a season since 2004, couldn't evade the law this time either. Police clocked Werth's vehicle at 105 mph in a 55-mph zone, and the 12-year veteran was charged with reckless driving.

The officer who pulled him over testified that Werth's ride sounded like a race car when the engine revved as he prepared to get on the Beltway. The cop floored the accelerator of his cruiser to keep pace with Werth and tailed him for the next half-mile at 105 mph, but the bearded wonder still managed to pull away.

When the officer pulled him over, he approached the Porsche with his gun unholstered but not pointed at Werth. The officer

Jayson Werth, who had to spend five nights in jail during 2015 because of reckless driving, is shown in better times, celebrating his walk-off home run to win Game 4 of the 2012 NLDS against the St. Louis Cardinals.

asked him what he was doing. Werth, who was on his way to Nationals Park for the team's 1:30 PM game against the Chicago Cubs, replied that he was "pressing his luck." Werth batted third and went 0-for-3 in the Nats' 2–1 victory against Chicago.

Virginia is notorious for the strict enforcement of its driving laws, and Werth was found guilty of misdemeanor reckless driving and sentenced to 10 days in jail. "Speed kills and does not discern what he or she does for a living," the judge told Werth. "[Interstate] 495 is not a racetrack." Werth eventually pleaded guilty to reckless driving. His license was suspended for 30 days, and he served five days in jail. In early 2015 he served his sentence in two weekend stints so he could continue rehabbing his shoulder before spring training.

While in jail Werth said he received a lot of support from guards and fellow inmates. "Nats Nation holds no bounds," he said. Werth played cards, used a treadmill, rode a stationary bike, and even joined a group CrossFit workout to keep in shape. A Reddit user posted a link with text that read: "Told Jayson Werth I was at game 4 back in 2012. My last day in the system was neat." The link opened in a new tab showing a photo of the Fairfax County Adult Detention Center's Inmate Handbook with Werth's signature. The slugger wrote: "George, Gm 4 was sick!!" Werth verified the legitimacy of it during spring training, telling *The Washington Post*, "That's authentic."

Werth explained his transgression. "It's a time in my life that I'm glad it's behind me," he said. "It's not something that was fun. It's not a destination you would choose. I don't want to be looked at as some renegade in the community...This doesn't look the best. It was a one-time event. I was on my way to work one day. It was a Sunday morning. There was no one around on the Beltway. At the same time, I felt like people may have the wrong idea of me."

Driving on a highway at such speeds is a serious matter, and Werth was punished for it with a jail sentence. "I wouldn't say it was the easiest thing to go through," he added. "I don't feel like my spirit has been broken or anything like that. It was something I went through. I put it behind me and moved forward."

97 Watch a Concert at Nationals Park

Yeah, you can see a baseball game 81 times a year at Nationals Park. That's a given. But spice things up a bit and try something different like a concert. Nationals Park has played host to more than 20 concerts over the last few years, including some of the biggest names in music.

Billy Joel and Elton John performed the inaugural concert at the one-year-old stadium on July 11, 2009, for their Face 2 Face tour. Dave Matthews Band and the Zac Brown Band took the stage in 2010. The Eagles, Dixie Chicks, and Keith Urban were supposed to perform together in June 2010, but the concert was cancelled. Lifehouse performed after the Nats beat the New York Mets 8–7 on September 3, 2011.

In 2012 the team introduced the NatsLive Postgame Concert Series, a summer-long promotion of free shows that take place in the outfield approximately 15 minutes after each game. The first lineup consisted of Dierks Bentley, the Wallflowers, and Third Eye Blind.

Bruce Springsteen & the E Street Band put on a show that September for his "Wrecking Ball" world tour. The 2013 post-game concert lineup featured Blues Traveler, Thompson Square, Gavin DeGraw, Montgomery Gentry, and Sammy Hagar. Sir Paul McCartney also rocked Nationals Park on July 12, 2013, as part of his "Out There" tour.

In 2014 the 41,888-seat venue played host to acts like Plain White T's, Austin Mahone, and Martina McBride as part of the team's postgame concert series. That was a big year for concerts at the stadium for fans of all ages. Billy Joel became the first two-time performer at Nats Park that July. Jason Aldean played his "Burn It Down" tour there. One Direction performed a sold-out show during their "Where We Are" tour with 5 Seconds of Summer as their opening act on a rainy night in Southeast D.C.

Another non-baseball event at Nationals Park kicked off 2015 the right way with the NHL's Winter Classic on New Year's Day. The Washington Capitals pulled off a 3–2 victory with 12.9 seconds left over the eventual Stanley Cup champion Chicago Blackhawks. Nationals general manager Mike Rizzo made an appearance and, much to the chagrin of Capitals fans, the Chicago native was wearing a throwback Blackhawks Bobby Hull jersey.

The team curtailed its Postgame Concert Series in 2015 to commemorate its 10-year anniversary with increased promotions and giveaways throughout the season, but big acts still put on a show at the young stadium constructed along the Anacostia River. Taylor Swift, the hottest name in music in 2015, performed two shows from "The 1989 World Tour" last July while the team was off for the All-Star break. The Zac Brown Band performed there for the second time in mid-August for their "Jekyll + Hyde" Tour with The Avett Brothers as their opening act.

Make sure to treat yourself and snag some VIP passes so you can see your favorite bands up close from the field. But please, for the sake of humanity, no selfie sticks. Also make sure you save yourself the $50 for parking. Either take the Metro, stay at a friend's place in the city, or rent a bike through D.C.'s bikeshare program. It should be a crime to pay that much just to park a vehicle anywhere.

Villains

When the following names are spoken to defenders of the Curly W, they instantly remember why they despise them.

Pete Kozma

Most Nationals fans had never heard of Pete Kozma before Washington embarked on their first playoff series. When the 2012 National League Division Series was over, those same fans would never be able to forget his name even if they tried. With a 6–0 lead against the St. Louis Cardinals after three innings in Game 5 of the 2012 NLDS, things were looking up for the Nats. It wasn't to be, as the Cards cut the lead to 6–5 by the eighth inning. With a security blanket run tacked on the bottom of the eighth, the Nats held a two-run lead with three outs to go.

A two-out, two-run single from St. Louis' Daniel Descalso tied the game at 7 in the top of the ninth inning. With two on and two out, seldom-used Pete Kozma, who played in just 42 games in 2011 and 2012 combined, came up to the plate. As fate would have it, he smacked a two-run single to right, giving the Cardinals a 9–7 win and ultimately the series victory.

Nationals fans still let Kozma know how they feel whenever he returns to D.C. "I got a pretty good booing the one [other] time I came back," said Kozma before the two teams met for their first series of 2015. "It kind of makes me feel like I did something. It wasn't like I hurt anybody. I just hurt their feelings. That was about it."

Cole Hamels

Aside from helping the hated Philadelphia Phillies win the 2008 World Series and posting a career record of 14–9, 2.67 ERA and a

.217 batting average against the Nats, he etched his place in villain-ous lore with his first pitch against rookie outfielder Bryce Harper in 2012.

On the May 6 broadcast of ESPN's *Sunday Night Baseball,* Cole Hamels decided to hit Harper in the small of the back as a way of sending the 19-year-old a message. "I was trying to hit him," Hamels admitted after the game. "I'm not going to deny it. It's something I grew up watching. That's what happened. I'm just trying to continue the old baseball."

Harper retaliated by stealing home several pitches later, and his general manager had his back as well. "I've never seen a more class-less, gutless chickenshit act in my 30 years in baseball," Nationals general manager Mike Rizzo said the next morning. "Cole Hamels says he's old school? He's the polar opposite of old school. He's fake tough."

Peter Angelos

You can't make a list of Nationals villains without including the Baltimore Orioles owner. Let's put it this way: even his own fanbase isn't fond of him. For many years Angelos worked hard to keep a baseball team out of Washington, D.C., stating that a team in the nation's capital would infringe on his team's territory. He also said in a July 2004 radio interview that "there are no real baseball fans in D.C."

When the Montreal Expos finally moved to Washington, most local fans couldn't even watch their new team on TV thanks to a holdup for a new local cable deal. When fans were finally able to see their team, Angelos profited heavily off of the TV deal that formed the Mid-Atlantic Sports Network (MASN).

Brandon Belt/Hunter Pence/Joe Panik

These three come in as a combo pack for their 2014 National League Division Series performances. In the 18th inning of Game

2's marathon matchup between the Nationals and San Francisco Giants, Brandon Belt broke the 1–1 tie with a 413-foot solo home run to right field, placing a dagger in the heart of every Nats fan who witnessed the longest playoff game in MLB history.

Nats fans were well aware of Hunter Pence's quirkiness at the plate and in the outfield from his brief stint in Philadelphia, but in their eyes, he made a name for himself in the NLDS. He tied Belt and Brandon Crawford for second on the Giants with five hits in the series. His reliable glove helped do the Nats in, including a leaping catch against the right-field fence to rob Jayson Werth of an extra-base hit in the sixth inning of Game 4.

Joe Panik led the Giants with three of the team's nine runs, including the go-ahead run on Aaron Barrett's bases-loaded wild pitch in the seventh inning of Game 4. The Giants won that game 3–2 and the series 3–1 on the way to their third World Series title in five years.

Jose Tabata

Perfection was just a pitch away for Nationals ace Max Scherzer. Having retired the previous 26 Pittsburgh Pirates, Scherzer was on the cusp of becoming the 24th pitcher to throw a perfect game. Then he faced Pittsburgh's Jose Tabata. On a 2–2 count in the top of the ninth inning, Scherzer tossed a pitch high and inside, striking Tabata on his left elbow pad. The debate raged on. Did Tabata drop his elbow intentionally or was it on instinct?

For Nats fans, the discussion was irrelevant. They argued that Scherzer's perfect game was ruined and that Tabata should have been thrown out. "Mad Max" still came out of it with a no-hitter, but fans feel the result is forever tainted. The home crowd booed Tabata vociferously as he took his base and even during his at-bats in the next game.

Tabata denied that he dropped his elbow intentionally. "I wanted to get a hit," he said in Spanish before the next game.

"People don't understand that those were the instincts people have. I wasn't looking to get hit. I wanted to get a hit. I wanted to get on base."

Tony Cingrani /Joey Votto
On May 29, 2015, in the top of the seventh inning against the Cincinnati Reds, Bryce Harper was in his fourth plate appearance and still looking for his first hit. With two outs in the inning, Reds pitcher Tony Cingrani relieved Jumbo Diaz on the mound. On Cingrani's first pitch, he delivered a 93-mph fastball straight into Harper's back. Harper bent over, wincing in pain, and took his time removing his equipment, tossing it toward the Nationals dugout and making his way toward first base.

Reds first baseman Joey Votto grew impatient and took exception to Harper leisurely advancing to first base as he walked off the pain. The two exchanged words, prompting Nationals analyst Ray Knight to say on-air: "I would shut up if I was Joey Votto."

Cingrani, though, took the same stance as Votto. "I threw it as hard as I could, and it ran up and in and hit him," Cingrani told reporters. "What are you going to do? He should have jogged, but what are you going to do? Be a baseball player. Sorry, I hit you. Run."

99 Hiring Dusty Baker

For the 2015 Washington Nationals, the year wouldn't have been complete without a wacky managerial search following the ouster of Matt Williams. It's not in the nature of D.C. sports for things to be seamless. After going with Williams, who had no managerial experience at the major league level, the team wanted someone with a track record as an MLB skipper.

Just more than three weeks after firing Williams, news broke that the club was set to hire Bud Black as their newest manager. Black was fired by the San Diego Padres in the middle of the 2015 season after eight and a half years of leading the club. The news was not official because Major League Baseball prefers major announcements to occur after the World Series, which was days away from ending.

Black, 58, had failed to produce a playoff bid during his time in San Diego while guiding a roster with a limited payroll for much of his tenure. Black, who spent 15 years as an MLB pitcher from 1981 to 1995, was expected to handle Washington's pitching staff and communicate with the players far better than Williams.

That, however, never materialized. The Nationals and Black had not yet discussed financial terms before the agreement and their first offer, which reportedly guaranteed one year and $1.6 million, left Black deeply offended. Negotiations faltered, and the Nats lost out on their guy. The Nats then shifted their focus to 66-year-old Dusty Baker, who managed a combined 20 years for the San Francisco Giants, Chicago Cubs, and Cincinnati Reds, making consecutive National League Championship Series appearances (2002, 2003) and a 2002 World Series appearance.

Baker eventually accepted a two-year deal, reportedly worth less than $4 million, a bargain for a manager with seven postseason appearances and three Manager of the Year awards in 20 years of experience. Baker acclimated himself to D.C. pretty quickly, attending the Washington Wizards-San Antonio Spurs the night before his introductory press conference and chewing on his trademark toothpick.

The next morning, Baker was introduced to the D.C. media as the sixth manager in team history and won over the media pretty quickly, namedropping Barack Obama, Stevie Wonder, Nelson

Mandela, the Doors, Bill Russell, and Bill Walsh, among others. He said his friends call him "the chameleon because they think I can adapt to any place, any time, anywhere."

Baker, who played 19 years in the bigs from 1968 to 1986, exudes confidence in his abilities as well as his aptitude to handle superstars like Bryce Harper. "I'm not really intimidated or anything by stars because *I* was a star," Baker said. "I wasn't as bright a star as some of these guys, but I was a star. I tell them I don't care how much money you make—don't plan on giving me any of your money; I'm not giving you any of mine. But when the game starts, it's not about money, it's about whether I kick your butt or you kick mine. It's as simple as that."

The Presidential Statistician

From 1901 to 1971, the Senators had strong ties to presidents during their tenure. Whether it was connections through owner Clark Griffith or the commander in chief's love of national pastime, the leader of the free world always had Senators baseball on his mind.

In 1970 that connection intensified when one certain presidential connection infiltrated the Senators front office. In spring training 22-year-old David Eisenhower visited the team and expressed an interest in working for the club during the summer before joining the Navy in September. Eisenhower is the grandson of the 34th president of the United States, Dwight Eisenhower, and son-in-law of the 37th president of the United States, Richard Nixon.

On April 6 Nixon was running late for the Opening Day game between the Senators and Detroit Tigers at RFK Stadium. He didn't show up until the fifth inning, so his son-in-law threw out the first pitch. While there David talked with Senators owner Bob Short and discussed his interest in further summer employment with the team.

Eisenhower, the namesake for the Maryland presidential retreat Camp David, joined the Senators in late May after graduating from Amherst. "This is something I particularly wanted to do for a long time," Eisenhower said at the time of his hiring. "I don't think I'd want to make baseball a career—even as a top executive. I just love the game and wanted to see this side of it."

He assisted Hal Keller, the team's farm director, tracking statistics of Senators players and the 120 players on their five minor league affiliates. He also performed odd jobs such as assisting press relations director and traveling secretary Burt Hawkins with making travel and hotel arrangements with the team.

The Eisenhowers were fond of the Senators long before his brief stay as a statistician. At a game in 1959, David's grandfather asked Senators slugger Harmon Killebrew to sign a baseball. Naturally, Killebrew asked for an autographed ball in exchange.

David didn't stay with the team for long. He went on a few road trips with the team, and a month later, he and his wife Julie represented President Nixon at Osaka, Japan's Expo 70 during United States Day. He is now a communications professor at the University of Pennsylvania.

Acknowledgements

In no particular order, I'd like to thank the following for their assistance, encouragement, and time when it came to the development of this book: Rick Snider, Phil Wood, Adam Kilgore, Barry Svrluga, Mel Proctor, Carol Flaisher, and Tripp Whitbeck.

Sources

Books

Bradlee, B. (2013). *The Kid: The Immortal Life of Ted Williams.* New York. Little, Brown and Company.

Carroll, J. (2008). *Sam Rice: A Biography of the Washington Senators Hall of Famer.* Jefferson, North Carolina. McFarland.

Ceresi, F., Rucker, M., and McMains, C. (2002). *Baseball in Washington, D.C.,* Charleston, South Carolina. Arcadia Pub.

Frommer, F. J. (2005). *The Washington Baseball Fan's Little Book of Wisdom.* Lanham, Maryland. Taylor Trade Pub.

Frommer, F. J. (2013). *You Gotta Have Heart: A History of Washington Baseball from 1859 to the 2012 National League East Champions.* Lanham, Maryland. Taylor Trade Publishing, an imprint of The Rowman & Littlefield Pub. Group, Inc.

Gorman, R., Weeks, D. (2007) *Death at the Ballpark: A Comprehensive Study of Game-related Fatalities, 1862–2007.* Jefferson, North Carolina. McFarland.

Honig, D. (1993). *Baseball Between the Lines: Baseball in the Forties and Fifties, As Told by the Men Who Played It.* Lincoln, Nebraska. University of Nebraska Press.

Kavanaugh, J. (1992). *Baseball Legends: Walter Johnson.* New York. Chelsea House Publishers.

Leavengood, Ted. (2011). *Clark Griffith: The Old Fox of Washington Baseball.* Jefferson, North Carolina. McFarland.

Mead, William B. (1993). *Baseball: The Presidents' Game.* Washington, D.C., Farragut Pub. Co.

Povich, S. (2010). *The Washington Senators.* Kent, Ohio. The Kent State University Press.

Smith, E. (2013). *Beltway Boys: Stephen Strasburg, Bryce Harper, and the rise of the Nationals.* Chicago. Triumph Books.

Snyder, B. (2003). *Beyond the Shadow of the Senators: The Untold Story of the Homestead Grays and the Integration of Baseball.* Chicago. Contemporary Books.

Svrluga, B. (2006). *National Pastime: Sports, Politics, and the Return of Baseball to Washington, D.C.* New York. Doubleday.

Thomas, H. (1995). *Walter Johnson: Baseball's Big Train.* Washington, D.C., Phenom Press.

Interviews

Flaisher, Carol. Phone interview. May 2015.

Proctor, Mel. Phone interview. August 2015.

Whitbeck, Tripp. Email interview. August 2015.

Newspapers
Chicago Tribune
The Gazette and Daily (York, Pennslyvania)
Los Angeles Times
New York Post
The New York Times
USA TODAY
The Washington Post
Washington Times

Publications
2015 Minnesota Twins media guide
2015 Washington Nationals media guide
2015 Washington Nationals yearbook

Websites
Baltimore.CBSlocal.com
BaseballAmerica.com
Baseball-almanac.com
Baseball-reference.com
Baseballhall.org
Books.Google.com
CIA.gov
DCConvention.com
ESPN.com
FederalBaseball.com
FoxNews.com
Gallaudet.edu
HardballTalk.com
HuffingtonPost.com
IMDB.com
LATimes.com
MASNsports.com

MILB.com
MLB.com
NatsEnquirer.com
NatsInsider.com
People.com
Reporterherald.com
Reuters.com
SABR.org
Senate.gov
SI.com
TwinCities.com
Twitter.com
USATODAY.com
Variety.com
Washington.CBSlocal.com
Washingtonian.com
YouTube.com

Wire Services
Associated Press
United Press International

Television
National Pastime: Baseball's Return to Washington, Mid-Atlantic Sports Network, April 14, 2015.